Later Muggletonian Interest: Academic, Literary and Scientific

Edited by Mike Pettit

Visit us online at www.muggletonianpress.com **and
view our entire range of Muggletonian Literature**

A Muggletonian Press Book

Copyright © Mike Pettit 2010

All rights reserved. No portion of this publication may be reproduced, stored in a retrieval system, or transmitted in any form or by any means, electronic, mechanical, photocopy, recording or otherwise, without prior written permission of the copyright owner. While many of the original texts which form the basis of this publication are to be found in the public domain the texts found herein have been typographically modernised and reformatted at great expense. Please respect the resulting copyright that such work has created.

ISBN 978-1-907466-05-2

Cover Image: The engraving of Lodowick Muggleton found in the 1794 edition of the "Lives and Portraits of Remarkable Characters"

Published by:
Muggletonian Press
129 Hebdon Road
London SW17 7NL
England

I would like to make it clear that in editing and publishing this volume I am not seeking to advocate any element of *Muggletonian* theology. I fully subscribe to historic orthodox Christianity as expressed in the Reformed Confessions of Faith and would plead with all the readers of this work to consider the claims of the triune God.

From the Heidelberg Catechism

Question 12. Since then, by the righteous judgment of God, we deserve temporal and eternal punishment, is there no way by which we may escape that punishment, and be again received into favour?

Answer: God will have his justice satisfied: and therefore we must make this full satisfaction, either by ourselves, or by another.

Question 13. Can we ourselves then make this satisfaction?

Answer: By no means; but on the contrary we daily increase our debt.

Question 14. Can there be found anywhere, one, who is a mere creature, able to satisfy for us?

Answer: None; for, first, God will not punish any other creature for the sin which man has committed; and further, no mere creature can sustain the burden of God's eternal wrath against sin, so as to deliver others from it.

Mike Pettit

CONTENTS

	Page
Introduction	5
Lives and Portraits of Remarkable Characters	9
Two Systems of Astronomy	13
Varia: Readings from Rare Books	99
The Origin of the Muggletonians	109
Ancient and Modern Muggletonians	133
Bibliotheca Anti-Quakeriana	175
The Prophet of Walnut-Tree Yard	213
Lodowick Muggleton: A Paper Read	233
English Sects: An Historical Handbook	277

INTRODUCTION

The early years of the Muggletonian church generated a large amount of polemical literature, a fluid dialogue both attacking and defending the movement. As time passed the Church became more inward looking, concentrating on republishing existing material, rather than interacting with the outside world.

The perceived wisdom was that the sect was extinct, a perception reinforced by the 1851 census that did not record a Muggletonian presence, even so there were isolated mentions of Muggletonianism in the literature of the nineteenth century. It was not until 1869 that the great Alexander Gordon published his ground breaking "The Origin of the Muggletonians", a work that so impressed the church that they invited Gordon (much to his surprise) to attend their meetings and study the church archives. Gordon published his invaluable "Ancient And Modern Muggletonians" in 1870 which represents the finest scholarly insight that we have into the church, a feat unlikely to be repeated in the absence of the first hand sources that were available to Gordon.

Rather uniquely the Muggletonians also published the splendid "Two Systems of Astronomy" in 1846 in order to disprove Newtonian physics, the Muggletonians last concerted attempt to interact in print directly with popular culture.

Further works of a lower quality emerged over time, still with (on occasion) some limited input from the church as well as a few inaccurate popular pieces.

We then come to the present day where the great Christopher Hill awoke interest in Muggletonianism with his 1983 "The World of the Muggletonians" which has been followed by the discovery of the Muggletonian archive and William Lamont's "Last Witnesses: the Muggletonian History, 1652-1979", the only work to date that has emerged to rival Gordon's 1870 work in its historical importance.

This volume contains the following:

Lives and Portraits of Remarkable Characters

The entry in respect of Lodowick Muggleton from the 1794 edition of the "Lives And Portraits Of Remarkable Characters" by James Caulfield is reproduced in this volume. This publication would be of limited interest if it were not for the print accompanying the work, the majority of the text comprising a reprint from the earlier Harleian Miscellany, which was itself a reprint of the 1676 original.

Two Systems of Astronomy

The full text of this 1846 Muggletonian work disputing Newtonian astronomy is reproduced in this volume, unfortunately I only hold image rights to six of the 11 plates from the original work therefore I have been unable to reproduce 5 of the original plates, and those that have been reproduced are unfortunately only reproduced in grayscale.

Varia: Readings from Rare Books

This 1866 essay on Lodowick Muggleton from J Hain Friswell's larger publication "Varia: Readings From Rare Books" is reproduced here. While the essay is based on a very limited selection of sources and is undoubtedly misleading in many ways (Alexander Gordon refers to it having "little or no value" in his 1869 "The Origin of the Muggletonians"), the work was at least an attempt (however poor) to consider Muggletonianism in its historical context.

The Origin of the Muggletonians

This paper presented to the Liverpool Literary and Philosophical Society in 1869 by the distinguished Unitarian Alexander Gordon represented what is possibly the first serious external attempt to appraise Muggletonianism.

Gordon ended this substantial essay with the statement that:

"In this slight sketch I have by no means exhausted the details of the Muggletonian system, or entered upon the history of the Muggletonian Sect. I have simply attempted to fulfil the promise of giving some account of the circumstances which led to its origination. The literature and philosophy of the Muggletonians may be thought perhaps to deserve further enquiry and study; and I may take a future opportunity of presenting to the members of the Literary and Philosophical Society the result of enlarged investigations into the writings and fortunes of this singular people."

The success of this work led to Gordon being approached by the Muggletonian Church and his being invited to examine the church archives and to attend some of their great meetings. This in turn led to the publication in the following year of Gordon's great work "Ancient and Modern Muggletonians"

Ancient and Modern Muggletonians

This 1870 presentation to the Liverpool Literary and Philosophical Society by Alexander Gordon is breathtaking in its achievement, it presents Muggletonianism as a living movement and dominates our knowledge of the later development of the movement, indeed the discovery of the Muggletonian archive (now to be found in the British Library) can be traced to this work.

Any serious understanding of Muggletonianism has to involve the study of this remarkable work, which is reproduced in this volume.

Bibliotheca Anti-Quakeriana

The extracts relevant to Muggletonianism from this rather eccentric 1873 volume are reproduced here.

This volume is of major importance in studying Muggletonianism, Joseph Smith had a remarkable knowledge of Muggletonian literature and his passing comments are often of immense interest, especially in relation to his details of Birchite influences on Muggletonianism in the nineteenth century.

The Prophet of Walnut-Tree Yard

This rather bombastic essay from the Rev Augustus Jessopp's 1884 work "The Coming of the Friars: and other historic essays" is reproduced in this volume.

William Lamont records that the great Muggletonian, Thomas Robinson, wrote to Jessop explaining his dissatisfaction with both the contents and tone of Jessopp's work. Jessopp is said to have responded in a "bluff and conciliatory way".

This essay is of little historic importance but it is not without its insights, especially the passage that reads:

> "There were two men in England who were quite certain - George Fox was one, Muggleton was the other. Everybody else was doubting, hesitating, groping for the light, moaning in the darkness. These two men knew, other people were seeking to know. George Fox went forth to win the world over from darkness to light. Muggleton stayed at home, he was the light. They that wanted it must come to him to find it."

Lodowick Muggleton: A Paper Read

This fascinating 1919 work by George Charles Williamson mirrors Gordon's earlier work in that Williamson visited with the Muggletonians and gained valuable insights from the then struggling church. You do get the feeling that they were having fun with him, his belief that the books he was allowed to buy were not usually available to those outside the church appears to be at odds with the efforts that had been made to sell such books to the general public.

This is however a valuable work, not least for the marvelous photographs that bring the Muggletonian meeting room to life once again. The original photographs are not of the best quality therefore the reproductions in this volume are similarly limited in quality.

English Sects: An Historical Handbook

This short extract relating to Muggletonians from Arthur Reynolds 1921 volume is an interesting but brief insight into the church, not least because Reynolds appears to have a working knowledge of the modern church and its organization.

Lives and Portraits of Remarkable Characters, Drawn from the most authentic sources

Lodowick Muggleton.
Dyed the 14.th of March 169$\frac{7}{8}$. then Aged 88 years 7 months and 14 days.

Published by Caulfield and Herbert 1794.

LODOWICK MUGGLETON.

LODOWICK MUGGLETON, who was by trade a tailor, was a notorious, schismatic, and father of the sect called after his name. He was a great pretender to inward light, which was to answer every purpose of religion.

He regarded himself as above ordinances of every kind, not excepting prayer and preaching. He acknowledged but one person in the Godhead, rejected creeds, and all church discipline and authority; but expected the greatest deference to be paid to what he taught and enjoined himself.

He esteemed the scripture, a dead letter, and resolved every thing into his own private spirit. He like other enthusiasts, made no scruple of damning all the world that differed from his own mode of faith. His disciples are said to have recorded many of his prophecies. He began to distinguish himself about the year 1650.[1] His books, for writing which he was pillored and imprisoned, were burnt by the common hangman.

To give an idea of the principles entertained by Muggleton and his followers, the annexed Stories are subjoined, extracted from the Harlean Miscellany, vol. i. p. 193.

A person one Sunday walking in the fields, and meeting there an old acquaintance of his, who had lately turned Muggletonian, with a young baggage in his hand, which he did more than suspect was light, he could not forbear expressing his admiration to this Muggletonion himself, in these or such-like terms: "I cannot but wonder to see you, my old neighbour, who have, for there many years, busied yourself in the study of religion, and was not long since like to have gone mad, because you knew not which opinion to stick to—I say I cannot but wonder to see you abroad, on the sabbath-day, in this brisk posture: you are altered both in countenance, apparel, and manners; so that I almost doubt whom I speak to."—"Ah!" answered the Muggletonian, "you know, friend, how I have heretofore troubled myself about religion indeed, insomuch that it had almost cost me my life; but all in vain, till about six weeks since; at which time I met with Lodowick

---

[1] George Fox, a journeyman shoemaker, and one of the great apostles of the Quakers, began to exert himself about the same time. He was a friend and associate of Muggleton; and they are said to have been "so deeply seized with despair, that they forsook all human conversation, and retired into desarts and solitary places, where they spent whole days and nights alone."—Leslie's "Snake in the Grass," edit. 1698, p. 331.—See also "Fox's Journal."

Muggleton, who has put me into the easiest way to heaven that ever was invented; for he gives us liberty, provided we do but believe in his commission, freely to launch into all those pleasures, which others, less knowing, call vices; and, after all, will assure us of eternal salvation.

A timish gentleman, accoutred with sword and peruke, hearing the noise, this man caused in the town, had a great desire to discourse with him, whom he found alone in his study; and, taking advantage of that occasion, he urged Muggleton so far, that, knowing not what to say, he falls to a solemn cursing of the gentleman; who was so enraged thereat, that he drew his sword, and swore he would run him through immediately, unless he recanted the sentence of damnation which he had presumptuously cast upon him. Muggleton perceiving, by the gentleman's looks, that he really intended what he threatened, did not only recant his curse, but pitifully intreated him, whom he had cursed before, to spare his life.

TWO SYSTEMS

OF

ASTRONOMY:

First

THE NEWTONIAN SYSTEM,

SHOWING THE RISE AND PROGRESS THEREOF, BY A SHORT HISTORICAL ACCOUNT;
THE GENERAL THEORY, WITH A VARIETY OF REMARKS THEREON.

Second

THE SYSTEM IN ACCORDANCE WITH

THE HOLY SCRIPTURES,

SHOWING THE RISE AND PROGRESS FROM ENOCH, THE SEVENTH FROM ADAM;
THE PROPHETS, MOSES AND OTHERS, IN THE FIRST TESTAMENT;
OUR LORD JESUS CHRIST, AND HIS APOSTLES, IN THE NEW OR SECOND TESTAMENT;
REEVE AND MUGGLETON, IN THE THIRD AND LAST TESTAMENT;
WITH A VARIETY OF REMARKS THEREON.

BY ISAAC FROST.

"NEVERTHELESS WE, ACCORDING TO HIS PROMISE, LOOK FOR NEW HEAVENS AND A NEW EARTH, WHEREIN
DWELLETH RIGHTEOUSNESS," 2 Peter iii. 13.

Entered at Stationers' Hall.

LONDON:
PRINTED BY CATCHPOOL & TRENT, 5, ST. JOHN'S SQUARE;
AND
PUBLISHED BY SIMPKIN, MARSHALL, & CO., STATIONERS' HALL COURT.

1846.

CONTENTS.

PART I.

NEWTONIAN, OR SOLAR SYSTEM OF ASTRONOMY.

CHAPTER I.

	Page
1. Introduction of the Two Systems. 2. The Theory and History of the Newtonian System, with several Remark	23

CHAPTER II.

The varied Distances of the Planetary Bodies, and their apparent Sizes	29

CHAPTER III.

1. The Positions of the Earth with the Sun and fixed Stars. 2. The Earth buried in the immense Rays of the Sun. 3. The Rays of the Sun gliding off the Sides of the Earth without effect	33

CHAPTER IV.

1. The impossibility of the Moon borrowing her Light from the Sun philosophically proved. 2. The Differences of Light and Dark Bodies in perspective	36

CHAPTER V.

1. Rising and Setting of the Sun, with the Descending Line of Sight. 2. Refraction shown by Experiments with Water. 3. How Water, in a global term, magnifies Objects	38

CHAPTER VI.

1. The Earth's position with the Sun and Polar Stars; 2. Showing the Degrees of Angles for Winter and Summer. 3. The Stars changing their position. 4. The Phases seen on Mercury, Venus, &c. 5. The Stars considered Suns, with Worlds revolving round them, and supposed to be peopled like this Earth. 6. The Error of such absurd Ideas	41

PART II.

SYSTEM OF ASTRONOMY ACCORDING TO THE SCRIPTURES.

CHAPTER I.

Page

1. The one unvaried Line of Knowledge as to the Rising and Setting of the Sun, from first to last. 2. Enoch's Declaration that the Sun, Moon, and Stars rise and set upon the Earth, in Four Chapters, taken from his Book   46

CHAPTER II.

1. Explanation of Enoch's meaning by the Six Gates, wherein the Sun and Moon rise and set. 2. Enoch acknowledged by the Prophets, Apostles, &c.   54

CHAPTER III.

1. The necessity of rightly understanding the Scriptures. 2. The Creation of the visible Firmament. 3. From whence the Water was obtained to drown the World. 4. The Building of the Tower of Babel. 5. The Visibility of God, and his Descending from Heaven above the Stars. 6. How God may be said to fill Heaven and Earth   59

CHAPTER IV.

1. The necessity of true Faith and true Knowledge to please God. 2. The rising and setting of the Sun proved by Scripture. 3. The different Glories of the Sun, Moon, and Stars. 4. Our Lord Jesus Christ's Ascent into his Kingdom above, &c.   64

CHAPTER V.

Containing a Quotation of Three Chapters from the Divine Looking-Glass of the Third Testament of our Lord Jesus Christ, by Reeve and Muggleton, concerning the Kingdom of Heaven, and the Creation of this World   68

CHAPTER VI.

A Discourse between John Reeve and Richard Leader, Merchant; recited by Lodowick Muggleton, one of the two last Witnesses and Prophets of the most high God, the man Jesus In Glory   76

CHAPTER VII.

Remarks as to the Result and Impossibility of the Truth of the Newtonian System   84

CHAPTER VIII.

Page

1. Concerning the Eclipse of the Moon. 2. The possibility of all things being fulfilled, as named in the Holy Scriptures, by this System according with Holy Writ   86

CHAPTER IX.

1. The Cause of the Tops of the Mountains being cold. 2. The Earth varying with the Stars. 3. The Firmament reflects the Sun's rays. 4. Five Points of both Systems opposing each other   90

ERRATUM.—Page 47, line 14, for Haggerter, read Flaggerter.

EXPLANATION OF THE PLATES.

Plate 1 represents part of the great universe, according to the Newtonian system; the stars as suns, with worlds revolving round them, as is *supposed*.

Plate 2 shows the sun as a fixed body in the centre of the system, with Mercury, Venus, and the Earth, with their various distances from each other; the other planets and stars in the distance.

Plate 3 shows the sun in the centre of the system: the Earth, Mars, and Jupiter, with their several distances from each other.— The Earth and Mars are put a little out of their proper place, for the purpose of explanation, in the same manner as *Plate 2*.

Plate 4 shows the impossibility of producing a perfect penumbra by one sun, even supposing the sun to be so much larger than the earth; and also that the short shadow of the moon could not eclipse the sun from the earth, even admitting that the shadow of the earth would terminate in a point according to the Newtonian system: it likewise shows the absolute necessity of two suns to produce a perfect penumbra, i.e. a shadow that is half light and half dark on each side of the shadow of the earth.

Plate 5 shows five positions for each of the polar stars, with the earth in four positions, and the sun in the centre-proving that, let the earth be placed in either of these four positions, and removed therefrom, it must deviate from any two given polar stars; and thus prove, beyond dispute, that the earth does not move from its situation, but keeps the polar stars continually at its poles, although the polar stars may appear to vary one or two degrees, by virtue of refraction, occasioned by winter and summer seasons.

Plate 6 is designed to show how it would be if the sun was a fixed body in the centre, and the earth revolving in its orbit round it—how the earth would vary with every fixed star on the equator, by degrees, throughout the whole of its orbit, and would not be in the same position with any one of those fixed stars two successive days throughout all the year, either in its diurnal or annual motion, but would be in one position with each star once in every year, and not oftener.

Plate 7 shows the earth in the centre, and the impossibility of the sun being more than about three diameters of our earth in distance from the earth, which would be about 24,000 miles, otherwise the sun would be seen in the distance far below the earth in the morning and in the evening, and we should see the sun for more than twelve hours on the equator out of the twenty-four hours; this will deduct from the:

Newtonian computation of of miles, the following number	95,000,000 94,976,000
Remainder	24,000

and will also show that should the sun be at that distance, we should then only have six hours darkness out of the twenty-four, as may be seen by the shadow of the earth.—The poles in the plate are placed east and west, for the purpose of showing the globe more perfectly.

Plate 8 shows three situations of the sun with the earth, and how the sun varies forty-seven degrees with the north and south polar stars, and the centre of our earth, in the height of summer and the depth of winter: also, the eclipse of the sun, by the moon passing between the earth and the sun, with the shadow of the moon thrown upon the earth, and the moon eclipsed by a planetary dark body passing between the moon and our earth, with its shadow thrown upon the earth: both the eclipses are shown on this plate to prove the similarity of effect; only the shadow of the moon from the sun is much the strongest, because it doth eclipse the greater light: it doth also point out the true form of the shadow of each eclipse as it really is, according to the principles of shadow expanding as it increases in distance.

Plate 9 shows that the six divisions of that part of the earth situate between the two tropic lines of Cancer and Capricorn, are the spaces which Enoch, the seventh from Adam, calleth six gates, wherein the sun goes forth in the visible heavens to shine upon the earth, and the sun going twice through each gate, makes twelve times (or twelve months), one whole year: the year originally commenced when the sun was on the equator, and then it traversed six months in the northern hemisphere and six months in the southern hemisphere; the year was then completed.

Plate 10 gives at one view the day and night scene of the sun, moon, and the stars shining upon the earth; and will at once strike the mind with the truth of those declarations of Moses, when he says in his declaration of the creation of the world (see Genesis), that "God made two great lights; the greater light to rule the day, and the lesser light to rule the night: he made the stars also. And God set them in the firmament to shine upon the earth." About one-half of the stars are to be seen, the others being hid from view by the light of the sun: the clouds are omitted, to show the luminaries more clearly.

Plate 11 will convey to the mind a grand view of a complete system according with the Holy Scriptures, showing the kingdom of the eternal God, infinite in length, breadth, and height, suitable to an infinite and glorious personal majesty, who is the source of truth and righteousness. Also, the eternal earth and waters, and the world which God created out of them, and which we now inhabit, with an atmosphere round it, and encompassed about with a firmament to divide it from those eternal earth and waters that are above the stars. And in this world the good and evil natures are mixed together in mankind, and will continue so until the last day, when God will separate them from each other for ever, as is declared in holy writ.

PREFATORY REMARKS.

GENEROUS READER,

I CONFESS myself an uneducated man, and, therefore, permit me to solicit your kindest indulgence accordingly. Allow me to say, the reason of my introducing this work is solely on the score of truth. I was taught to believe the Holy Scriptures to be the word of God, as delivered to the people by his Prophets and Apostles, who declare themselves commissioned of God so to do; and, on examination, I could not find one word,—from Enoch, Moses, and the Prophets in the First Testament; our Lord Jesus Christ and his Apostles in the New or Second Testament; and Reeve and Muggleton in the Third Testament;—that the earth revolved or went round the sun; but, always, that the sun rose and set upon the earth, &c.

When I had occasion to speak of my faith in the Holy Scriptures, I was invariably more opposed therein by those who had made astronomy their study, than I was by any others. I accordingly learned the science of astronomy in its great principles; and having completely satisfied myself on the subject, I feel inclined to place the two systems before the whole world, together with a little of my own experience, and leave them in the hands of the readers to judge for themselves as to which is the right or true system; for both cannot be correct, as the reader will readily perceive, when he shall understand the two lines of knowledge that have ran counter to each other from the earliest period; as, namely, the faith in the living Cod of Israel, and the heathen worship.

The Newtonian System is, confessedly, of heathen origin, as may be seen by its history; having passed through so many vicissitudes or changes and conflicting opinions.

It will appear that Ptolemy of Egypt, who was considered the prince of astronomers in his day, took a great liking to the most ancient system, of the earth being stationary, as acknowledged from the days of Enoch, the seventh from Adam, and he made his theory accordingly, partly of one system, and partly of the other: this was the cause why his system ultimately failed, although it had lasted for about eight hundred years. Ptolemy did this good, by his system of the earth being fixed, and the sun rising and setting upon it: he has proved the possibility of calculating all the rises and setting of the heavenly bodies, eclipses, &c., which he did for six hundred years in advance, as related in the history of astronomy (see "Smith" on astronomy); therefore that part of the science, so far as calculating the rising, setting, northing, and southing of the various heavenly lights, eclipses, &c., is good and acceptable with God, inasmuch as God hath set them in the firmament of heaven for that, purpose, and to be a benefit to his creation on this earth. But that part of the science which treats on the magnitude and vast distance of the sun, moon, and stars, and that the stars are suns having worlds revolving round them, as shown in Plate 1; so that the whole infinity of distance, in height, depth, length, and breadth; that is, the whole infinite space, is filled with sons, and worlds revolving round them. This portion of the scienceappears very unacceptable unto God, because it tends to abstract, or destroy that true faith and confidence which the people ought to have in his Prophets and Apostles, &c., and seems to be the chief cause of all the various opinions with regard to the sayings in the Holy Scriptures.

Having in this work given the Newtonian System, and the System according to the Holy Scriptures, I shall leave my readers to draw their own conclusions.

I remain your very humble and most obedient Servant,

ISAAC FROST.

PART I.

NEWTONIAN,

OR,

SOLAR SYSTEM OF ASTRONOMY.

NEWTONIAN,

OR,

SOLAR SYSTEM OF ASTRONOMY.

COURTEOUS READER,

I will place before you, for your consideration, two systems concerning the works of our Almighty God, so far as regards the visible firmamental heavens, and the celestial lights therein—sun, moon, and stars; also, the earth, which we now inhabit; and heaven, the throne or kingdom of God.

The first system which I shall introduce to your notice is that which is commonly known as the Newtonian or Solar System of Astronomy. Mark, and particularly observe, that this system takes its rise and progress from the reason and imagination of man.

The second system is that which is in accordance with the Holy Scriptures, and takes its rise and progress from those who declare themselves to be commissioned of God; that is, all the prophets and apostles, who have made known the wonderful works of the true God. The reader will then judge for himself which of the two systems is based upon truth.

The Newtonian System of Astronomy, which is almost universally acknowledged, represents the sun to be a globe of vast magnitude, nearly 900,000 miles in diameter (or through its centre, that is, from one side to the other); that it is fixed in one place, not moving from its situation, but simply turning round upon its own axis. This system also represents that there is a certain number of, what appears to us, stars—say 11 in number[1]—which are moveable, acid revolve in circles round the sun, which is called the centre of our system.

All other stars that we see are considered fixed stars, not moving from their situation; and it is supposed that they are as suns in the vast distance: it is also imagined that there are planetary bodies, like this our world, revolving round them as our world does round the sun, although, from the immense distance, it is impossible we can behold them—so that the whole infinity of space in height, depth, length, and breadth, is filled with these supposed suns, and various

---

[1] Including the earth, which is also considered a planet.

worlds revolving round them, as may be seen in Plate 1; and the darkness is only interspersed or become visible, where the rays of the various suns do not reach. Were it not for these suns to illuminate the infinite space, all would remain perfectly dark.

The planetary bodies appertaining to our own system, varying in their distance from the sun, are as thus:

Mercury is supposed to pass in its orbit, ring, or circle, at a distance from the sun of 37 millions of miles; is supposed to be 3224 miles in its diameter, and travels through the whole of its orbit; that is, it arrives in the same situation, after completing its circle, once in 87 days, 23 hours, 14 minutes, 33 seconds.

The next planet is that which is called Venus, a distance of 68 millions of miles from the sun, and consequently its circle or orbit is much larger than that of Mercury; its diameter is supposed to be 7687 miles; its revolution in its circle round the sun is completed in 224 days, 16 hours, 41 minutes, 27 seconds.

The next planet is supposed to be this earth, (with one moon or satellite,) the diameter of which is 7911 miles; its distance from the sun is 95,000,000 miles; its revolution, or completion of its circle, is 365 days, 5 hours, 48 minutes, 49 seconds, as may be seen in Plate 2.

The next planet is Mars, which is distant from the sun 144 millions of miles, and which requires nearly 687 days to complete its annual revolution; its diameter is about 4189 miles.

The next is Vesta; it is about 238 miles in diameter, and is distant from the sun 215 millions of miles; it performs its revolutions round the sun in 1335 days.

The next is Juno; its diameter is 1425 miles; it is distant from the sun 243 millions of miles, and performs its revolutions round the sun in 1590 days.

The next is Ceres Ferdinandea; its diameter is only 163 miles; its distance from the sun 263 millions of miles; its revolution, as calculated by Laplace, is performed in 1681 days, 17 hours, 57 seconds.

The next is Pallas; its diameter is only 80 miles; its distance from the sun is nearly 264 millions of miles; its revolution in its sidereal year is 1681 days, 17 hours, and 57 seconds.

The next is Jupiter; its diameter is 89,170 miles; its revolution round the sun is once in 4330 days, 14 hours, 39 minutes, and 2 seconds; its distance from the sun is 490 millions of miles.

The next is Saturn, the diameter of which is 79,042 miles; its revolution round the sun is performed in 10,746 days, 19 hours, 16 minutes, 15 seconds; its distance from the sun is 900 millions of miles.

The next is Herschel, or, Georgium Sidus, whose diameter is 35,112 miles; its annual revolution 30,637 days, 4 hours (being about 84 of our years); its distance from the sun is 1800 millions of miles.

The following are a few of the historical remarks of "Smith," in his account of the rise and progress of astronomical knowledge, which will show how men have laboured to discover the works of the Almighty God, by the power of their own reason, and not by faith in commissioned men, sent of God:

"It appears that astronomy was much cultivated among the Chaldeans. From Chaldea astronomy passed into Egypt, acid was soon afterwards carried into Phoenicia.

"Thales, the Milesian, who flourished about 700 years before the Christian era, brought the science of the stars from Phoenicia into Greece, where he taught the theory of the motion of the sun and moon, by which he accounted for the length and shortness of the days, and determined the number of the days, of the solar year, &c.

"To Anaximander, one of the disciples of Whales, is ascribed the invention of the terrestrial globe.

"To Pythagoras, another disciple of Thales, is attributed the discovery of the system which, after the lapse of many centuries, was revived by Copernicus.

"Pythias taught the method of distinguishing climates by the length of days and nights, &c.

"Eudoxus, a disciple of Plato, not satisfied with what he could learn at Athens, repaired to Egypt to cultivate astronomy at its source [1]. On his return, he compiled several books on astronomy, and, among others, a description of the constellations. He also attempted to explain the celebrated circle of 19 years, which had been imagined by Meton, in order to conciliate the solar and lunar motions.

"Aristotle, a disciple of Plato, and the contemporary of Eudoxus, made use of astronomy for improving physics and geography.

"It appears that in the school of Alexandria the stars first began to be minutely determined, the course of the planets to be traced with care, and the inequalities of the solar acid lunar motions to be better known.

"Hipparchus of Bithynia, who flourished at Alexandria about the year 162 before Christ, is particularly famous for the excellence of his observations; and he determined the length of the tropical year with a

---

[1] Here there appears a contradiction, as Chaldea was first said to be the source, and from thence to Egypt.

precision never attained before.

"Ptolemy, an Egyptian, who has always been considered the prince of astronomers among the ancients, flourished in the second century of the Christian era. He has preserved and transmitted to us the observations and principal discoveries of the ancients, much enriched and enlarged by his own labours, in a treatise called "The Great Syntaxis," in which he gave the theory and tables of the motion of the sun and moon, the planets and the fixed stars. He adopted the most ancient system, which supposed the, earth to be in the centre of the universe; and this system, to distinguish it from others, has been called the Ptolemaic System. The (considered) defects of his system did not, however, prevent him from calculating all the eclipses that were to happen for six hundred years to come.

"About the year 826, Ptolemy's great work was translated by the Arabians into their language, in which it was called the Almagist.

"About the year 1230, it was translated from the Arabic into Latin, under the auspices of the emperor Frederic the Second, who was willing that the Christians should understand astronomy as well as those whom they styled Barbarians. Alphonso, king of Castile, went further, for he assembled the most able astronomers from all parts, who composed new tables, called after him the Alphonsine tables.

"Nicholas Copernicus, a native of Thorn, in Prussia, born 1472, revived the ancient Pythagorean system, which had been set aside since the time of Ptolemy; and the only opposition of any consequence which the theory of Copernicus ever met with from science and argument, proceeded from Tycho Brahe, a celebrated Danish astronomer, who attempted to set up against it a theory of his own. His system is not very different from the Ptolemaic, but is generally called by his name: he supposed the earth to be immoveable in the centre of the universe, and the sun to revolve about it every twenty-four hours: the planets, he thought, went round the sun in their periodical time, &c.

"Kepler was one of the pupils of Tycho Brahe, and a man of a truly original and admirable genius.

"Hipparclius, Ptolemy, Tycho Brahe, and even Copernicus himself, were indebted for a great part of their knowledge to the Egyptians, Chaldeans, and Indians.

"Galileo was contemporary with Kepler, and while the latter was tracing the orbits of the planets, and settling the laws of their motions, he was investigating the doctrine of motion in general, which had been neglected for two thousand years; and from the result of their united labours Newton and Huygens were afterwards enabled to establish the most complete theories of all the planetary motions.

"From the time of Newton, who carried the theoretical part of the science to perfection[1], astronomy has never been without an illustrious phalanx of supporters."

A gentleman once said he would convince me of the error of my (what he termed) foolish notions; in about ten minutes, and for this purpose, he introduced "Bonnycastle on Astronomy." Opening the book, he showed me the following passage, and requested me to read it, and say what I thought of it:-

"The celebrated Huygens carried his thoughts so far upon this subject, as to believe that there might be stars at such an inconceivable distance from our earth, that their light, though it is known to travel at the rate of ten millions of miles in a minute, has not yet reached us, since the creation of the world."

When I had read the aforesaid, I asked him if it had ever crossed his mind to think how many of the other stars' light the light of such stars would interfere with in their progress to our earth, seeing their light expands as they travel: when he closed the book, saying that such an idea had never entered his mind before.

Astronomers say this our earth receives no light from any of the stars, because of the vast distance they are from the earth, and that

---

[1] I was once invited to hear read over "Guthrie on Astronomy," and when the reading was concluded, I was asked my opinion thereon; when I said, "Doctor, it appears to me that Sir Isaac Newton has only given two proofs in support of his theory of the earth revolving round the sun: all the rest is assertion without any proofs." "What are they?" inquired the doctor." "Well," I said, "they are first the power of attraction, to keep the earth to the sun; the second is the power of repulsion, by virtue of the centrifugal motion of the earth: all the rest appears to be assertion without proof." The doctor considered a short time, and then said, "It certainly did appear so." I said, "Sir Isaac has certainly obtained the credit of completing the system; but really he has only half done his work." "How is that?" inquired my friend the doctor. My reply was this: "You will observe his system shows the earth traverses round the sun on an inclined plane; the consequence is, there are FOUR powers required to make his system complete:

1st.	The power of ATTRACTION.
2ndly.	The power Of REPULSION.
3rdly.	The power of ASCENDING the inclined plane.
4thly.	The power of DESCENDING the inclined plane.

You will thus easily see the FOUR powers required, and Newton has only accounted for Two: the work is therefore only half done." Upon due reflection the doctor said, "It certainly was necessary to have these FOUR points cleared up before the system could be said to be complete."

they are suns, whose rays terminate at about nineteen hundred millions of miles from our earth, which is their nearest distance, so that the light of the stars can never reach us. For the truth of this I will only suggest to the reader the propriety of going into the open air on a beautiful starlight night, when the sun and moon are both absent from us, and then let him judge for himself whether he can see any better for the stars shining or not: on the contrary, it is usual for us to say (when there are not many stars) how very dark it is.

"Some of the comets make excursions of ten thousand millions of miles beyond the orbit of Saturn; and yet at that amazing distance they are incomparably nearer to the sun than to any of the fixed stars, as is evident from their keeping clear of the stars, and returning periodically by virtue of the sun's attraction. Since the fixed stars, therefore, are prodigious spheres of fire, like our sun, and at inconceivable distances from each other as well as from us, it is reasonable to conclude that they are made for the same purposes with the sun; to bestow light, heat, and vegetation on a certain number of planets and satellites revolving round them[1]."

Compare this statement with others, and then say, ten thousand millions; pray how much is that, with regard to the attractive power of the sun? Then, again, incomparably nearer to the sun than to any of the fixed stars; what can we make of this? Consider these two points well, and then ask, at what distance does the attractive power of the sun terminate from itself? Again, is the power of the attraction of the sun as great in the distance as it is near at hand? If not, how will it be when the comet is attracted and brought so near to the sun? By what power is the comet taken again to such a great distance from the sill, and from its attractive grasp?

---

[1] See "Bonnycastle."

CHAPTER II.

THE VARIED DISTANCES OF THE PLANETARY BODIES, AND THEIR APPARENT SIZES.

BEFORE we can place implicit reliance on the Newtonian system, it is highly necessary to consider the following various points:—First, the numerous and contradictory statements and calculations made by those who have been engaged in that science from its earliest period. It is calculated that the distance of the heavenly bodies from our earth is the cause of their appearing so small to us. It is therefore necessary to examine this portion of the science, to see how far it can be borne out by the above system. Respecting the varied distances of the planetary bodies from this earth, it will be seen that when the sun is between this our earth and the planet Mercury, the distance of Mercury from the earth would be about 132 millions of miles; and when Mercury is between the sun and our earth, the distance of Mercury from our earth would be about 58 millions of miles, making a variation in its distance from this earth of 74 millions of miles, with all its intermediate variations: also the planet Venus, when the sun is between our earth and Venus, would be distant from the earth 163 millions of miles; and when Venus is between our earth and the sun, its distance would be only 27 millions, making a variation of 136 millions of miles; also with all its intermediate variations. Now it will again be highly requisite to show how it is, if distance is the cause, why it appears so small; that by removing of five-sixths of its distance from our earth, we do not then see five-sixths more parts of its natural size, according to the laws of perspective. See Plate 2.

A gentleman once made an observation at one of my lectures, that the laws of perspective did not extend beyond our atmosphere, which he said was calculated at about 45 miles distance from the surface of the earth, beyond which, in the empty space, the laws of perspective had no effect, and beyond which the heavenly bodies did not alter in their apparent size. I asked him if he thought that if the sun was brought to the distance of 45 miles from this earth, whether it would not appear larger than it now does; when he directly gave up the point, and acknowledged his error. Another gentleman made an observation to this effect, that the planets Mercury and Venus, being in the inner orbits, were so much buried in the sun's rays, that we had not a fair opportunity of judging of their real or apparent size, in consequence of the sun's rays having an effect on our vision or sight; when I drew his attention to Mars, whose greatest distance from the earth would be 239 millions of miles; that is, when the sun is between Mars and our earth, and when the earth is between the sun and Mars, the distance would be only 49 millions, making a variation in its distance from the earth of 190 millions of miles; and when we were turned from the sun, we should have a perfect view of Mars at its nearest distance, uninterrupted by the sun's rays. See Plate 3. I asked him how it was that it did not appear then, in comparative size, any larger when so near to us, than when removed so much further from us; when he, also, gave up the point, saying he had never heard such questions put before. And so on by the other planetary bodies, varying in their distances as above.

The reader will do well to compare the magnitudes and distances of Mars, poor little Pallas, and Jupiter, and see if there appears to us anything like what you would naturally expect, according to the laws of perspective, at their nearest and furthest distance from the earth.[1]

---

[1] See "The Panorama of Science and Art," by James Smith, from which I quote.

Two Systems of Astronomy

	Miles in diameter.	Nearest distance.	Furthest distance.
Mars ..	4,189	49,000,000	239,000,000
Pallas ..	80	169,000,000	359,000,000
Jupiter..	89.170	395,000,000	585,000,000

By this it will be seen that Jupiter, at the nearest distance, is little more than twice the distance from the earth that Pallas is; and at the greatest distance is not quite half as far again, and yet it is calculated to be 1114 times larger in its diameter than Pallas is: how different in their apparent size ought they to appear to us, if this calculation is a correct one!

```
Miles         Miles                                    Cubic or Solid
Diameter of   Diameter of      Superficial                Measure
Pallas.       Jupiter.            1114                   1,240,996
  80)           89,170            1114                     1114
(1114
                80
                ──                ────                   ─────────
                                  4456                   4,963,984
                90                1114                   1,240,996
                80                1114                   1,240,996
                ──                1114                   1,240,996
                117              ─────────
                 80              1,240,996
                ──                                       ─────────────
                370                                      1,382,469,544
                320                                      ─────────────
                ──
    Remainder    50
```

It will appear by the above calculation, that Jupiter, in its diameter (simply across its centre) is 1114 times larger than Pallas; in its superficial measure, 1,240,996 times larger; and in its solid measure, 1,382,469,544 times larger; and at no time is it three times the distance from us that Pallas is. The nearest distance is about one-half as far again as Pallas: compare the vast difference of their size, and the small difference in their distance, and then judge accordingly, and see if you can find such difference in their apparent size as you might be naturally led to expect.

As, also, Mars is but little more than one-half the distance from us that Pallas is, and 52 times larger in its diameter.

Miles Miles	Superficial	Cubic or Solid
Diameter of Diameter of	52	Measure
Pallas. Mars.	52	2704
80) 4189 (52	———	52
400	104	———
———	260	5408
189	———	13.520
160	2704	———
———		140,608
Remainder 29		

Compare these things, and then judge for yourself as to the truth of these calculations; and more especially, when Mars is at its nearest distance, which is only 49 millions of miles from the earth, and the nearest distance of Pallas would be 169 millions of miles; so that Pallas, in addition to being so very small, would be more than three times as far from us; and yet see how little difference there is in their apparent size. The greatest distance of Pallas from the earth would be (according to these calculations) 369 millions of miles when the sun is between our earth and Pallas.

See and compare how far distant you may observe a candle burning on a clear dark night, and then take a common marble the same size as the flame of the candle, and try how far distant you can perceive it on a clear day; then measure their several distances, and you will be able to form a better idea of the difference in the appearance of the celestial luminaries and terrestrial bodies.

CHAPTER III.

1. THE POSITIONS OF THE EARTH WITH THE SUN AND FIXED STARS. 2. THE EARTH BURIED IN THE IMMENSE RAYS OF THE SUN. 3. THE RAYS OF THE SUN GLIDING OFF THE SIDES OF THE EARTH.

I WILL now draw the attention of the reader to another point of consideration, namely, the sun is stated to be a fixed body, immoveable from its situation, simply revolving upon its own axis; and all the stars we behold from the earth, except the planetary bodies, are said to be fixed also, and immoveable from their situations, and that this, our earth, revolves round the sun once a year. Now, if such actually were to be the case, the effect produced would be this:

The earth, on the first of January, when turned to the sun, would be mid-day, and we should not see the fixed stars beyond or on the other side of the sun; and when we are turned from the sun, it would be midnight, and we should see the fixed stars on this side of the sun; then our earth would traverse its orbit for six months, and arrive at the opposite side of the sun, which would be on the first of July; when we should be turned to the sun, it would be mid-day, we should not then be able to see the fixed stars we saw on the first of January, six months before; and when we are turned from the sun, it would be midnight, we should then be looking in an opposite direction to what we were, and see other fixed stars which we could not see on the first of January previous.

Now, consider, is this the case? if it is not so, then this system cannot possibly be correct. Again, it will be extremely necessary that this next point should make a deep impression, and not be erased from the mind; that is to say, if the sun be as this system states, nearly 900,000 miles in diameter, and whose rays of light and heat make but one vast volume of light, extending in every direction from the sun itself, to the distance of 2,000,000,000 of miles; and that our small speck of earth, in comparison of size to so great a body of fire as to gain our summer heat, and buried in such a volume of light, whether we should not be so encompassed by such immense rays of light as to preclude us from perceiving any darkness on the surface of our globe; for, be assured of this, it is a principle in nature, that any small object or mass before a fire so considerably larger than itself, would be heated thoroughly; and, on the contrary, if you place a large mass or globe before a fire that is proportionably small, it will be heated in part or portion, and the remaining part will be proportionably cold: as, for instance, place a small piece of meat before a fire much larger than itself, it will be completely warmed through; but, on the contrary, if you place a large piece of meat before a small fire, it would be only partly cooked, while the remainder would be perfectly raw; this principle will show that the sun cannot be so large as it is said to be.

I once asked a gentleman, a professor of the science of astronomy, how it was, that the earth being so much in the sun's rays, our poles remained so very cold, when, at the same time, it was so intolerably hot at the equator: his reply was, that the centre of the earth, or the equator, was full towards the sun, and interrupted or stayed the rays of it, which falling upon it, could not pass, but lodged there; but the rays of the sun falling upon the poles, glide off without effect, in consequence of the global form of the earth; so that the rays of the sun could not possibly remain oil them, was the cause of the poles remaining quite cold; because the rays of the sun could make no lodgment upon the sides of the earth: when I said, if it be a principle for the sun's rays to glide off the sides of a globe without effect, would not the same principle be applicable to the moon, which is also considered to be a globe; that the rays of the sun would glide off the sides of the moon also, without effect; and, consequently, we should have very weak, or no bright horns, to the phase of our moon; when he replied, that he had not given that a thought.

I once had a conversation with a gentleman on this subject, when he said, although the rays of the sun might glide off the plain surface of the sides of the moon, in all probability the atmosphere which surrounds the moon may hold the rays of the sun, and thus be the cause of our seeing the bright horns; I then said, if we admit that to be the cause, we know that the sun's rays will penetrate into the atmosphere far beyond the centre of the moon, and the consequence would be, that we should have more than half a moon; he replied, that most certainly would be the case, and gave up the point.

It is also very important to consider the next point following:-

It is calculated, according to the solar system, that the size of the moon is about 64 times smaller than the earth; if such be a correct calculation, it would be requisite to see how that will stand in regard to the earth and the moon eclipsing each other from the sun.

It is also calculated, that, in consequence of the sun being so much larger than the earth, and that the rays of the sun concentrate to a point or apex, as may be seen in Plate 4, and that the moon passes in its orbit round the earth, at such a distance from it as to pass immediately through the point of the shadow of the earth, which is said to be the cause of the eclipse of the moon; if such be the case, it would appear, in consequence of the earth being so much larger than the moon, its shadow must necessarily be much longer, and the shadow of the moon proportionably short, in comparison with the size of the earth; the result would be, that when the moon arrives in that part of her orbit, which is situated between the earth and the sun, its short shadow would terminate in a point at an immense distance from the earth; and, consequently, it would not be able, according to this principle, to eclipse the earth from the sun, and thus render this calculation impossible to be borne out in practice: here there appears to be a very great mistake, and contrary to natural philosophy.

The readiest mode to prove this point will be to place a lighted candle on the table, and take a small ball, say about the size of a pea; then go a distance from the candle, take a sheet of white paper and place the ball just against it, opposite to the candle, acid you will observe the shadow of the ball on the paper will be precisely the same size as the hail; then remove the ball from the paper towards the candle, and you will see the shadow become larger on the paper, thus showing, that although the light of the candle is much larger than the ball, yet the shadow will not terminate in a point, which will prove that, supposing the sun to be in the centre of our system, and (as said to be) so much larger than the earth is, yet its shadow would not terminate in a point.

It is a point or principle in nature, that the rays flowing from any one single light, flow from its centre and expand to fill the space in the greater distance; and that any thing opposed to or placed before it, whether large or small, its shadow will also expand in the greater distance, or increase in width. Upon this principle it is impossible that the shadow of the earth really can terminate in a point. It may be shown, by practical experiment, the impossibility of producing a perfect penumbra without having two suns, or lights, placed near unto each other in the distance, the rays of which flowing from each of their centres and crossing each other, will show a perfect penumbra; which cannot be done like it by the rays from one sun or light, although the light may be much larger than the object placed before it. See Plate 4.

CHAPTER IV.

1. THE IMPOSSIBILITY OF THE MOON BORROWING HER LIGHT FROM THE SUN, PHILOSOPHICALLY PROVED. 2. THE DIFFERENCES OF LIGHT AND DARK BODIES IN PERSPECTIVE.

AGAIN, it will be extremely requisite to consider this point. It is said that the moon borrowing its light from the sun, reflects its borrowed rays upon this earth, which is termed the moon's light.

It is necessary here to examine, in a philosophical manner, how this can be effected. In the first place, it is a principle in nature, that whatever is borrowed, must be repaid or reflected in the same quality, if not quantity, as thus: if we apply a reflector to the sun, it will reflect a warm heated ray of light suitable to the sun's rays; and if we apply a number of reflectors, and bring their reflected rays to one focus, it will absolutely set a thing on fire.

Now when we consider the two different qualities of the rays of light of, or from the sun and moon, the rays of the sun are heating, and the rays of the moon are cold and freezing, as may be seen by the following example:—When the snow lies on the ground, and the sun shines in its strength, you may easily perceive that where the sun's rays fall, the snow will be melted or thawed, and in the shadow it will remain perfectly unthawed; on the other hand, where the moon's rays fall, the water will freeze, and in the shadow it will remain unfrozen for some time; so that it will appear absolutely impossible that the moon's rays can be borrowed from the sun, seeing it is of so opposite a nature, one body being of a fiery and hot nature, while the other is of a watery and cold body or nature. Again, if the moon be a world like our own, it would not be unreasonable to think, that she would have quite enough to do to rule and govern her own waters, without having to rule the waters of this globe; for it is acknowledged that she does rule the waters of this earth, and the things appertaining to the night. Besides, the astronomers, arid also astrologers, when they think fit, can ascribe to the moon, the comets, and stars or planets, great influence on this earth or not, as best suits the times and seasons; but if we consider them created lights for the benefit of this world, then it would be their duty to attend to this globe only, and not to be considered as worlds in themselves.

By this philosophical rule it is clearly proved that Moses spoke the truth when he said that "God had made two great lights; the greater light to rule the day, and the lesser light to rule the night, and the stars to shine upon the earth;" neither is it right to suppose that God would commission a man like unto Moses to be the great commissioner of his law unto man, and not to furnish him with knowledge of his works, that he might declare them unto the people. There is also another point that is very interesting to know, and which ought to be especially remarked; that is, no opaque or dark body in a globular form (or ball) will reflect any borrowed light upon another globe in the distance, because of the innate principle of all globular bodies to extend their rays in every point of direction, and riot to any object in particular, as may be proved in the manner following: place a lighted candle in a dark room, and then take two balls of a dark (opaque) complexion, and pass them round each other, at a distance from the candle; you cannot then see any reflection of light cast from one globe upon the other, similar to our moonlight (as astronomers do assert that our earth acts as a moon to the supposed inhabitants of the moon, by giving back its borrowed rays from the sun to them, in the same manner as it is imagined the moon gives its light colour will cause a slight reflection, because its rays are directed to one object, which is not the case with any globular body; the reason for this is, there being a sympathy of nature between light and light, which is not the case with dark bodies and light, because of the opposition of their natures; darkness will always reject light as much as possible, as you will often perceive when professors lecture on astronomy, they use a white or light-coloured ball (such as chalk, &c.) to show the phases of the moon, (but never show any reflected rays therefrom upon another ball,) and then explain that the moon is not a light body, but a dark opaque body—thus showing the effect by one principle, and certifying the thing to be another, which, according to truth, ought not to be done; for it ought to be explained by the same principle as it is shown to be. There is also another thing that has been overlooked by those who have studied the science, of astronomy according to the Newtonian system; that is, light and dark bodies, in their appearance as to the laws of perspective, appear thus: light bodies do not diminish in their apparent size, in the distance, as dark bodies do; for instance, a simple lighted candle, in a clear dark night, may be observed many miles distant; whereas a dark body, of a much larger size, at the same distance, by day-light, or even a house, is scarcely so visible.

Thus those who have studied astronomy agreeably to this system have erred in their judgment, by making their calculation as to the distance of the heavenly bodies, or celestial lights, according to the principles that are applicable to terrestrial or opaque substances or bodies.

CHAPTER V.

1. RISING AND SETTING OF THE SUN, WITH THE DESCENDING LINE OF SIGHT. 2. REFRACTION SHOWN BY EXPERIMENTS WITH WATER. 3. HOW WATER, IN A GLOBAL FORM, MAGNIFIES OBJECTS.

THERE is another point to, which I claim your very particular attention; that is, with respect to the rising and setting of the sun. See Plate 7. It must be obvious to our understanding, that if a person stands on the globe at the equator, his line of sight descends to meet the sunrise, when it arrives on the right line, which passes through the centre of the earth, to meet the sun in its ascent in the morning at sunrise. Again, the line of sight must descend to see the sun, when it descends to the right line, at sunset in the evening, which must be the case, otherwise we should not be able to see the sun for twelve hours out of twenty-four hours when on the equator; so that it is quite clear that the line of sight on the equator takes a descending position; the question then will be, at what distance from the earth does the descending line of sight meet or cut through the right hue that passes through the centre of the earth, because the sun cannot possibly be further from the earth than that point, even without the power of refraction; and if the sun was any vast distance from the earth, it would be seen far below the earth itself in the morning, and also in the evening: consequently the sun would be seen much more than twelve hours by the person so standing on the top of the globe, and the greater the sun's distance from the earth, the further it would be seen in the distance below the earth itself; as, for instance, a man standing on a hill may not be able to see another man who is close under the brow of the hill; but when he is removed a little distance from the hill, he becomes visible to him that stands on the top, in consequence of his line of sight descending from the top to see him: this will show that the sun need not be very far distant from the earth, to be seen on the equator when it ascends half-way up the globe. The reader will do well to give very particular attention to the descending line of sight, and see at what distance it meets the right or straight line, that passes through the centre of the earth, and which will be seen by Plate 7, that it cannot possibly be more than about three diameters of the earth in its distance from the earth; so that the result will be, that the sun cannot be more than about 24,000 miles from the earth, supposing the earth to be 8000 miles in its diameter, which will cut off from the Newtonian computation (of 95,000,000 of miles) 94,976,000 miles, leaving only 24,000 miles, which the reader will easily perceive is no small variation to begin with. The power of refraction is not included in this view of the matter, but I will notice it next in order. I would not have the reader to think that I believe the

Two Systems of Astronomy   39

sun to be so far as 24,000 miles distant from the earth, or anything near it, for when we consider the following little experiment, it will tend to show that the sun may be very near to the earth, and yet be seen by refraction. Let the reader take a seat a short distance from a table, and let an empty shallow basin be placed upon it; then let a penny (or any other coin that will not float) be placed in the bottom of the basin: next let the reader elevate his sight into the basin, as near as possible, so as to escape seeing the coin at the bottom, and not moving his eye from that situation; let a second person pour the basin gently full of water, and the coin will be seen by degrees, and then perfectly. If it should be said that the coin is raised by pouring in the water, let, the water (for proof) be gently drawn from the basin by a small tube, with the mouth (or a syphon), when the coin will gradually disappear from the sight of the reader, who has not, during the time, changed his position in the least; thus showing that it has not been forced up into view by the pouring in of the water, but only rendered visible by the natural effects of the water.

Upon seeing this little experiment, shall any man say that the water on the surface of our globe will not have a similar effect on the sun at its rising and setting, and thus be seen, although the sun shall not be very far from the earth. Should this be the case, I would suggest that it might in all probability account for what is termed the sun's dip, when it arrives at the meridian, observed by navigators, which takes place precisely at twelve o'clock in the day, that being the crisis when it turns from the morning's ascent to the evening's descent; and as a further illustration, that the water will have an effect on our vision of the sun from our globe, we know by common experience that after a hot summer's day, in particular when the sun's rays have had a much greater influence on the earth, and warmed it a little more than usual, a larger quantity of mist will arise from the surface of the earth, through which the sun, as it sets in the evening, will appear to be magnified full three or four times larger than its usual size, but not so in the morning, because the mist condenses during the night. Here it may not be altogether amiss, or at least very unacceptable to the reader, to direct his attention to the following, which will tend to , show that water, when in a globular form, will have a different effect on our sight than when in a flat, level, or even surface: as, for instance, see a small fish as it swims in a glass globe of water, it appears much larger than it really is of itself; but if you remove it from the globe, and put it into a small pond of water, it will then appear much smaller than it really is. The aforesaid will show that it is not because the sun appears larger on one evening than on another, that it is much nearer to us: as also in our winter, when the sun is nearer the horizon, that is, the sun appears lower in the firmament, that the sun shall be any nearer to the earth on that account; if it were so, it would be observed by the inhabitants of the south; it is only because we see it through a larger quantity of damp vapour or mist that arises from the surface of our globe. Now if it should be objected, with regard to the fish in the globe, that the fish when in the furthest part of the globe from us, while we are looking at it, appears larger than when it is near to us: this will show that the fish is simply magnified by the water in the globe; but let the water be removed, and the fish will appear more in its natural size: so, by the same rule, is the sun when the mist is removed from the surface of the earth.

The following question is certainly very capable of being infallibly proved to our understanding; that is, whether the sun can, or cannot, be seen by a person when he shall be on the top of the globe, or at the equator, for precisely twelve hours, either at the end of March or the end of September, when the sun would be also on the equator? I have heard it stated on more than one occasion, by persons who have said they have been at the equator about that time of the year, and that the sun itself is only seen for rather less than twelve hours, but that the twilight in the morning and evening, when included, will make up all the difference, and that the twilight at that time is but of very short duration. I will not vouch for the truth of the above assertions, because I have not been there myself, which, if the above statements should prove to be correctly made, they most surely will tend to show more fully the correctness of the system according with the holy scriptures. Indeed the proving of this is so very simple in itself, that every individual who may visit that part of the globe at those times of the year, may see with his own eyes whether he can see the sun for twelve hours or not; and if only seen for twelve hours precisely, then it will prove the correctness of Plate 7, that the sun would be seen more than twelve hours, if it should be further from the earth than the distance marked thereon, where the descending line of sight meets the right line.

CHAPTER VI.

1. THE EARTH'S POSITION WITH THE SUN AND POLAR STARS; 2. SHOWING THE DEGREES OF ANGLES FOR WINTER AND SUMMER. 3. THE STARS CHANGING THEIR POSITION. 4. THE PHASES SEEN ON MERCURY, VENUS, &c. 5. THE STARS CONSIDERED SUNS, WITH WORLDS REVOLVING ROUND THEM, AND SUPPOSED TO BE PEOPLED LIKE THIS EARTH. 6. THE ERROR OF SUCH ABSURD IDEAS.

I WILL call your marked attention to another point of the utmost importance to be clearly comprehended. It is stated that the two polar stars are fixed stars, not moving from their situation; the same as the sun, not moving from his position; and that our earth is the only moving body (that is to say, moving from its situation) out of the four; as, namely, the sun, the two fixed polar stars, and our earth. It would be highly advisable to understand, with mathematical precision, how it is that our earth shall vary 47 degrees in its position with the sun, and not vary 47 degrees from the two polar stars likewise, they being also fixed bodies, as the sun is stated to be: see Plate 5, amid explanation of Plates: also, why not all the fixed stars within the two tropic lines appear to vary as far north and south to us as the sun doth, if they are equally fixed as our sun is said to be?

You will observe that when the sun arrives on the tropical line of Cancer, that it then forms an acute angle of 66½ degrees with the north polar star and the centre of our earth, as may be seen in Plate 8; and then our days are 16 hours, acid our nights 8 hours, making the day twice as long as the night, in the northern hemisphere, at about 50 degrees from the equator; and when the sun retires southward, and arrives at the equinoctial line, then the sun forms right angles with the north and south polar stars; that is to say, it forms an angle of 90 degrees with each star; then our days and nights are equal, being 12 hours each; the sun then extends his rays equal—north, south, east, and west; and continues to retire southwards, always rising in the east and setting in the west, until it arrives on the tropical line of Capricorn; then the sun forms an obtuse angle of 113½ degrees with the north polar star and the centre of our earth, and at the same time an acute angle of 66½ degrees with the south polar star and the centre of our earth, as near as may be; then our day, that is, in our northern hemisphere in England, is about 8 hours, and our night 16 hours, making our night twice as long as our day; whilst in the southern hemisphere, where they are the same number of degrees from the equator as ourselves, their days would be 16 hours, and their nights 8 hours, forming their summer and our winter; and so alternately reversed, once in every year, winter and summer: see Plate 8. I have asked this question of many, but it is a question that has always been given up, as unanswerable according to the Newtonian system, because all the number of degrees upon the circle must be accounted for; and if we turn a certain number of degrees from any object near at hand, we at the same time, turn the same number of degrees from any other object, let the distance be ever so great; as, for instance, if we turn our face from any person standing close before us, we at the same time, by the same rule, turn as many degrees from any other object that is much further off; so that it is (as will appear) utterly impossible that we can vary 47 degrees from the sun, without also varying 47 degrees from the polar stars, which certainly cannot be the case, supposing them to be fixed bodies, and the earth the only one in motion: but if we reverse the system, and allow the earth to be a fixed body, not moving from its situation, and the two polar stars fixed, not moving from their situation, and allow the sun to be a moving body, revolving over and under the earth, advancing into the northern hemisphere to give us our summer, and then retiring into the southern hemisphere, thereby leaving us our winter season, and so giving them their summer in the southern hemisphere—then all can be fulfilled, and the Scriptures be proved true; see Plates 8 and 9; and those stars nearer the polar stars, moving in small circles round the polar stars, and so on, increasing in the size of their circles, according to the distance they are from the polar stars, until they arrive at the equator; that is to say, those stars that are on the equator make the larger or largest circle round the earth, than those stars do that are near the polar stars, and the polar stars may appear to vary one or two degrees, by virtue of refraction, during the winter and the summer, occasioned by the wet and dry seasons: also the other stars differ in their speed, some quicker and some slower than others in their motion, which is the cause why one rises and sets earlier or later than another, and so alternately changing their position to our view, and some stars may even shoot from one part of the heavens to another in an instant.

I have been asked, on several occasions, that if I deny the moon being a dark body, and say it does not borrow its light from the sun, how I could account for the phases that are observed by a telescopic view on Mercury, Venus, &c. My reply was, that they being lights in themselves, although of a very humble character compared with the sun, the sun's vast rays being so superior to the light of the stars, will cause that side of the star which is from the sun to appear much darker than what it would if left to shine in its own light, as must be admitted when viewed through a telescope, (and this might cause persons to suppose that it borrowed its light from the sun,) as may be proved in the following manner: if you take a red-hot ball into a dark room, it will partially illuminate that room; if you then introduce another ball heated in a much greater degree — say at what a blacksmith terms a welding heat — and place them in contact with each other, the rays of light, flowing from the highly heated ball, will shine upon the lesser light, and cause that side which is turned from the heated ball to appear much darker than it did before the introduction of the highly heated ball; then remove the highly heated ball from the room, and the lesser light will appear more visible; so that it will appear by this rule, that the further the stars are from the sun, the brighter they appear in their awn light. On the contrary, if they borrowed their light from the sun, then the nearer they were to the sun, the brighter they would appear: as, for instance, if you take a dark or opaque ball, and hold it at a distance from a lighted candle, it would appear very dim, and be scarcely seen in the distance; but the nearer you advance it toward the light, the more plainly you perceive it, which would be the same case with the stars, or planets, were they to borrow their light from the sun, instead of which they appear brighter in the distance: this clearly shows that they are not dark bodies, borrowing their light from the sun, but are distinct lights in themselves: thus it is only in the absence of the sun that the stars can be seen by the naked eye. As a further proof that the lesser light may be eclipsed by the greater, place a lighted candle in the sun's rays, and its light will be scarcely (if at all) visible; but when the sun's rays depart, you can then see the candle burning in all the brilliancy of its own natural light. The parties asking these questions have, upon due consideration, thought what I have here stated to be highly probable, and they, could not gainsay it.

I will now conclude this first System, and my brief remarks thereon. Much more might be said than what I have here written, and many more points and proofs might be urged equally true; but I think I have written sufficient to call the attention of those who willingly search into the merits of the Newtonian System. If necessary, I will say more on a future occasion.

As regards the calculations on the rising and setting of the heavenly luminaries, eclipses, &c., they are right, and perfectly justified of God, inasmuch as God hath designed these changes for the benefit of his creation on this earth; that men may use them for a guide, in navigating their vessels from shore to shore, for the benefit of commerce, &c.; even to the ends of the earth, that is to say, all parts of the globe.

But herein lies the error, which amounts to a wickedness, and cannot be acceptable unto God, and that is the imaginative branch, which is introduced into this science; such as imagining that the planets are worlds, and the whole infinite space is an innumerable mass of worlds, revolving round suns, and those worlds peopled like unto this globe, which is nothing more than imagination, and which leads the people to forsake the revealed word of the true God, and his prophets and apostles, commissioned of God to declare his mind unto the people, and teaching them to say that "the prophets and apostles lived in the dark ages, and consequently they did not understand the works of God concerning the celestial bodies; that therefore they only wrote those things with a view of pleasing the people," &c., &c.

It also is the root or cause of so much division of opinion concerning the holy Scriptures.

I have been asked the question, what could induce me ever to interfere with the Newtonian System of Astronomy? My reply was, that I firmly believed the holy Scriptures were written by divine inspiration from God, through the medium of his prophets and apostles, and therefore to be the word of God, and which taught a different line of knowledge to that which the professors of astronomy teach. The holy Scriptures are taught from the pulpit to be the word of God, and that it is the duty of the people to believe them as such, if they wish to obtain eternal life: also it is taught to be death eternal to those who despise God's holy truth, as it is spoken in the Scriptures: while at the same time there are some who teach this, and yet they became professors of the science of astronomy, and have taught that science, which amounted to a contradiction of the Scriptures, inasmuch as it led men to doubt whether the prophets and apostles really understood the works of God, although we know by faith they were commissioned to declare it. This contradiction in practice became a matter of surprise to me, how men could assert such opposite principles, that I determined to go into the merits of astronomy, to see wherein it so materially differed from what my faith in the Scriptures really was, concerning the wonderful works of the Almighty God, as I had always found myself opposed in my faith in the Scriptures by those who studied astronomy.

But having now thoroughly satisfied myself that the knowledge of Enoch, Moses, &c., is true, and ought to be believed, I shall next proceed to show the System according unto their testimony, which is recorded for the benefit of mankind—at least to those who receive it.

END OF THE FIRST, OR NEWTONIAN, SYSTEM.

PART II.

THE SYSTEM OF ASTRONOMY
IN ACCORDANCE WITH THE
HOLY SCRIPTURES.

… Academic Literary and Scientific Interest

THE SYSTEM OF ASTRONOMY

IN ACCORDANCE WITH THE

HOLY SCRIPTURES.

CHAPTER I.

1. THE ONE UNVARIED LINE OF KNOWLEDGE AS TO THE RISING AND SETTING OF THE SUN, FROM FIRST TO LAST. 2. ENOCH'S DECLARATION THAT THE SUN, MOON, AND STARS RISE AND SET UPON THE EARTH, IN FOUR CHAPTERS, TAKEN FROM HIS BOOK.

IN the first place I shall invite the attention of the reader to the one unbroken line of knowledge, or evidence, from Enoch, (who was the seventh from Adam,) Moses, Joshua, and all the rest of the Prophets under the law of Moses, in the First Testament or Bible; our Lord Jesus Christ, and the Apostles, in the New or Second Testament; also Reeve and Muggleton, in the Third and last Testament from the Holy Spirit, to prove that the sun rises and sets upon the earth, and that there is a heaven (the residence of God) above the stars, but not one single word that the earth rises and sets upon the sun, or revolves round it. I will commence with the testimony of Enoch, whose words are as follow:-

LXXI. [SECT. XIII.][1]

1. The book of the revolutions of the luminaries of heaven, according to their respective classes, their respective powers, their respective periods, their respective names, the places where they commence their progress, and their respective months, which Uriel, the holy angel who was with me, explained to me; he who conducts them. The whole account of them, according to every year of the world for ever, until a new work shall be effected, which will be eternal.

---

[1] See the Book of Enoch the Prophet, translated by Richard Laurence, LL.D., Archbishop of Cashel; printed at Oxford by J. H. Parker; and published by J., G., and F. Rivington, London, 1833.

2. This is the first law of the luminaries. The sun and the light arrive at the gates of heaven, which are on the east, and on the west of it at the western gates of heaven.

3. I beheld the gates whence the sun goes forth; and the gates where the sun sets;

4. In which gates also the moon rises and sets; and I beheld the conductors of the stars, among those who precede them; six gates were at the rising, and six at the setting of the sun.

5. All these respectively, one after another, are on a level; and numerous windows are on the right and on the left sides of those gates.

6. First proceeds forth that great luminary, which is called the sun; the orb of which is as the orb of heaven, the whole of it being replete with splendid and flaming fire.

7. Its chariot, where it ascends, the wind blows.

8. The sun sets in heaven, and, returning by the north, to proceed towards the east, is conducted so as to enter by that gate, and illuminate the face of heaven.

9. In the same manner it goes forth in the first month by a great gate.

10. It goes forth through the fourth of those six gates, which are at the rising of the sun.

11. And in the fourth gate, through which the sun with the moon proceeds, in the first part of it, there are twelve open windows; from which issues out a flame, when they are opened at their proper periods.

12. When the sun rises in heaven, it goes forth through this fourth gate thirty days, and by the fourth gate in the west of heaven on a level with it descends.

13. During that period the clay is lengthened from the day, and the night curtailed from the night for thirty days. And then the day is longer by two parts than the night.

14. The day is precisely ten parts, and the night is eight.

15. The sun goes forth through this fourth gate, and sets in it, and turns to the fifth gate during thirty days; after, which it proceeds from, and sets in, the fifth gate.

16. Then the day becomes lengthened by a second portion, so that it is eleven parts; while the night becomes shortened, and is only seven parts.

17. The sun now returns to the east, entering into the sixth gate, and rising and setting in the sixth gate thirty-one days, on account of its signs.

18. At that period the day is longer than the night, being twice as long as the night; and becomes twelve parts;

19. But the night is shortened, and becomes six parts. Then the sun rises up, that the day may be shortened, and the night lengthened.

20. And the sun returns towards the east, entering into the sixth gate, where it rises and sets for thirty days.

21. When that period is completed, the day becomes shortened precisely one part, so that it is eleven parts, while the night is seven parts.

22. Then the sun goes from the west, from that sixth gate, and proceeds eastwards, rising in the fifth gate for thirty days, and setting again westwards in the fifth gate of the west.

23. At that period the day becomes shortened two parts; and is ten parts, while the night is eight parts.

24. Then the sun goes from the fifth gate, as it sets in the fifth gate of the west; and rises in the fourth gate for thirty-one days, on account of its signs, setting in the west.

25. At that period the day is made equal with the night; and, being equal with it, the night becomes nine parts, and the day nine parts.

26. Then the sun goes from that gate, as it sets in the west; and returning to the east proceeds by the third gate for thirty days, setting in the west at the third gate.

27. At that period the night is lengthened from the day during thirty mornings, and the day is curtailed from the day during thirty days; the night being ten parts precisely, and the day eight parts.

Two Systems of Astronomy

28. The sun now goes from the third gate, as it sets in the third gate in the west; but returning to the east, it proceeds by the second gate of the east for thirty days.

29. In like manner also it sets in the second gate in the west of heaven.

30. At that period the night is eleven parts, and the day seven parts.

31. Then the sun goes at that time from the second gate, as it sets in the second gate in the west; but returns to the east, proceeding by the first gate, for thirty-one days.

32. And sets in the west in the first gate.

33. At that period the night is lengthened as much again as the day.

34. It is twelve parts precisely, while the day is six parts.

35. The sun has thus completed its beginnings, and a second time goes round from these beginnings.

36. Into that gate it enters for thirty days, and sets in the west, in the opposite part of heaven.

37. At that period the night is contracted in its length a fourth part, that is, one portion, and becomes eleven parts.

38. The day is seven parts.

39. Then the sun returns, and enters into the second gate of the east.

40. It returns by these beginnings thirty days, rising and setting.

41. At that period the night is contracted in its length. It becomes ten parts, and the day eight parts. Then the sun goes from that second gate, and sets in the west; but returns to the east, and rises in the east, in the third gate, thirty-one days, setting in the west of heaven.

42. At that period the night becomes shortened. It is nine parts. And the night is equal with the day. The year is precisely three hundred and sixty-four days.

43. The lengthening of the day and night, and the contraction of the day and night, are made to differ from each other by the progress of the sun.

44. By means of this progress the day is daily lengthened, and the night nightly shortened.

45. This is the law and progress of the sun, and its turning when it turns back, turning during sixty days, and going forth. This is the great everlasting luminary, that which He names the sun for ever and ever.

46. This also is that which goes forth a great luminary, and which is named after its peculiar kind, as God commanded.

47. And thus it goes in and out, neither slackening nor resting; but running on in its chariot by day and by night. It shines with a seventh portion of light from the moon; but the dimensions of both are equal.

LXXII. [Sect. XIV.]

1. After this law I beheld another law of an inferior luminary, the name of which is the moon, and the orb of which is as the orb of heaven.

2. Its chariot, which it secretly ascends, the wind blows; and light is given to it by measure.

3. Every month at its exit and entrance it becomes changed; and its periods are as the periods of the sun. And when in like manner its light is to exist, its light is a seventh portion from the light of the sun.

4. Thus it rises, and at its commencement towards the east goes forth for thirty days.

5. At that time it appears, and becomes to you the beginning of the month. Thirty days it is with the sun in the gate from which the sun goes forth.

6. Half of it is in extent seven portions, one half; and the whole of its orb is void of light, except a seventh portion out of the fourteen portions of its light. And in a day it receives a seventh portion, or half that portion, of its light. Its light is by sevens, by one portion, and by the half of a portion. It sets with the sun.

Two Systems of Astronomy

7. And when the sun rises, the moon rises with it; receiving a half portion of light.

8. On that night, when it commences its period, previously to the day of the month, the moon sets with the sun.

9. And on that night it is dark in its fourteen portions, that each half; but it rises on that day with one seventh portion precisely, aid in its progress declines from the rising of the sun.

10. During the remainder of its period its light increases to fourteen portions.

LXXIII.

1. Then I saw another progress and regulation which He effected in the law of the moon. The progress of the moons, and every thing relating to them, Uriel showed me, the holy angel who conducted them all.

2. Their stations I wrote down as he showed them to me.

3. I wrote down their months, as they occur, and the appearance of their light, until it is completed in fifteen days.

4. In each of its two seven portions it completes all its light at rising and at setting.

5. On stated months it changes its settings; and on stated months it makes its progress through each gate. In two gates the moon sets with the sun, viz, in those two gates which are in the midst, in the third and fourth gate. From the third gate it goes forth for seven days, and makes its circuit.

6. Again it returns to the gate whence the sun goes forth, and in that completes the whole of its light. Then it declines from the sun, and enters in eight days into the sixth gate, and returns in seven days to the third gate, from which the sun goes forth.

7. When the sun proceeds from the fourth gate, the moon goes forth for seven days, until it passes from the fifth gate.

8. Again it returns in seven days to the fourth gate, and completing all its light, declines, and passes on by the first gate in eight days;

9. And returns in seven days to the fourth gate, from which the sun goes forth.

10. Thus I beheld their stations, as according to the fixed order of the months the sun rises and sets.

11. At those times there is an excess of thirty days belonging to the sun in five years; all the days belonging to each year of the five years, when completed, amount to three hundred and sixty-four days; and to the sun and stars belong six days; six days in each of the five years; thus thirty days belong to them;

12. So that the moon has thirty days less than the sun and stars.

13. The moon brings on all the years exactly, that their stations may come neither too forwards nor too backwards a single day; but that the years may be changed with correct precision in three hundred and sixty-four days. In three years the days are one thousand and ninety-two; in five years they are one thousand eight hundred and twenty; and in eight years two thousand nine hundred and twelve days.

14. To the moon alone belong in three years one thousand and sixty-two days; in five years it has fifty days less than the sun, for an addition being made to the one thousand and sixty-two days, in five years there are one thousand seven hundred and seventy days; and the days of the moon in eight years are two thousand eight hundred and thirty-two days.

15. For its days in eight years are less than those of the sun by eighty days, which eighty days are its diminution in eight years.

16. The year then becomes truly complete according to the station of the moons, and the station of the sun; which rise in the different gates; which rise and set in them for thirty days.

LXXIV.

1. These are the leaders of the chiefs of the thousands, those which preside over all creation, and over all the stars; with the four days which are added and never separated from the place allotted them, according to the complete computation of the year,

2. And these serve four days, which are not computed in the computation of the year.

3. Respecting them, men greatly err; for these luminaries truly serve, in the mansion of the world, one day in the first gate, one in the third gate, one in the fourth, and one in the sixth gate.

4. And the harmony of the world becomes complete every three hundred and sixty-fourth state of it. For the signs,

5. The seasons,

6. The years,

7. And the days, Uriel showed me; the angel whom the Lord of glory appointed over all the luminaries

8. Of heaven in heaven, and in the world; that they might rule in the face of the sky, and, appearing over the earth, become

9. Conductors of the days and nights; the sun, the moon, the stars, and all the ministers of heaven, which make their circuit with all the chariots of heaven.

10. Thus Uriel: showed me twelve gates open for the circuit of the chariots of the sun in heaven, from which the rays of the sun shoot forth.

11. From these proceed heat over the earth, when they are opened in their stated seasons. They are for the winds, and the spirit of the dew, when in their seasons they are opened; opened in heaven at its extremities.

12. Twelve gates I beheld in heaven, at the extremities of the earth, through which the sun, moon, and stars, and all the works of heaven, proceed at their rising and setting.

13. Many windows also are open on the right and on the left.

14. One window at a certain season grows extremely hot. So also are there gates from which the stars go forth as they are commanded, and in which they set according to their number.

15. I saw likewise the chariots of heaven, running in the world above to those gates in which the stars turn, which never set. One of these is greater than all, which goes round the whole world.

CHAPTER II.

1. EXPLANATION OF ENOCH'S MEANING BY THE SIX GATES, WHEREIN THE SUN AND MOON RISE AND SET. 2. ENOCH ACKNOWLEDGED BY THE PROPHETS, APOSTLES, &c.

THOSE portions of our globe that are situated between the two tropic lines from Cancer unto Capricorn, are divided into six parts or divisions, and are called by Enoch six gates; the first gate being situated next unto the tropic line of Capricorn, in the southern hemisphere; the sixth gate is situated next unto the tropic line of Cancer, in the northern hemisphere; the other four gates are between them: and in these six gates or divisions of the said space, the sun passes twice in each of them, to make up twelve, which are the twelve months, and which make the year complete. You will observe that the year is reckoned to commence when. the Sun is on the equator in spring; the sun then commences advancing into the northern hemisphere, northward, during April, May, and June, and then returns from the north during July, August, and September, the sun having passed twice in each (in going and returning) of those three gates or divisions, and are called by Enoch gates Nos. 4, 5, and 6. The sun then advances into the southern hemisphere, southward, during the months of October, November, and December; arid returns back to the equator during the months of January, February, and March: these gates are called Nos. 1, 2, and 3, and when the sun arrives on the equator, the year is completed. See Plates 9 acid 10.

Since writing the above, I have accidentally met with the following remarks (on the seventy-first Chapter) by the translator of the Book of Enoch, the Rev. Richard Lawrence, LL.D., Archbishop of Cashel, which will fully bear out my explanation. His remarks are as follow:

"The system of astronomy, detailed in this and in the subsequent chapters, is precisely that of an untutored but accurate observer of the heavens. He describes the eastern and western parts of heaven, where the sun and moon rise and set, as divided each into six different gates, through which those orbs of light pass at their respective periods. In the denomination: of these gates he begins with that, through which the sun passes at the winter solstice; and this he terms the first gate. It of course answers to the sign Capricornus; and is the southernmost point to which the sun reaches both at rising and at setting. The next gate, at which the sun arrives in its progress towards the east at rising, and towards the west at setting, and which answers to the sign Aquarius, he terms the second gate. The next, in continuation of the same course of the' sun, which answers to the sign Pisces, he terms the third gate. The fourth, gate in his description is that which is situated due east at sun-rising, and due west at sun-setting, and which, answering to the sign Aries, the sun enters at the vernal equinox. With this fourth gate he commences his account of the sun's annual circuit, and of the consequent change in the length of day and night at the various seasons of the year. Verse 12, &c. His fifth gate is now to be found in the sun's progress northwards; and answers to the sign Taurus. And his sixth gate is situated still further north; which answering to the sign Gemini, concludes at the most northern point of heaven, to which the sun, arrives, and from which it turns at the summer solstice, again to measure back its course southwards.

"Hence it happens, that the same gates which answer to the six signs alluded to in the sun's passage from the winter to the summer solstice, necessarily also answer to the remaining six of the twelve signs of the zodiac in its passage back again; viz, the sixth gate answers to Cancer, as before it did to Gemini; the fifth to Leo, as before to Taurus; the fourth to Virgo, as before to Aries; the third to Libra, as before to Pisces; the second to Scorpio, as before to Aquarius; and the first to Sagittarius, as before to Capricornus."

Thus the reader may clearly see that it is the declaration of Enoch that the sun does rise in the east and set in the west; and at the same time advancing northwards, to give the northern hemisphere its summer, and make the day twice the length of the night; and then retires southward into the southern hemisphere, to give the southern hemisphere its summer, and make its day twice as long as the night; and leave the northern hemisphere to its winter, and make its night twice as long as the day, and thus proceeds alternately, and that continually.

I shall now request the marked attention of the reader to, the following point; that is to say, Enoch states the days of the year, when the year is completed, to be 364 days; whereas the Newtonian or Solar System of Astronomy, states that there are 365 days, 5 hours, 48 minutes, 49 seconds.

Here it will be necessary for the reader to consider whether or not the different mode of calculating the year by the solar system, is a sufficient authority, to put aside a declaration of the prophet Enoch. It will also be requisite for the reader to consider that there are prophets who are prophets of God by inspiration and revelation only, as Enoch was, he not being commissioned to set up a visible form of worship as Moses was, yet God inspired him with the knowledge of his works. There are prophets by commission; as, for instance,—to show the difference,—king David was a prophet, inasmuch as he did prophecy of the coming of Christ, and also of his own victories, &c.; yet he was not equal with the prophet Nathan, who was commissioned of God to go tell David of his fault with respect to Uriah and his wife; and David hearkened and repented, and was forgiven of God for his fault, as to his eternal life.

1 will here state, for the information of the reader, the estimation in

which Enoch has been held as a righteous man by our righteous forefathers, the sons of Jacob, as may be seen in the "Testament of the Twelve Patriarchs" at their death, &c., translated by Robert Grotshead.

Simeon saith, "For I have seen in Enoch's writings, that you and your children shall be corrupted with whoredom, and do levy wrong by the sword," &c.—p. 27.

Levi saith, "Nevertheless, the house which the Lord shall choose, shall be called Jerusalem, as the book of Enoch the righteous containeth" —p. 41. "And truly, - my children, I know by the writings of Enoch, that in the: end ye shall do wickedly, laying your hands most spitefully upon the Lord, and through you. Your brethren shall be confounded, and made a scorning stock to all nations," &c.—p. 44. Furthermore, " I know by the book of Enoch, that ye shall go astray, by the space of threescore and ten weeks, and defile the priesthood, stain the sacrifices, destroy the law, despise the sayings of the prophets," &c.—p. 46.

Judah saith, "But I have read in the books of Enoch the righteous, that ye shall work wickedness in the latter days. Therefore, my children, keep yourselves from lechery and covetousness, and give ear unto your father Judah; for those things withdraw men from God's law, and blind the understanding of their minds, and teach them pride," &c.—p. 66.

Zabulon saith, "Therefore, in the sceptre of Enoch's law it is written," &c.—p. 85.

Dan saith, "For I have read in Enoch, that Satan is your prince, and that all the spirits of fornication and pride shall ply themselves in laying snares for the children of Dan," &c. —p. 98.

Nephthalim saith, "My children, I say these things because I have read in the holy writings of Enoch, that you also shall depart from the Lord, and walk in all the wickedness of Sodom; and the Lord shall bring thraldom upon you, so as you shall serve your enemies," &c.—p. 107.

Benjamin saith, "And I perceived by the sayings of the righteous Enoch, that there shall be evil deeds among you," &c. —p. 158. "Then shall ye see Enoch, Noah, Shem, Abraham, Isaac, and Jacob, sitting at his right hand with joyfulness. Then shall we rise also every one of us to his own sceptre, worshipping the king of heaven, which appeared on earth in the base shape of man," &c.—p. 160.

Now it will appear by the aforesaid evidence, that Enoch was held in very high esteem by the righteous forefathers of old, before God did give a commission to Moses to be a law-giver unto the people: and what saith Moses concerning Enoch, Gen. v. 24, "And Enoch walked with God; and he was not, for God took him." See also what the apostle Jude (verses 14 and 15) saith, in the New or second Testament, "And Enoch also, the seventh from Adam, prophesied of these, saying, Behold, the Lord cometh with ten thousand of his saints, to execute judgment upon all, and to convince all that are ungodly among them of all their ungodly deeds which they have ungodly committed, and of all their hard speeches which ungodly sinners have spoken against them."

It is desirable that the reader should understand the visions and revelations of Enoch, so as to know when Enoch is speaking of the sun, moon, and stars in the visible firmamental heaven, and when he is assimilating men to stars, angels, &c., as the apostle Jude did when he said (verse 6), "And the angels which kept not their first estate, but left their own habitation, he hath reserved in everlasting chains under darkness unto the judgment of the great day;" and (verse 13), "Raging waves of the sea, foaming out their own shame; wandering stars, to whom is reserved the blackness of darkness for ever."

It is very evident by the before-mentioned, that Jude understood the writings of Enoch, when he shows what Enoch's prophesies meant, and thereby acknowledges the existence of Enoch, and the truth of his book.

The meaning of "the angels which kept not their first estate," is clearly this: the first state of men is innocency; and when they forsake that first innocent state, and become guilty of wickedness against God, then are they reserved for punishment unto the great day of judgment.

St. Paul also acknowledges the righteousness of Enoch, and of his translation, so that he should not see death, Heb. xi. 5, "By faith Enoch was translated that he should not see death; and was not found, because God had translated him: for before his translation he had this testimony, that he pleased God."

See also what the prophet Lodowick Muggleton says in a Letter to Elizabeth Haggerter, of Cork, in Ireland, June 22nd, 1682, as recorded in the third and last Testament, in the book of Letters, p. 516:

"That God doth choose and ordain some particular man, and doth furnish him with revelation to declare unto the people what the true God is, in the time of his commission.

"The first man God chose after the fall of Adam, was Enoch; and God did furnish him with revelation to write books, wherein he did declare to the succeeding fathers of old, that were of the seed of faith, or seed of Adam his father; and this revelation of his walking with God, and what God was; he left this revelation to Noah, and Noah left it to Shem, and Shem left it to his sons, until it came to Abraham, Isaac, and Jacob.

"So that Enoch's revelation and declaration to the fathers of old, and all that did believe the books of Enoch, they were as a parliament, to enact it as a statute law to their children, from generation to generation, for ever. And so it was with Moses and the prophets, and with Christ and the apostles."

I shall here conclude the evidence as to the truth of Enoch's character and existence; for that there was such a person is beyond dispute, seeing it is testified of by so many witnesses.

CHAPTER III.

1. THE NECESSITY OF RIGHTLY UNDERSTANDING THE SCRIPTURES. 2. THE CREATION OF THE VISIBLE FIRMAMENT. 3. FROM WHENCE THE WATER WAS OBTAINED TO DROWN THE WORLD. 4. THE BUILDING OF THE TOWER OF BABEL. 5. THE VISIBILITY OF GOD, AND HIS DESCENDING FROM HEAVEN ABOVE THE STARS. 6. HOW GOD MAY BE SAID TO FILL HEAVEN AND EARTH.

PERMIT me here to request the very particular attention of the reader to the great necessity there is for a right understanding of the holy Scriptures, in order that he may know how to distinguish the sayings of the prophets and apostles when they speak of the earth we tread upon, and the earth (so called) when they speak of the earthy heart of man, who minds earthly things in preference to spiritual things; as thus, for example: David says, "rejoice, O ye heavens, and sing praises unto the Lord, O earth;" as if he should say, rejoice, O ye heavenly-hearted saints, who mind heavenly things, for great will be your reward in the kingdom of Gad, which is in heaven above the stars; and sing praises unto the Lord, O ye earthly-minded men, for all the good things of this earth which the Lord hath given you.

You will observe there are three heavens spoken of in scripture: one heaven is the heart of man, wherein God dwells by faith; the second heaven is the visible firmamental heaven, wherein God has set the sun, moon, and stars to shine upon the earth; the third heaven is the kingdom of God, above or beyond the stars, which is infinite in height, length, and breadth, suitable to an infinite majesty, and from which kingdom He has descended, to visit his creature man upon the earth, either to reward them with temporal blessings for their faith and good works, or to bring the evil of punishment upon them for their misdeeds, so often mentioned in the holy Scriptures. See Abraham was blessed, and Sodom and Gomorrah were destroyed, &c.; and the kingdom of God is infinite in height, length, arid breadth: where there is earth and water under foot, infinite in length, breadth, and depth: see Plate 11.

I shall now proceed with the declarations of the prophet Moses, and other prophets in the commission of the law or holy Bible:

"In the beginning God created the heaven and the earth. And the earth was without form and void; and darkness was upon the face of the deep. And the Spirit of God moved upon the face of the waters," Gen. i. 1, 2. "And God said, Let there be a firmament in the midst of the waters, and let it divide the waters from the waters. And God made the firmament, and divided the waters which were under the firmament from the waters which were above the firmament: and it was so. And God called the firmament Heaven. And the evening and the morning were the second day," 1. 6-8.

The firmament is made of water, congealed, cemented, or knit together as firmly as ice is on the surface of a pond of water that we can walk upon, and made so by the powerful word of Almighty God, and therefore called the firmament; to keep those waters that are above the firmament from the waters that are on our earth beneath the firmament; and God can, when He pleases, divide those waters above, and open the firmament and descend upon earth, and ascend again at his pleasure, and which He will do at the last day, even as Moses divided the Red Sea, when the children of Israel passed through in safety, but the water closed in upon their enemies, and they were destroyed.

Some curious mind might ask me, how thick is the firmament? To which I should reply, it is sufficiently thick to answer, the purpose for which God has made it.

"And God said, Let there be lights in the firmament of the heaven to divide the day from the night; and let them be for signs, and for seasons, and for days, and years: and let them be for lights in the firmament of the heaven to give light upon the earth: and it was so. And God made two great lights; the greater light to rule the day, and the lesser light to rule the night: he made the stars also. And God set them in the firmament of heaven, to give light upon the earth, to rule over the day and over the night, and to divide the light from the darkness: and God saw, that it was good. And the evening and the morning were the fourth day," Gen. i. 14-19. See Plate 10.

The reader will here observe, that the sayings of Moses are clear to show that God in the beginning of the world did make a firmament in the midst of the eternal waters in the kingdom above, to divide the waters that are on this earth from the waters which are in heaven above the visible firmament, where the supply of water was obtained when the world was drowned, as may be seen by the following passages:

"And it came to pass after seven days, that the waters of the flood were upon the earth. In the six hundredth year of Noah's life, in the second month, the seventeenth day of the month, the same day were all the fountains of the great deep broken up, and the windows of heaven were opened. And the rain was upon the earth forty days and forty nights," Gen. vii. 10-12:

"The fountains also of the deep and the windows of heaven were stopped, and the rain from heaven was restrained; and the waters returned from off the earth continually: and after the end of the hundred and fifty days the waters were abated," Gen. viii. 2, 3.

So that the reader will clearly perceive that the waters were actually sent from heaven to drown the creation on this earth, and were retaken to their former position when the work of destruction was completed.

I shall next draw your attention to the very important subject of the building of the tower of Babel, whose top was intended to reach up to heaven, as recorded by Moses, and said to have taken place after the flood; when the world had been drowned, and when men had multiplied on the earth; this is stated to have taken place, in very plain words to our understanding; and the question is simply, is it so, or is it not so? If we take the Newtonian system of astronomy for our guide, we cannot for a moment see the possibility of such a thing ever having taken place; for you must know, should that system be the true one, there is no such place as the kingdom of heaven, as recorded in the holy Scriptures, but that we must be in the infinite space already, instead of a bounded space, as the holy Scriptures declare us to be. But if, on the contrary, we take the Scriptures for our guide, we shall then see that God has made a firmament to encompass this globe all round about; even as with a brazen wall, and suitable for mortal men for a time only, and that the firmament cannot be very far from the surface of our globe; therefore it is necessary to choose the one, and refuse the other, for both cannot be the truth. The text is this:

"And they said, Go to, let us build us a city and a tower, whose top may reach unto heaven; and let us make us a name, lest we be scattered abroad upon the face of the whole earth. And the Lord came down to see the city and the tower, which the children of men builded. And the Lord said, Behold, the people is one, and they have all one language; and this they begin to do: and now nothing will be restrained from them, which they have imagined to do. Go to, let us go dawn, and there confound their language, that they may not understand one another's speech," Gen. xi. 4-7.

The next thing to which I claim the particular notice of the reader is, where the prophet Moses says that "God descended upon mount Sinai, and not only so, but that God spake unto him in plain words, even as a man speaks to his friend; " and that "Moses saw the person of God in part, even while God appeared in his glory;" and also that God said unto him, "Thou canst not see my face and live;" evidently meaning, that Moses being in mortality, and God being in immortality and glory, he could not see the face of God, in his bright burning glory, and live; although Moses was much strengthened to be able: to be with or near unto God, while in his glory. Now with regard to the difference of Moses not being able to look in the face of God, it will appear thus: we all know that there is naturally a very great difference between looking at a superior personage in the face, to what there is when he is walking away from us, because of the piercing quality of the sight, although in mortality.

Now it appears by the holy Scriptures, that the Almighty God has on many occasions veiled his glory, and appeared unto men on this earth, as when He spake to Moses face to face, and also as unto Abraham, &c.; even as a mighty earthly king might veil his stately glory, and appear incog. among his people; and if it were impossible for God to do so likewise, then would God be inferior in power to the earthly kings; and how far that would be right, judge ye.

That the aforesaid statements are made by those who declare themselves to be commissioned of the true and living God of Israel, is apparent to all who read the Scriptures. Then the only question is, shall we believe them to be the, truth or, not? I must say that if we believe the Newtonian system of astronomy to be the correct one, then we must of necessity turn those sayings in scripture to some very mystical meaning, which no man can thoroughly comprehend; but if we look to the system according to the prophets' writings laid down, then it is quite possible that all these things could have taken place even as they are written.. I will record the passages, which are as follow:

"And mount Sinai was altogether on a smoke, because the Lord descended upon it in fire: and the smoke thereof ascended as the smoke of a furnace, and the whole mount quaked greatly," Exod. xix. 18.

"And the Lord spake unto Moses face to face, as a man speaketh unto his friend," xxxiii. 11.

"And the Lord descended in a cloud, and stood with him there, and proclaimed the name of the Lord," xxxiv. 5.

I shall now request your serious consideration to the one uniform faith and declaration of all the prophets and holy men of old, or in the early period of the world; as also the apostles in the gospel; and the last two witnesses of the Holy Spirit, John Reeve and Lodowick Muggleton, in the third or last Testament of God, in these last days, when the mystery of God is finished, according to the Revelation of Saint John the Divine. The whole of their testimony is, that the sun doth rise and set upon the earth; and not one word do they say that the earth rises and sets upon (or goes round) the sun. Also they have one uniform declaration that there is a kingdom of glory, or place of residence, (which is called Heaven,) for the eternal God personally to dwell in; and that whenever God did visit his creature man on this earth, it is always represented that He descended (or came down) from heaven, which is above the stars. This is the language of the prophets of God when they speak of his personal habitation: therefore observe the distinction when the prophets speak of God's personal dwelling, and when they speak of his dwelling by faith in the heart of man, or by his power only; for you must know that it is the true understanding of God and his works, that alone can give peace and satisfaction to our souls; as, for instance, where the Scriptures say, "Do not I fill heaven and earth, saith the Lord?" What does this saying mean, other than that God, by his almighty power, fills the kingdom of heaven above, and the earth beneath the firmament; even as a mighty king on earth doth by his power fill his kingdom where he personally resides, and also his foreign possessions, where his laws are in force also.

CHAPTER IV.

1. THE NECESSITY OF TRUE FAITH AND TRUE KNOWLEDGE TO PLEASE GOD. 2. THE RISING AND SETTING OF THE SUN PROVED BY SCRIPTURE. 3. THE DIFFERENT GLORIES OF THE SUN, MOON, AND STARS. 4. OUR LORD JESUS CHRIST'S ASCENT INTO HIS KINGDOM ABOVE, &c.

IT is written, that "without faith it is impossible to please God." The Scriptures tell us of two faiths—a true faith and a false faith. Now it is the true faith in the true God that is pleasing to Him; and all false faiths are an abomination to Him: therefore this will show the necessity of arriving at the knowledge of truth for lasting satisfaction, and will cause the reader to consider carefully, and compare all things with great moderation, if he wishes to enjoy true knowledge and satisfaction in his mind.

I shall here give various quotations for the reader's perusal, which I have selected to show that the sun does rise and set upon the earth; and also that there is a kingdom of heaven above the stars, the place or residence of the eternal God:

"The sun was risen upon the earth when Lot entered into Zoar," Gen. xix. 23.

"Look down from thy holy habitation, from heaven, and bless thy people Israel, and the land which thou hast given us, as thou swarest unto our fathers, a land that floweth with milk and honey," Deut. xxvi. 15.

"Then spake Joshua to the Lord in the day when the Lord delivered up the Amorites before the children of Israel, and he said in the sight of Israel, Sun, stand thou still upon Gibeon; and thou, Moon, in the valley of Ajalon. And the sun stood still, and the moon stayed, until the people had avenged themselves upon their enemies. Is not this written in the book of Jasher? So the sun stood still in the midst of heaven, and hasted not to go down about a whole day. And there was no day like that before it or after it, that the Lord hearkened unto the voice of a man: for the Lord fought for Israel, Josh. x. 12-14.

"And Gideon the son of Joash returned from battle before the sun was up, Judg. viii. 13.

"Before the sun went down, &c., Judg. xiv. 18.

"And the sun went down, &c., 2 Sam. ii. 24.

"And he shall be as the light of the morning, when the sun riseth, &c., 2 Sam. xxiii. 4.

"And this shall be a sign unto thee from the Lord, that the Lord will do this thing that he hath spoken; behold, I will bring again the shadow of the degrees, which is gone down in the sun-dial of Ahaz, ten degrees backward. So the sun returned ten degrees, by which degrees it was gone down, Is. xxxviii. 7, 8.

"Who laid the foundations of the earth, that it should not be removed for ever, Ps. civ. 5.

"Hearken unto me, O Jacob and Israel my called; I am he; I am the first, I also am the last. Mine hand also hath laid the foundation of the earth, and my right hand hath spanned the heavens: when I call unto them, they stand up together, Is. xlviii. 12, 13.

"Behold, the day of the Lord cometh, cruel both with wrath and fierce anger, to lay the land desolate: and he shall destroy the sinners thereof out of it. For the stars of heaven and the constellations thereof shall not give their light: the sun shall be darkened, &c., Is. xiii. 9, 10.

"Thus saith the Lord, Learn not the way of the heathen,, and be not dismayed at the signs of heaven; for the heathen are dismayed at them. . . He hath made the earth by his power, he hath established the world by his wisdom, and hath stretched out the heavens by his discretion, Jer. x. 2 & 12.

"And it came to pass; when the sun did arise, that God prepared a vehement east wind; and the sun beat upon the head of Jonah, that he fainted, &c., Jonah iv. 8.

"The sun and moon stood still in their habitation, Habakkuk iii. 11.

"That ye may be children of your Father which is in heaven: for he maketh his sun to rise on the evil and on the good, and sendeth rain on the just and on the unjust, Mat. v. 45.

"And when the sun was up, they were scorched; and because they had no root, they withered away, Mat. xiii. 6, and Mark iv. 6.

"And at even, when the sun did set, &c., Mark i. 32.

"Now when the sun was setting, &c., Luke iv. 40.

"There is one glory of the sun, and another glory of the moon, and another glory of the stars: for one star differeth from another star in glory, Cor. xv. 41.

"Be ye angry, and sin not: let not the sun go down upon your wrath, Eph. iv. 26.

"For the sun is no sooner risen with a burning heat, but it withereth the grass," &c., James i. 11.

It is thus positively shown, that it was the faith of all the prophets, that the sun did actually rise and set upon the earth.

"And Elijah went up by a whirlwind into heaven, 2 Kings ii. 11.

"So then after the Lord had spoken unto them, he was received up into heaven, and sat on the right hand of God, Mark xvi. 19.

"And it came to pass, as the angels were gone away from them into heaven, Luke ii. 15.

"And it came to pass, while he blessed them, he was parted from them, and carried up into heaven, Luke xxiv. 51.

"And he saith unto him, Verily, verily, I say unto you, Hereafter ye shall see heaven open, and the angels of God ascending and descending upon the Son of man, John i. 51.

"Whom the heavens must receive until the times of restitution of all things, which God hath spoken by the mouths of all his holy prophets since the world began, Acts iii. 21.

"For as I passed by, and beheld your devotions, I found an altar with this inscription, To THE UNKNOWN GOD. Whom therefore ye ignorantly worship, him declare I unto you. God that made the world, and all things therein, seeing that he is Lord of heaven and earth, dwelleth not in temples made with hands, Acts xvii. 23, 24.

"Him that overcometh will I make a pillar in the temple of my God, and he shall go no more out: and I will write upon him the name of my God, and the name of the city of my God, which is new Jerusalem, which cometh clown out of heaven from my God: and I will write upon him my new name," Rev. iii. 12.

The reader will here observe, that St. John the Divine is shown by way of vision and inspiration; heaven, that is to say, the kingdom and throne of God, and the conclusion of God's work, with regard to this world, and all the consequence of righteousness and wickedness, as to eternity.

The interpretation of the Revelations has been given by the two last witnesses of the holy Spirit, John Reeve and Lodowick Muggleton.

"After this I looked, and, behold, a door was opened in heaven: and the first voice which I heard was as it were of a trumpet talking with me; which said, Come up hither, and I will show thee things which must be hereafter. And immediately I was in the Spirit: and, behold, a throne was set in heaven, and one sat on the throne. . . And before the throne there was a sea of glass like unto crystal, Rev. iv. 1, 2, and 6.

"And I say unto you, that many shall come from the east and west, and shall sit down with Abraham, and Isaac, and Jacob, in the kingdom of heaven, Mat. viii. 11.

"The field is the world; the good seed are the children of the kingdom; but the tares are the children of the wicked one ... Then shall the righteous shine forth as the sun in the kingdom of their Father. Who hath ears to hear, let him hear, Mat. xiii. 38 and 43.

"Then shall the King say unto them on his right hand, Come, ye blessed of my Father, inherit the kingdom prepared for you from the foundation of the world, Mat. xxv. 34.

"But I say unto you, I will not drink henceforth of this fruit of the vine, until that day when I drink it new with you in my Father's kingdom, Mat. xxvi. 29.

"And Jesus came and spake unto them, saying, All power is given unto me in heaven and in earth, Mat. xxviii: 18.

"But rather seek ye the kingdom of God; and all these things shall be added unto you. Fear not, little flock; for it is your Father's good pleasure to give you the kingdom, Luke xii. 31, 32.

"Jesus answered, My kingdom is not of this world: if my kingdom were of this world, then would my servants fight, John xviii. 36.

"So then after the Lord had spoken unto them, he was received up into heaven, and sat on the right hand of God, Mark xvi. 19.

"And when he had spoken these things, while they beheld, he was taken up; and a cloud received him out of their sight. And while they looked stedfastly toward heaven as lie went up, behold, two men stood by them in white apparel; which also said, he men of Galilee, why stand ye gazing up into heaven? this same Jesus, which is taken up from you into heaven, shall so come in like manner as ye have seen him go into heaven, Acts i. 9-11.

"Nevertheless we, according to his promise, look for new heavens and a new earth, wherein dwelleth righteousness," 2 Pet. iii. 13.

Having given these few remarks out of the many that are written in holy writ, namely, the Old and New Testament, to show that it was the faith of the prophets and apostles that there was such a place as heaven, and that our Almighty God could and did descend from, and ascend to it, again at his pleasure, I shall now proceed with various extracts from the third and last Testament, to show the belief of the last prophets was a continuation and substantiation of the same faith, in every particular, as in olden time, only more clearly developed, and therefore justly entitled "the Commission of the Holy Spirit."

CHAPTER V.

CONTAINING A QUOTATION OF THREE CHAPTERS FROM THE DIVINE LOOKING-GLASS OF THE THIRD TESTAMENT OF OUR LORD JESUS CHRIST, BY REEVE AND MUGGLETON, CONCERNING THE KINGDOM OF HEAVEN, AND THE CREATION OF THIS WORLD.

PART OF THE SECOND CHAPTER OF THE DIVINE LOOKING-GLASS.

"1. Again, in the next place, by inspiration from the unerring Spirit, I positively affirm, that the substances of earth and water were from all eternity in the Creator's presence, uncreated, senseless, dark, dead matter, like unto water and dust, that have no kind of life, or light, or virtue in them at all.

2. Also I declare from the holy Spirit, that darkness, death, or devil and hell, lay secretly hid in that earth above this perishing globe, and in the sight of the Creator were eternally naked and bare, both in their root and in their fruit.

3. Again, I declare from the true light of life eternal, that that world or kingdom where the Creator's glorious person is visible, is a place or throne infinite in length, breadth, or height, answerable unto an infinite majesty.

4. Moreover, for your information that are spiritual, from the true God I declare, that in this heavenly city there is no firmament, sun, moon, or stars: so that you may understand that it is an infinite open place for divine personal ascending or descending at pleasure, only under foot is fixed a spiritual earth, and a crystal sea. (See Plate 11.)

5. Furthermore, you that are spiritual may know, that it stands to very good sense that an infinite majesty cannot be confined to a finite world or kingdom as this is; I mean when He possesseth the throne of immortality as at this time, or before He became a body of unspotted flesh.

6. Again, concerning that glorious earth and crystal sea aforesaid, I would not have you to think that I mean it was eternally so, but after, or in the finishing of the creation of angels, and variety of other creatures, the infinite virtue of the Creator's word produced that crystal spirituality in them, that both visible as well as invisible, every thing or creature appointed to abide in the presence of the divine majesty, might be all glory in their kind and measure, answerable to the unmeasurable variety of unspeakable glory in the Creator Himself.

7. My spiritual brethren, you know that it is an opinion of the learned, that those substances, earth and water aforesaid, were not eternal; but they have long imagined that the Creator spake the word, and so they came to be; and after He had given them their being, He formed all things that were made out of them.

8. My beloved brethren, you may know that this must needs be an

error, because you know that the word create is to make formless dead matter into sensible living forms.

9. Besides this, you know, as for creating of those elements of water or dust, there is no scripture maketh mention of any such thing; therefore a mere imagination; but more of this in the seventh chapter."

THE SEVENTH CHAPTER OF THE DIVINE LOOKING-GLASS.

"1. Seeing a right understanding of the mysteries of the true creation or redemption, or any spiritual truth whatsoever, consists only in the knowledge of Him which gave them their beings; therefore, by divine assistance, in the next place, I shall treat again of that glorious Being concerning whom there is and hath been in this world such innumerable dark disputes.

2. My beloved brethren in the truth, you may remember that unto any sober man's understanding it is cleared already, that earth and water were an eternal chaos of confused matter, essentially distinct from the Creator.

3. Also you may remember, that out of those elements I have told you by inspiration from an unerring Spirit, that the divine majesty hath created all things that were made, into that heavenly order they appear to be, whether for a time or for eternity.

4. Moreover, it is clear also, that without those eternal materials was nothing made that was made, neither possibly could be, only that serpentine devil in the learned men of this world have long imagined a confused creation of more seeming wisdom, power, and glory, than that of the Creator, as abundantly beforesaid.

5. Again, concerning the word create, make or form, I shall write a little of the sense of it.

6. My beloved brethren, the very true meaning of that word create is to compose confused dead matter into complete living forms; or that word create is light and life, producing dark dead dust or water into sensible living beings; or it is a powerful word proceeding from a glorious form of sensible light and life, into a chaos of confused formless matter of senseless darkness and death, and from thence producing variety of sensible living bodies, according to their kind, for the demonstration of the Creator's infinite wisdom, power, and glory, in creation unto some of these living forms.

7. Again, seeing unlearned spiritual men wrest the scripture to their own destruction, therefore for our more clearer understanding of the true Creator in order thereunto, I shall speak somewhat of the visible heavens, and the lights formed in them for man's natural comfort, next unto the Creator's glory.

8. My beloved spiritual brethren, you know concerning the deep waters throughout the scripture records, no man can find one word or

tittle in reference to its beginning; therefore of necessity it must be eternal.

9. Likewise you know that the waters covered the earth before the creation; wherefore the earth being as it is in the deep waters, of necessity must needs be one essence eternally with those deep waters aforesaid.

10. Therefore though it be said, In the beginning God created the heavens end the earth, and the earth was without form and void, and darkness was upon the deep, and the Spirit of God moved upon the waters,

11. My spiritual brethren, you cannot be deceived by literal interpretations, as to think that the deep waters might be eternal, but that lump of hid earth within those waters had a beginning by the word of the Lord:

12. No, you know that is against all sober sense or reason itself; for if that earth which was within the water proceeded from the word of the Lord, then the dark deep water must of necessity have its beginning also at that time the earth received its being, because in the lump they were essentially one.

13. Wherefore whatever men in darkness have dreamed, as to say that God created all things of nothing, or that God created that confused chaos of water and earth, it is so far from having any truth in it, that it is all one as if they should say, there is no Creator at all but earth and water, and such like stuff as they are.

14. Again, by inspiration from an unerring Spirit I positively affirm, against men or angels, that the earth and the deep water were eternally one chaos of confused matter distinct from the ever God.

15. And whereas it is said, In the beginning God created the heaven and the earth, that is, out of that matter of water and earth that were formless and void, God did by a word speaking create a formable world, as a place of convenient residence for mortals to inhabit.

16. I also declare from the holy Spirit, that God created no light nor darkness at all without bodies;

17. Wherefore, concerning those words, Then God said, Let there be light, and there was light; that is, the Spirit of God being all light, moving or speaking into the deep dark waters, his word caused a light to appear throughout those waters, to make a distinction between light and that utter darkness that was both in the deep water and the earth, inclosed as a prisoner in the womb of darkness:

18. So that the Lord called this created light day; not only because it was all darkness before, or that 1Ie did not purpose to form a more eminent natural light than that was; but, as aforesaid, an ordinary created light is worthy to be called day, as well as ordinary darkness is called eight.

19. Or you may know that the very word light signifieth day, as the word darkness signifieth night.

20. Likewise you know, that darkness was not darkness without its

body; therefore you may know, that light can be no light unless it be in a body also.

21. It is not the word light, nor the word darkness, is or possibly can be any thing at all, unless they be in distinct bodies, that they might become absolute beings of light, or beings of darkness.

22. It is written again, God said, Let there be a firmament in the midst of the waters, and let it separate the waters from the waters.

23. My spiritual brethren, I declare from the holy Spirit, that this visible firmament called heaven, was formed by the powerful word of the Creator, out of those very waters in which it is now fixed, to keep them asunder.

24. Moreover, it is written, And God said, Let there be lights in the firmament of the heaven to five light upon the earth: and it was so. God then made two great lights; the greater light to rule the day, and the lesser light to rule the night. He made also the stars, and God set them in the firmament of heaven, to shine upon the earth.

25. My spiritual brethren, whatsoever hath been written formerly from men's imaginations concerning the vastness of the bodies of the sun, moon, and stars, it arose in them from their utter darkness of that glorious Creator from whence all true light proceeds.

26. Wherefore, from that light by whom no man ever was deceived, in some measure I shall demonstrate why the Lord called the sun and moon two great lights, and of that matter of which they were made.

27. My spiritual brethren, though the sun, moon, and stars transcend each other in glory, yet you may know that they were all created of that element of water, and are distinct bodies of light fixed in the heavenly firmament.

28. I do not mean that they are so fixed as to be incapable of motion; but of the contrary, from the Lord I affirm, that the firmament itself is not capable of motion; but by the word of the Lord that formed it, it is made unmoveable until the day of its dissolution; and those bodies of sun, moon, and stars, motions in that firmamental heaven in their seasons, to fulfil that ward of government in them.

29. For you that are spiritual may know that the firmament of heaven, and those rulers of sun, moon, and stars set in them, as to govern both the day and the night, may be compared to a prince, with his nobles, throne, and other inferior rulers:

30. For you know that his kingdom, whereon they have their living being, is unmoveable; but the governors do the work unto which they are appointed.

31 My brethren, you may understand also, that the firmamental body above us, or below us, if you think it so, for its appointed season, is as firmly fixed as the earth we tread on; and as things in power are motional on this earth, so likewise those created lights are only motional in that heavenly body aforesaid.

32. Again, it is said that God set them in the firmament of heaven to shine upon the earth.

33. My brethren, hearken no more unto vain astronomers or stargazers, concerning the bulk of the suit, moon, and stars; for I positively affirm from that God that made them, that the compass of their bodies are not much bigger than they appear to our natural sight.

34. O empty vain liars! how long have you been suffered to deceive the people with your monstrous imaginary bodies of sun, moon, and stars, which are not, and of your great knowledge concerning them? Your things are too big to be good or true, and the time of your serpentine sophistry is almost finished.

35. Again, I declare from the holy Spirit, that the bodies of the sun, moon, and stars are all distinct beings from each other, and possess their own created light alone, neither borrowing nor lending their light to one another, whatever hath been imagined to the contrary, concerning new moons or eclipses.

36. Again, you know the scriptures do not say that the sun and moon are two great bodies, but two great lights only: neither doth the scripture say that the bodies of the global earth and heavenly firmament are covered with the vastness of the sun, moon, or stars, or that they enclose any other bodies within their own bodies; or that any other bodies are fixed in them:

37. But, on the contrary, the scripture saith, that the sun and moon were set in the firmament of heaven to shine upon the earth: wherefore it is as clear as the light, that that which is fixed is of a less bulk than that wherein it is enclosed.

38. Yet you know that the greater bulk may receive its principal light from that lesser body within its circumference, as a rich diamond in a ring, or a candle or torch in the night in a wide room, or the like.

39. My spiritual brethren, you may understand that the glory of the most high God consists not in bulk of things, but in the exceeding brightness of them.

40. Nay, moreover, you cannot but know that the infinite wisdom of the divine majesty doth the more abundantly appear in an extraordinary light shining from a very little body.

41. My brethren, it is not the bulk of the sun or moon which causeth so great a light; but, as aforesaid, it is the transcendent brightness of their created purities which displayeth those beams of light through the visible heaven and earth.

42. Whatever hath or shall be said to the contrary, from the Lord I positively affirm, that the bodies of the sun, moon, and stars are all fixed beings, only in one firmament.

43. Moreover, from the Lord of glory I declare, that this visible heaven is all the firmament that ever was formed by the Creator.

44. Furthermore, though the bodies of the sun and moon were both formed out of that element of water, yet they were made as contrary in their natures as fire and water.

45. Because you know their government were over contrary beings,

the one to rule the day, and the other to rule the night; so that as the sun is a fiery glorious light for consolation unto the natural things of the day, so likewise the moon is a qualifying, cold, watery light, answerable to the watery things of the night:

46. Wherefore, though the body of the sun is of a more eminent brightness than that of the moon, yet they being of contrary natures, it is against all sober reason that the one should receive any light from the other in the least.

47. Again, you know that when the bodies of the sun and moon seem close together, instead of any agreement between them, there is such a fiery contest, as if they would absolutely destroy each other. And what, think you, is the just occasion of it? Is it not the difference of their natures?

48. Can fire acid water, or light and darkness, agree, if they be united together? Is there any rest unto either of them until one of them is dissolved?

49. My beloved friends in the pure truth, whatever men have long declared concerning the eclipse of the sun, through the near appearance of the moon, you may understand that the true occasion of the sun eclipsed, whether in part or whole, is according to their appearing at a further or nearer distance unto each other;

50. For, as beforesaid, the nature of the one being fiery, hot, and dry, and the nature of the other being watery, cold, and moist, if the most high God had not decreed the time of their contest, when they are nearly conjoined, there would be no communion between them until one of them were utterly dissolved.

51. Again, is it not as clear as the light itself unto us, that the true occasion of all variance between created beings, whether sensible or insensible, ariseth only from a difference of natures or spirits in them?

52. Moreover, when any kind of natures are suitable to each other, is there not a sweet harmony between them?

53. Wherefore if the moon received her light from the sun, as natural wise men have long imagined, is it not against all sense or reason that there should be no union between them but at a distance?

54. Doth it not rather agree with all true sense, that if the one received her light from the other, that the more nearer they are in bodily appearance, the more greater harmony would ensue, and occasion the lesser light rather to shine more clearly, than darken each other's brightness?

55. I think 7373at William Lilly, and his learned brethren in astrologian figures, dare not say, that either the sun or the moon were ever at variance with their own selves; or, that the eclipses of the sun or moon proceedeth from any harmony between that which occasioneth the eclipse, and the thing so eclipsed.

56. Well, then, if they acknowledge this rational truth, without controversy, when the light of the sun is eclipsed from us, it is through its near conjunction with the natural light or ruler of things of the night.

57. And when the light of the moon is eclipsed from us, though it be in the night, or early in the morning, it is through her near conjunction with the natural light or ruler of the day, or a planetary fire answerable to his nature.

58. My beloved spiritual brethren, as for the time and effect of eclipses, I leave them unto the figurative merchants of a sun, moon, and stars, which they rightly understand not, because no man can truly know them but by inspiration from Him that made them."

THE EIGHTH CHAPTER OF THE DIVINE LOOKING-GLASS.

"1. Again, if there was but one heavenly firmament created in all, some men may say unto me, what is the meaning of that third heaven in the scriptures?

2. From that light which cannot lie, to this I answer, the Spirit of God speaketh of a third heaven in scripture, that some men might be capable to declare unto his redeemed ones how many heavens there are, and where those heavens are, and what those heavens are.

3. My spiritual brethren, which have ears to hear, hearken unto the pure light of life eternal: there are three created heavens spoken of in scripture records, and no more; no, nor never was any more, whatever vain men have imagined.

4. The first is that third heaven of visible and invisible ravishing glories which are eternal: this is that vast kingdom where the persons of the mighty angels, and glorified bodies of Moses and Elias, do now inhabit, beholding the face of that most excellent majesty, whose divine nature unto his elect is crowns of unutterable excellencies.

5. This is that habitation, third heaven, throne, or kingdom of ravishing glory, above the starry heavens, spoken of so frequently in scripture records, which is needless to nominate unto you which are spiritual.

6. But lest some vain-glorious men should say, where is the word of God for what I speak? seeing the letter is their God whom they adore, instead of the holy Spirit which spake them; therefore to stop their carnal mouths, if it may be, I shall write down two or three scripture records: Heaven is my throne, and earth is my footstool, Acts vii. 49; O God, thy throne is for ever and ever, Heb. i. 8; That we have such an High Priest, that sitteth at the right hand of the throne of the Majesty in the heavens, Heb. viii. 1.

7. The second heaven which the Lord created was not a spiritual, but a natural, therefore of necessity it must fade away.

8. This heaven is this visible firmament, adorned with majestical lights above us, and a fixed earth beneath us, beautified in its seasons with variety of delights, which is nature's only desired haven, through the secret: decree of the most wise God, to manifest the variety of his

most infinite wisdom unto elect men and angels, in the creating of such natural glory to perish, and the angelical merciless rulers thereof, after they have enjoyed their momentary glory.

9. Give me leave to cite two or three scriptures, as a visible testimony to this second heaven also. It is written, in the beginning God created the heaven and the earth, Gen. i. 1.

10. My beloved spiritual brethren, you know that there could not be any beginning unto the Creator; therefore it may be understood, that saying did include that immortal throne above; and this mortal world beneath, as having a beginning, was spoken for the capacity unto men or angels which knew their being was from another, and understood also their continuance in those several heavens for a time or for eternity.

11. In Hebrews i. 10, 11, it is thus written: And, Thou, Lord, in the beginning hast established the earth, and the heavens are the works of thine hands; they shall perish, but thou dost remain; and they shall wax old as doth a garment.

12. Again, the third and last created heaven is that within the bodies of men, or the first man Adam, the which spiritual creation being in natural bodies, and within this perishing globe, it is made capable, through its union with changeable nature, to enter into mortality, that by the most secret decree of the most high God, after a moment's tasting of silent death, as He Himself did, it may quicken again, through death itself, spiritual bodies full of divine glories, that as one man naturally, as a flame of fire, all the elect may (as swift as thought) ascend to meet their Lord in the air, and with his divine person of bright burning glory, enter into that prepared throne of eternal pleasures.

13. This created or inspired light in man you know hath variety of scripture expressions for the setting forth its excellencies that it shall enjoy in the life to come; as, namely, The kingdom of heaven is within you; Christ in you the hope of glory; know you not that the Spirit of Christ is in you, except ye be reprobates? It is a true saying, For if we be created together with him, we also shall live together with him, 2 Tim. ii. Thus God created the man in his image, in the image of God created he him; he created them male and female, Gen. i. 27.

14. Thus briefly I have touched upon the three created heavens nominated in the literal records, unto an invisible, yet visible infinite being of all finite beings, blessed for ever, viz, a throne of eternal ravishing glories: secondly, a throne of natural perishing glories: lastly, an invisible spiritual throne leading them to eternity.

15. From that spiritual majesty by whom was formed the heavens aforesaid, and all, in them, I positively affirm against all mortals that ever were or shall be, that though men have written or shall speak of more worlds than what is forewritten, those additional heavens proceeded from their own imaginary confused reason, and not from that holy Spirit of all heavenly order."

CHAPTER VI.

A DISCOURSE BETWEEN JOHN REEVE AND RICHARD LEADER, MERCHANT; RECITED BY LODOWICK MUGGLETON, ONE OF THE TWO LAST WITNESSES AND PROPHETS OF THE MOST HIGH GOD, THE MAN JESUS IN GLORY.

"THIS Richard Leader, notwithstanding he was well satisfied in spiritual things, as to his eternal happiness, yet there was some things as to temporal. matters, which we had declared that he could not as yet consent unto, because it was contrary to the rule and art of astrology and philosophy, for I asked him what it was: he said, you declare the sun is not much bigger than it seemeth to be, and our art saith, it is threescore times bigger than the earth: also, said he, you say the moon doth not borrow any light of nor from the sun: likewise you say, that the heavens is not much above six miles high from the earth; and we by our art do say, the heavens are thousands of miles high from the earth; these things, saith he, seemeth something strange.

"Then I answered and said unto him, you are a man that have travelled through many parts of the world, and you have been in that place called the equinoctial line, where the sun is nearest to the earth of any other place, where the heat is so great that no creature can scarce live, the sun is so hot; did the sun seem any bigger to your sight when it was near to the earth, than at other times when you were at a distance? You saw the full proportion of it, did you not? He answered and said, he did. Then, said I, did the sun seem any bigger to your eye-sight, where it was near to the earth, than at other times? He answered, no, not any bigger, as he could discern. Why then, said I, will you believe your lying figure, before you will believe your own eye-sight? You must either say the sight of your eye is false, or the traditional figure you depend upon is false; now hath not God appointed the sight of the eye to be judge of that it sees? But men hath chose rather to believe their lying imagination, which they never saw, nor never can see, nor knows not what it is; therefore it hath erected a figure, that man might be led into darkness, imagine things that are not, and make people believe that the natural sight that God hath given men in their creation, to be judge of what it sees, to be a false sight and a false judge; and your dark imagination and figure to be a true light and a true judge of the bigness of the sun. For consider,

"That the imagination of reason in man doth always judge God to be bigger than He is, or lesser than He is; likewise imagination being blind, it judgeth God's power to be greater than it is, or lesser than it is, and so it doth in the works of creation; as, for example, the imagination of man judgeth that God made this vast earth and waters of nothing; which is more than God could do, for He never made any thing of substance of nothing, for of nothing comes nothing; for what thing or creature, that God made of nothing, God will turn it to nothing again. Then would it be well for all wicked men if the earth was made of nothing, and men made of the dust of the earth; then, when this earth is turned to nothing, its original also; but this earth was an eternal dark chaos, and shall return at the last day into darkness again, and wicked reprobate man shall live upon this earth in eternal torments, in utter darkness, for ever and ever.

" So that, neither the earth, nor wicked man, the seed of the serpent, shall neither of them both be turned to nothing, but shall be in utter darkness to eternity. Again, the imagination judgeth the, sun, moon, and stars, to be of vast greater bigness, though they seem to be small bodies to us; so that the imagination of man, being blind, judgeth every thing bigger than it is, or less than it is; though God hath made the sun, moon, and stars little bodies, to give light unto the earth and waters, and in their light the creatures here on earth do see light; and God hath made these lights bodies in heaven, to answer to that light that is in little bodies here on earth. And shall a man say, the light of his eyes is no true light, but the imagination, that seeth not at all, is called true light; thus it is with astrology and philosophy, that judgeth God to be bigger than He is, or lesser than He is, and his power to be greater than it is, to create this vast earth and waters of nothing; and the sun, moon, and stars of such a vast bigness, all out of nothing: so that the lying imagination hath created to itself a bigger God than the true God, and this God hath a greater power, and hath created things of a more bigger magnitude than the true God ever did and could do, as to make this earth of nothing, and the sun, moon, and stars of such a vast bigness, far bigger than ever the true God made them: but to tell the imagination of man of the true God, that created man in his own image, He became flesh, and became a little child, and grew to a man, and suffered death by his own creatures. Oh! no, saith the reason in man, God could not die, it is impossible for God to die; here God's power is looked upon, by the imagination of men's hearts, to be less than it is.

"Objection 1. Said he, the sun may seem to be but a little body, because of the great distance from us; as, for example, seta man upon the top of St. Paul's, and at a distance he will show as little as a crow. To this he answered and said, indeed a dark body at a distance doth show less than it is. But, said I, let a light body, as a torch or candle, be but a mile above the earth, if it were possible, and it shall show bigger a hundred miles distance from it. As for example:

" When a beacon is set on fire, it seemeth a greater blaze forty miles distance than it doth near at hand, for it is but a little thing of itself; yet, nevertheless, it is the nature of all light bodies, to show rather bigger at a distance than they are of themselves; and it is the nature of all dark bodies to seem less at a distance than they are in themselves. When he heard this, he was convinced, and did acknowledge that it must needs be so in nature, that light bodies did show bigger at a distance, and dark bodies less; so that the sun being a bright fire, light body, acid running so swift in its course, it could not be much bigger than it seemeth to be, notwithstanding he had long imagined the contrary.

"Objection 2. Saith he, we by our art doth judge that the moon doth borrow her light of the sun; because, saith he, so far as the sun is right against the moon, so far the moon is light, and when the moon is at the full, the face of the sun is right over it; so that sometimes the moon seems to have a dark. body, only a little piece of it forked; why is it then, said he? Because the sun is right against no more of the moon, and so much of it as the sun is against it, it receiveth light from the sun, and the rest of the body of the moon seemeth dark. To this I answered and said,

"If this should be so, then that saying of scripture, Gen. i. 16, must be laid aside, where it is said, God made two great lights; the greater light to rule the day, and the lesser light to rule the night. Certainly the moon hath light in itself to rule the night, else those words cannot be true; for if God made the moon a dark body, and that it hath no light in itself but what it receiveth from the sun, then God made but one great light and one dark body, and not two great lights; for if the moon hath not light in herself, but doth borrow of the sun, then the moon had no light in her creation: a man may as well say, that a man is a living man that hath no life in him; for if a man path not life in himself, he cannot move no further than a man that hath life doth carry him; so likewise if the moon were a dark body, and had no light in itself, how could it move to rule the night? The sun, that hath always light in itself, must carry the body of the dark moon, and move it about the firmament of heaven, to rule the night, which would be a great trouble to the sun to do two bodies' works; for God hath set every thing in order, and every particular thing shall do its own work; the sun shall rule the day, and the moon shall rule the night, and the stars shall give their light; so that every thing that God hath made shall do their own works, according to the law God hath placed in their natures. If the moon must rule the night according to God's command, certainly He gave the moon a light in itself to rule with, else it could not rule; for borrowed lights never ruleth well. A man that is stone blind may as well say to another man that can see, I would borrow your eye-sight, that I may see the light of the sun as you do: this cannot be done, for in light we see light; for there must be two lights, else a man cannot tell that there is any light at all.

" For that man that was born blind could not tell that there was any sun or light at all in the day-time, but as he heard others say; but when Christ opened his eyes, then he saw light, because he saw light in himself; and when he received his light, was not this light of his eyes in himself? Was it any borrowed light, or light for Christ? I trove not, for God hath made every creature, that hath light in itself, to see another light that is out of itself; so that in light we see light; there must be two lights, else things cannot be distinguished; for dark bodies, that hath not life and light in itself, cannot borrow light and life of any other; neither can the moon borrow any light of the sun at all, for it hath an inherent light in itself in its creation, as the sun hath in its creation; so that the words of Moses are true, that God made two great lights, the sun to rule the day, and the moon to rule the night; only the moon hath a lesser, but both hath a light in themselves, and doth not borrow one light of the other; else how could the moon fight with the sun in the eclipse sometimes; if the moon were a dark body, and had no light in itself, could it oppose the sun as it doth, that the moon even darkens the sun in the fight? Can a dark body fight with the light of the sun? You may as well say that a dead body may fight with a living man: but these fictions of men's imaginations hath deceived the whole world, and keepeth the people in darkness, and putteth out their own light of their eyes, and calleth darkness light, and light darkness, even in things that are visibly seen.

"Objection 3. Then, said he, how comes it to pass that there is - so many new moons, and sometimes we see but a piece of the new moon, and do discern the rest of the body to be dark, and so the moon doth intrace the dark bodies filled up with light; so that in a matter of fifteen days the moon is full and all light, and in a little time it is quite gone, and seen no more in our horizon. To this I answered and said,
"Were you ever up in the firmament of heaven? Do you know by your imagination how God hath framed it, and how many chambers He hath made in it, and how many planets, stars, and lights He hath put in every chamber in the firmament of heaven. You astrologers yourselves say there is twelve houses and four housons. Are you sure there is no mere houses in the firmament of heaven but twelve? and do you know how many lights there is in every house, and when these lights do remove out of one house into another? or do you know whether one star doth take its light from another star? or hath every star light in itself? or doth the light of the stars and planets remain in their own bodies, and neither increase nor decrease their light, since they were made and sit in the firmament of heaven? Is there any of those stars or lights in the firmament of heaven missing that were made at first? or hath any of them lost their light God put in them at first, when God created the heavens and the earth?
"If you can tell this, then you can say something, as the moon borroweth light of the sun but to give you a little further satisfaction; God hath placed the sun, moon, and stars in the firmament of heaven, and every one of these, houses of their own, that is, the place where they first began to give light, and to shine upon the earth, that

is, the house of the sun, moon, and stars: now God that made them knoweth the house and the place of the firmament of heaven, where they first began to give light; because He had measured out the firmament of heaven, because He made it; but man doth not know, nor cannot know by his imagination, art, and figure: also God hath given these lights power to go out of their own house, into any of the chambers of heaven, even as a man doth out of his own dwelling-house, into more remote parts; yet the man retaineth his own wisdom and knowledge, when he is remote from his own dwelling-house, as at home; so it is with the sun, moon, and stars, though they go out of their own house, yet they retain the same light in themselves wherever they go. And if God hath made the sun so swift and bright to run through all the houses of the firmament of heaven in twenty-four hours, yet that is the sun's own house, where it went first from, and it is the work God hath appointed the sun to do every day and night; and when the sun is absent, in its place the moon supplieth her light, and the moon not being so swift as the sun, it cometh not so soon into our horizon as the sun doth; besides, it passeth throughout the same region as the sun doth, but in a lower region of a degree in the firmament of heaven than the sun doth; and the cause why the moon showeth the light, but a little piece of her, when she is but a quarter old, so by degrees she increaseth till she is at the full, so that the full face and light of her may be seen by the light of the eye. The cause why we see her by a little and a little is, she cometh out of one chamber or house of heaven into another; and as the houses and the firmament of heaven be at such a distance one from another, so we see her light the more, and we see her sometimes half light and half dark: now the piece that seemeth dark, it is because she is not come out of that house or region; but when she is come to that horizon where she was at the full, then she is all light, and no darkness at all; not but that she was all light in herself before at all times, but she was in some chamber of heaven which shadowed her so, that we could not see her whole light of her whole face: as, for example, suppose a man stand in a bottom, and there be two high hills before him, at a distance one from the other; the man standing in the bottom discerneth a man upon the top of the further hill, so seeing him come down the hill a pretty way, but a little lower he loseth the sight of the man, until such time as the man cometh up that hill nigh to him, and when he cometh to the top of this hill before me, I do discern first his head, then after his face, then after his body, so that I see it is a perfect man which I saw at first, but this hill before me hindered the sight of him till he came to the top of it: so it is with the moon—a man cannot discern the full face of her till she hath passed in her journey through all those houses of the heavens which lieth lower in that region where she is, so that the hill and mountain of the earth doth hinder the sight of her until she cometh to the top of the hill of our horizon, then can we see her whole face; for the earth is as a ball,

Two Systems of Astronomy   81

standing upon and in the air; that is, the power of God's word hath made the air a foundation for the earth to stand upon; therefore it is that the earth standeth upon nothing as a man can see; and this is the foundation God hath laid this vast earth upon: and who could lay the foundation of this earth upon such a foundation as the air? None but God only, whose power is infinite and unspeakable. Likewise the earth about with the element, then the earth must needs interpose acid shadow the light of the moon, so that she cannot be seen in her perfect light until she stands upon the top of the ball; but those that are on every side and underneath the ball cannot see her, for she is always at the full in herself, though a man cannot see her so perfectly but when she is at the full; yet the moon is the same light in herself always as when she is at the full, though those on the sides and underneath cannot see her; neither is there any newness in her, but she is the same to-day, yesterday, and same for ever, as long as the world lasteth; ever the great light which God created and appointed to rule the night in one place or other of this world continually: this is truth, and Moses' words are truth, whatever men by their imaginations do say to the contrary.

"Objection 4. Well, said he, how will you make it appear that the heavens are not above six miles high from the earth?

"I answered and said, that I will make it appear by scripture and reason. That will do well, said he. Then said I, see that scripture, Gen. xi. 4, And they said, Go to, let us build us a city and a tower, whose top may reach unto heaven: and in the 5th verse, And the Lord came down to see the city and the tower which the children of men builded: and the 6th verse, And the Lord said, Behold, the people is one, and they have all one language, and this they begin to do, and now nothing will be restrained from them which they have imagined to do. Here, said I, it is plain that there was a possibility for the sons of men to build a tower up to heaven: now if heaven had been thousands of miles high, as the lying art of astrology saith, there could have been no possibility to build up to heaven, and that these men's reason knew well enough; neither could they have laid a foundation to build thousands of miles high: now the imagination of reason in these men were more right which went by no figure, nor rule of art, but by the sight of the eye, and their reason and sense; and they did imagine by the sight of the eye, that it could not be above three miles to the clouds, which the philosophers grant by their art, the clouds to be but three miles high from the earth; so they imagined that the firmament could not be above three miles higher; and we do imagine, said they, in themselves, that they might lay a foundation to build six miles; and, thought they, when we come up to the clouds in building, we shall see then how far it is to the firmament, and so build up unto it. Now the Lord Himself said it was possible for them to do what they had imagined; for, saith He, Nothing will restrain them for what they have imagined to do: so that God knew there was a possibility to build up to heaven, else He would never come down from heaven himself, to prevent them, in confounding their language, if the heavens had been thousands of miles high: besides, said I, do you think when Christ ascended up to heaven, after He was risen from the dead, that He ascended with that body thousands of miles high, from where He ascended up to heaven? It is said, Acts i. 9, While the men beheld, a cloud received him out of their sight: that is, they saw Him ascend up as far as the clouds, which is halfway to the firmament of heaven; for the clouds opened for Him to pass through, and closed together again, out of their sight, for they could not see no further than the clouds: likewise, when the prophet Elijah went up to heaven in a fiery chariot with horses of fire, do you believe that he had thousands of miles to heaven? He said No: besides, there is a possibility to build up to heaven now, as there was then, only it is forbidden of God: but this I say, if it were lawful, and that a man was sure to live seven or eight hundred years upon this earth, as they did then, then a man might as easily build up to heaven now as then, were it lawful, as I said before.

" So that God hath not made the heavens so high as the lying imagination of reason hath; for reason imagineth the heavens to be higher than they are, and reason imagines hell to be lower than it is; so that heaven is so high that reason can never ascend up to it, and hell so deep that reason can find no bottom, therefore called a bottomless pit, when indeed hell is but six miles distance from heaven to this earth, where men acted all their wickedness, shall be that place of hell for all the damned, and the place where the devil acid his angels, which are wicked men and women, shall be tormented to eternity.

"But the seed of faith knoweth the height of the heavens are but a few miles high, and can easily ascend up to it; and faith knoweth the bottom of hell, and knoweth it is upon this earth, and no deeper than this earth, and that the bottomless pit, so much feared by man, it is in a man, and not without a man: therefore, said I unto him, your figure, rule, and art, must be laid down; but arithmetic and numbers is necessary only for things on this earth, to measure land, and other accounts between man and man here on earth; your arithmetic and figures is not to measure the height of the heavens, nor the depths of hell; that belongeth only to the seed of faith, being God's own nature.

"Faith measureth the height of heaven, and the deepness of hell: therefore in these things you are to lay aside your figure and art, and depend wholly upon belief of what we have said in these things, because your reason, skill, and art, let it be never so great, cannot disprove a stedfast faith.

"When he heard this discourse, with much more than is here written, he was very well satisfied in these things and many others, and he grew very mighty in wisdom and knowledge, both in natural wisdom and heavenly; so that every great man of his acquaintance did submit to his wisdom, and loved him for his knowledge; so he continued in it all his life: but about a year or two: after, John Reeve died; he died at Barbadoes[1]."

---

[1] The foregoing Discourse is taken from a book entitled. "A. Stream from the Tree of Life," by the Two last Witnesses, of the Holy Spirit.

CHAPTER VII.

REMARKS AS TO THE RESULT AND IMPOSSIBILITY OF THE TRUTH OF THE NEWTONIAN SYSTEM.

HAVING touched briefly upon the two systems, and given, in as concise a manner as possible, their general outlines in as plain terms as I can do, and divested them of all technicalities in order to make them comprehensible to the most humble mind—being well aware that the learned can at all tunes understand the humble language, whereas the less educated mind cannot so well understand or comprehend the language of the learned - permit me to reason a little on these two most important points:

First, whether the Newtonian system be the true one or not.

Secondly, whether the system according to the holy Scriptures be true or not.

Allow me, with all humility of soul, to ask, in the first place, if we believe the Newtonian system as laid down in Plate 1? Was this system so from eternity, or was it not? If it was so from all eternity, then what hope can we have for a change? If we are to believe the stars are suns, round whom are revolving in circles millions of worlds all like our own globe, and inhabited with human beings, &c., the same as our globe is, are we to consider the inhabitants to be composed of righteous and wicked people as this earth is, or otherwise? And if we are indeed to believe these things, how or where shall the innocent be wholly protected from the guilty hand?

Have we any record from that system, that all mankind were perfectly happy at any one period whatsoever? or are we to consider that all those unknown worlds are peopled with happy beings, and this world the only one where good and evil are mixed together, and has been so from eternity? or if there was a beginning to evil amongst the good, does that system show such beginning, or when there will be an end to it? and does that system point out, to our comprehension, whether the high, almighty, supreme God, shall suffer these things to remain so for ever or not? or what final result does that system convey to our understanding? does it show any way that will lead us really to think or believe that all mankind will be eternally happy after they have had their portion of misery, more or less, in this or any other of the worlds, as set forth by that system? Then, if all mankind is to be for ever happy, is it shown where any such place of happiness is, or otherwise, or even the possibility of the existence of such a place? And if we are led to believe that there is no such place for eternal happiness for the innocent, when they have suffered at the hands of the guilty, but that all things are now as they ever were, and will continue so for ever—one generation passing away, and another coming in its room, &c.

If that system were really correct, then it must be very obvious to the most common understanding, that there cannot be such a place as heaven, (as the Scriptures make mention of,) for there is no room left for such a place, seeing the whole infinite space is filled with worlds, which, they say, you may travel unto all eternity, and yet not reach the furthest one.

Now if we believe this to be so, what shall we think of the divine mercies, and the retributive justice of Almighty God? Shall we, in the greatest reasoning of our minds, say it is perfectly right and just that the helpless and innocent shall be for ever in a situation to be taken advantage of by the evil and wickedly disposed? or shall we say that God will one day deliver the righteous from the wicked, and cause them to be kept apart from each other—the one to rejoice that his sufferings are past, and gone for ever; and the other to regret that all the pleasure he had in this world, and which he unjustly obtained, is gone from him for ever; and in the room thereof, the mortification to know, that those he injured are rewarded with peace, in compensation for their great sufferings; for who shall say that there are not injuries inflicted, and wickedness committed? What should we say if a man and his family be destroyed, and his estate be possessed by his destroyer? What possible advantage can it be to him if a third party come and destroy the destroyer, if he has not his life and estate restored to him? Indeed it will appear far better that we believe the Almighty God is all-powerful in mercy, as also in justice, which if we do believe, then let us look seriously, and consider how far the Newtonian system can be conducive to carry out this faith; and thus let us bear in mind, that it is truth alone that will establish the soul in peace and rest.

CHAPTER VIII.

1. CONCERNING THE ECLIPSE OF THE MOON. 2. THE POSSIBILITY OF ALL THINGS BEING FULFILLED AS NAMED IN THE HOLY SCRIPTURES, BY THIS SYSTEM ACCORDING WITH HOLY WRIT.

THE eclipse of the moon is most certainly a wonderful work of our Almighty God; but when we look and behold how many great and marvellous things there are in the magnificent work of the most high God, we shall then no longer be more astonished at this, the eclipse of the moon, than we are at many other of his great and marvellous works; for it does appear very possible that God can and does cause effects to be wrought upon one object with or without its having any effect upon another, as it may please Him; and so it appears to be the case in this instance, for that which doth eclipse the moon doth not appear to eclipse any of the stars (and only on one occasion did it eclipse the sun); and to show the possibility of the moon being eclipsed by a planetary body passing between the moon and the earth without interfering with the stars, I will refer the reader to the following:

It is well worthy to be remarked, that in the report given by Sir James South, and published in the newspapers, as to the superior qualities of the gigantic telescope belonging to the Earl of Rosse, and by which he says he perceived a star apparently of about the seventh magnitude, which he says appeared to pass between the moon and our earth, or else the moon must have been perfectly transparent, so that the star was seen through it.

This will tend to show that the stars are not so far from the earth as astronomers have so long supposed them to be: consequently it will go to prove much in favour of the system according to the Holy Scriptures; and thus show the possibility of there being a planetary body beyond those stars, and yet be between the earth and the moon.

With regard to the eclipse of the moon, it is one of the very many wonderful works of the Creator to cause the moon to be eclipsed by a planetary body of darkness passing between the moon and our earth, in a similar manner as the moon passes between our earth and the sun; and yet the same planetary body passing between the moon and our earth, eclipses none but the moon only, arid was never seen at any other time, except on that ever to be remembered occasion, the death of our Lord and Saviour Jesus Christ, when the sun was eclipsed while the moon was is at the full. See "the Concordance of the Holy Scriptures, by Alexander Cruder, M.A.," where he speaks of the three great miraculous things relating to the sun, (viz.) the sun's going back ten degrees; also its standing still; and the eclipse of the same at the crucifixion, "when the moon was at the full."

I will say it was that which God had appointed for the eclipse of the moon only; it was then reversed, and eclipsed the sun, as a proof that the Lord of life, who had authority over the heavenly luminaries, had been put to death; and for this cause was that great miracle performed, that men might be ashamed, acid repent or suffer for their guilt of shedding innocent blood.

In the next place I shall show to the reader how all things that are spoken of in the holy Scriptures, may be fulfilled by the system according with the declarations contained in them. See Plate 11.

It is said, In the beginning God created the heaven and the earth; but it is not said that He created them out of nothing, for out of nothing comes nothing, and no thing can be formed. The consequence is, that earth and water must have been from all eternity, although not in a global form; so that when God created or made this world, He divided it from that eternal earth and water above the stars, and He made it in a global form, which was not so before, and thus through faith we understand that the world was ordained by the word of God; so that the things which we see are not made of things which did appear[1]," Heb. xi. 3.

By this system it may clearly be seen how the Lord God of heaven could descend from his kingdom above, to visit the righteous fathers of old, Adam, Enoch, Noah, Abraham, &c. Also by this system it will appear that the Lord could drown the world from that eternal reservoir of water that is in heaven, beyond this visible firmamental heaven, and then take the waters back to the place from whence they came, and re-people the world from the generation of Noah. It will likewise appear possible that men might build up to the visible heavens; and will also appear that the Almighty God might descend from his glorious kingdom, with power and great glory, on the top of Mount Sinai, and give Moses authority to set his laws and commandments before the people, and to speak unto the people Himself; for it is declared that God hath the power of speech as man hath; indeed if it were not so, then man could say he was able to do more than God: whereas it is written, Is any thing too hard for God to do, when his will moves Him thereunto? Is not speech an excellent endowment? and shall He who hath power to give us this great gift not be able to do so Himself? Let all men judge.

By this system it is very perceptible that the immortal God, who made the sun to run its course in the visible heavens, could give such power unto a mortal man, as to command the sun and moon to stand still while He gained the victory over his enemies, and to convince the nations that He was the living God above all other gods. Also God could authorize his prophet Isaiah with a similar great power, so as to command the sun to go back, ten degrees, as a sign to king Hezekiah

---

[1] This quotation is taken from a copy of the Scriptures printed in the year 1608. Some of the modern translations say worlds, evidently being a mistake in adding the letters, since they both agree that God made heaven and earth, not earths.

that, God would add fifteen years to his life; and at the same time to convince the nations of the Jews that Isaiah's God was the true God, and to warn them against idolatrous worship, but to worship the true and living God of Israel, and to keep his commandments and statute law, and at the same time to believe the sayings of his prophet, who had power to prophesy concerning the redemption, which he does in several places in a very powerful manner, concerning God becoming flesh, &c. It will likewise show the possibility of God descending from his heavenly throne of glory, and taking upon Himself the form of a son and a servant, by transmuting his glorious spiritual body into a pure natural body, and be born of a virgin, and be called Emmanuel, which is (by interpretation), God with us; and suffered wicked men, his own creatures, to put Him to death, that He might know by experience how far innocency will be a protection against the evil mind of man, and give a reward accordingly; and that after death He could ascend up into that heaven from whence He came, until the restitution of all things, and from thence come at the last day to the judgment of the quick and the dead, as may be seen by what He says Himself as recorded in the New Testament by the apostles, Matt. xxv. 31-34, and Mark xiii. 23-27.

"When the Son of man comes in his glory, and all the holy angels with him, then shall he sit upon the throne of his glory: and before him shall be gathered all nations: and he shall separate them one from another, as a shepherd divideth his sheep from the goats: and he shall set the sheep on his right hand, but the goats on the left. Then shall the King say unto them on his right hand, Come, ye blessed of my Father, inherit the kingdom prepared for you front the foundation of the world."

So that it will be seen, according to this system, that it is quite possible that all things recorded in holy writ are perfectly able to be fulfilled as they are declared, either past, present, or to come. By this it will also be seen God can descend from heaven at the last day of this world, for mercy and justice, and call all mankind out of death into life, as it is written, the sea and the grave shall give up their dead, at the great judgment; and God can separate the righteous from the wicked, and take the righteous with Him into his eternal kingdom above, to have joy everlasting; and having removed all the glory and the water from this earth, and joined the water to those waters above the firmament, and left this earth quite dry, He can put out the light of the sun, moon, and stars, and leave the wicked in darkness to reflect upon their own evil deeds for ever, as is declared by the prophets and apostles, and more especially in the New Testament. See 2 Pet. iii., and Jude.

The question may arise as to the place called hell, and where it is, if in being. I would have the reader to understand that in the Scriptures, hell is often spoken of as if in present existence: at other times it is frequently observed, that the wicked are reserved for judgment until the great day; so that the scriptures sometimes mention things as if in present being, when they are yet to come; as, for instance, Isaiah (ix. 6) spoke of the birth of Christ about six hundred years before it took place, in the manner following: "For unto us a child is born, unto us a son is given: and the government shall be upon his shoulder: and his name shall be called Wonderful, Counsellor, The mighty God, The everlasting Father, and the Prince of Peace." Also in the Revelation of St. John, He says, He "saw the end of the world," which we know is not yet accomplished.

So also by hell, it is often spoken of, as by the rich man and Lazarus, as if hell was then in being; faith always looking at such things to come, as if so already, time not being reckoned to the dead; for we know it is only recorded that God created the two places, namely, heaven and earth, so that hell will not be until the end of all things come to pass, according to the spirit of the scriptures.

Then there will be a conclusion of all happiness to the wicked, and also an end to all misery to the righteous; which is called in holy writ, the end of the world.

CHAPTER IX.

1. THE CAUSE OF THE TOPS OF THE MOUNTAINS BEING COLD. 2. THE EARTH VARYING WITH THE STARS. 3. THE FIRMAMENT REFLECTS THE SUN'S RAYS. 4. FIVE POINTS OF BOTH SYSTEMS OPPOSING EACH OTHER.

A QUESTION is frequently asked, why it is that the tops of the mountains are so much colder than it is down in the valleys, although the tops of the mountains are most exposed to the sun's rays, to know how this could be—if the sun's rays are of a heating quality? My answer to this would be, that God having caused a cold atmosphere or air to blow round the earth, or pass over the surface of the globe, it overpowers or weakens the strength of the sun's rays, more especially upon those exposed points; whereas in the valley, or hollow parts of the earth, the air does not descend to keep them so cool; yet notwithstanding the cooling quality of the air, it does not prevent the sun's rays from descending to warm the earth; common experience shows us the truth of this; for we all know that it is at all times cooler on an eminence, than in a valley or lower situation; and the higher the eminence, the colder it is, in consequence of being always more exposed to the moving atmosphere.

As a further proof of this, suppose a piece of meat be roasting before a fire, if you allow the wind to blow upon it, it will tend to counteract the heat of the fire from having its full effect upon the meat so roasting, although so near the fire; but if you shield the meat from the wind, the fire will then have its full effect upon the meat.

Another question is, with regard to the fixed stars: it will be quite necessary to consider how the earth will be situate towards all those on the equator, as also the polar stars and all the others that intervene; for if they are fixed and immoveable from their places, together with the sun, and should our earth be the only one in motion (except the planets), in this case it will be seen that the earth will vary in a very regular manner, from one fixed star to another on the equator, every day throughout the whole year; and none would be exempt, as may be seen by Plates 5 & 6.

I have given five positions of the polar stars for your choice in Plate 5. If you cannot move the earth in its orbit, without leaving the polar stars, or altering in its position with them, then it will prove the Newtonian system to be quite incorrect, and not a true one.

Another observation I intended to make before closing, and which has probably not struck the attention of many, is, that the firmament being global, the concavity acts as a reflector to the sun's rays, and causes that light called twilight, being where the direct rays of the sun do not reach.

Here I will suggest to the reader the propriety of calmly considering both systems, as I have done, before he takes upon himself the responsibility of pronouncing his judgment, as it is utterly impossible that by argument we can make a truth to be a falsehood, or make a falsehood truth; therefore it requires great caution, lest we condemn that which is the truth.

It is not my wish to treat of the precise distance of the sun from the earth in the present instance, as I am only treating of the two systems in their great principles of faith and reason; that is, the faith of the prophets and apostles, and the reason of man's own heart: therefore it matters not to me in this case whether the sun be six, sixteen, sixty, or even six hundred miles distance from the earth. I am quite assured that the sun is near enough to the earth to do the work that God has appointed it to do, and not further from the earth than is necessary to answer all purposes. The plain question is this, whether the Newtonian system of astronomy is true, or the Holy Scriptures? for both cannot be right, because they are contrary in their principles. My faith is, that the Holy Scriptures are true, and the system I have laid down according therewith is the correct one, as may be seen in Plates 7, 8, 9, 10, and 11. I will leave others to consider for themselves, as every one must have the responsibility of his own judgment when he undertakes to give it upon this or any other question.

I will here note down a few of the great points, and show how the two systems are completely opposed to each other in their principles:

Newtonian System:	System in Accordance with Holy Writ:
1. That the sun is fixed in the centre, and that the earth rises and sets, or revolves the sun	1. That the earth is fixed in the centre, and that the sun rises and sets upon or revolves round the earth.
2. That the sun is by far the largest in bulk or size when compared with the earth.	2. That the sun is by far the largest in bulk or size when compared with the sun.
3. That the moon is not a light, and hath no light in herself to shine forth upon this earth.	3. That the moon is a light in herself, and doth give forth her own light to shine upon this earth.
4. That the stars are set in the firmament to shine upon this earth but are suns, made to illuminate thousands of other worlds, and not to shine upon this earth at all.	4. That the stars are set in the firmament to give their light to shine upon this earth only; and are not suns to illuminate any other worlds, but are for this earth only.
5. That when we look from the surface of this earth or globe, we then behold the infinite space.	5. That when we look from the surface of his earth or globe, we do not behold the Infinite space, because the firmament prevents us from doing so.

CATCHPOOL AND TRENT, PRINTERS, 5, ST. JOHN'S SQUARE, WEST SMITHFIELD

Plate 1

Plate 3

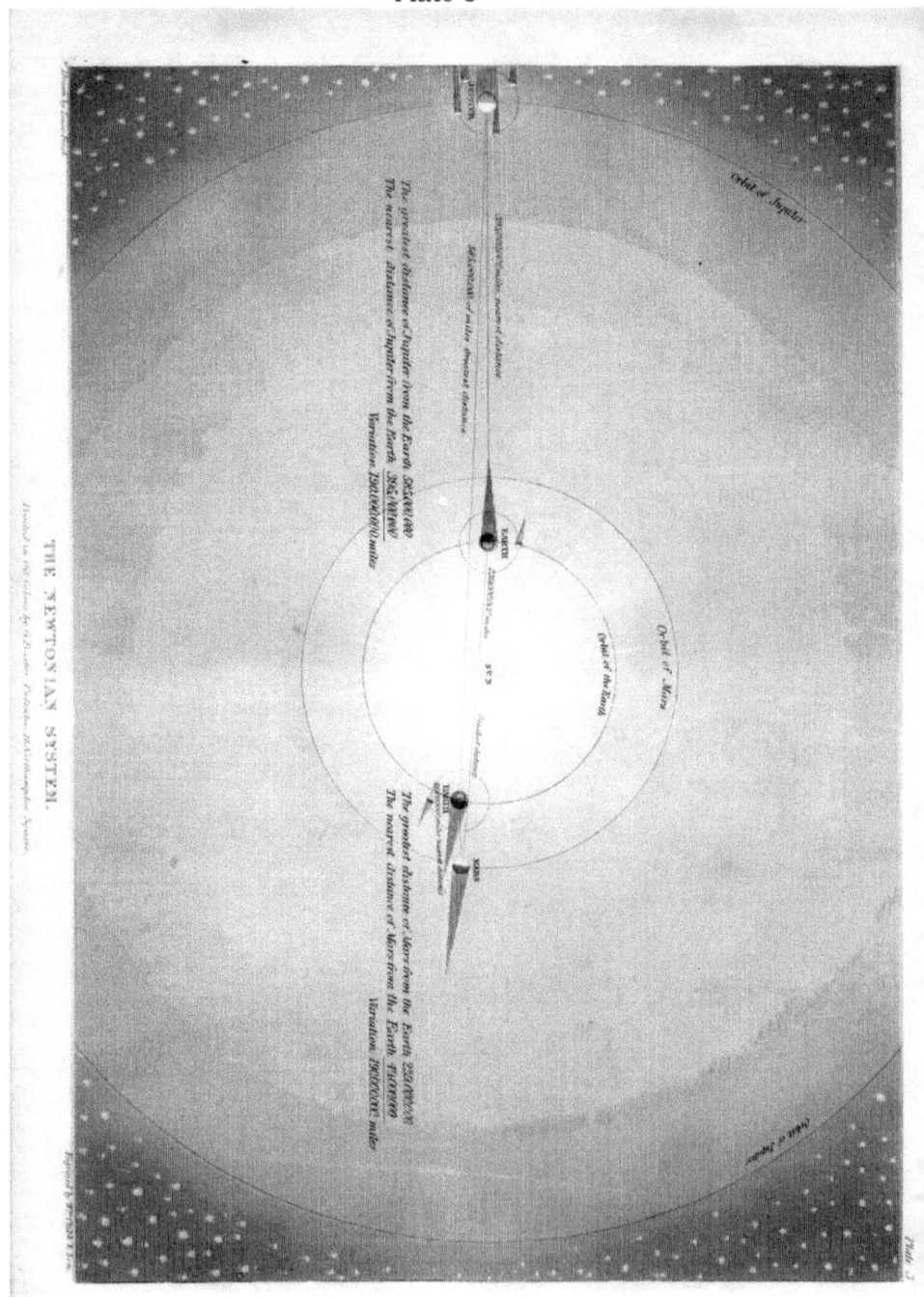

Two Systems of Astronomy

Plate 6

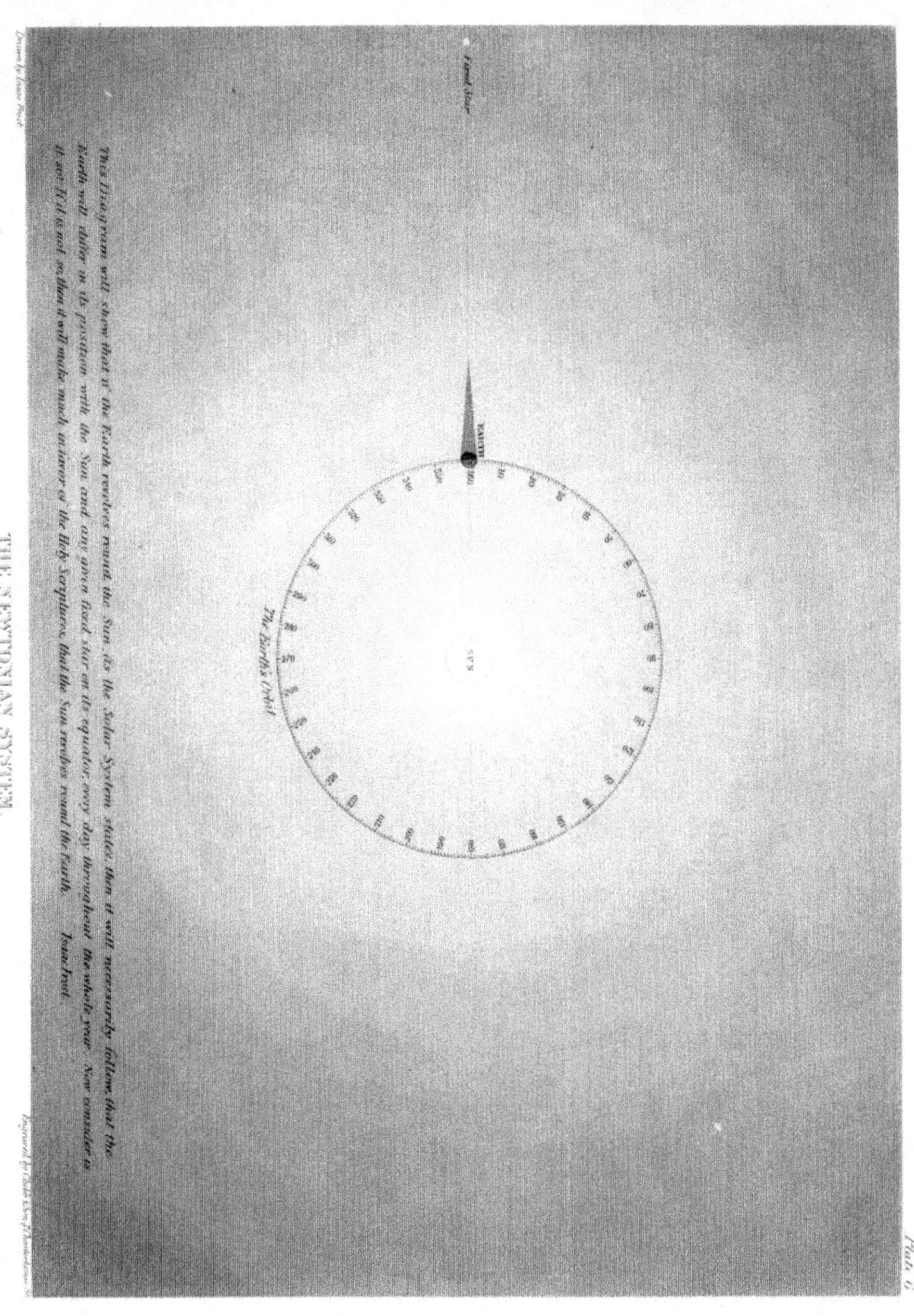

Plate 7

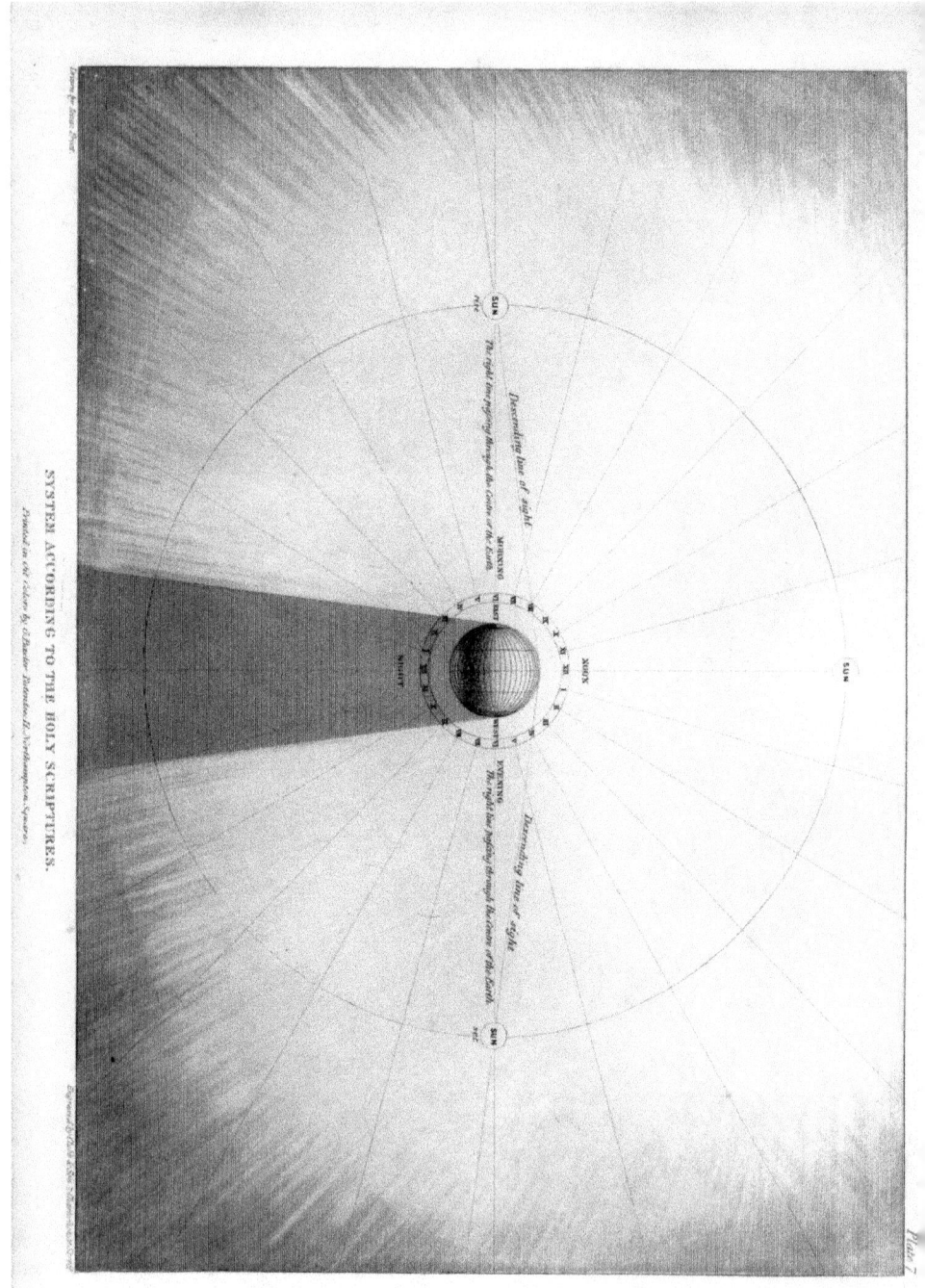

Plate 9

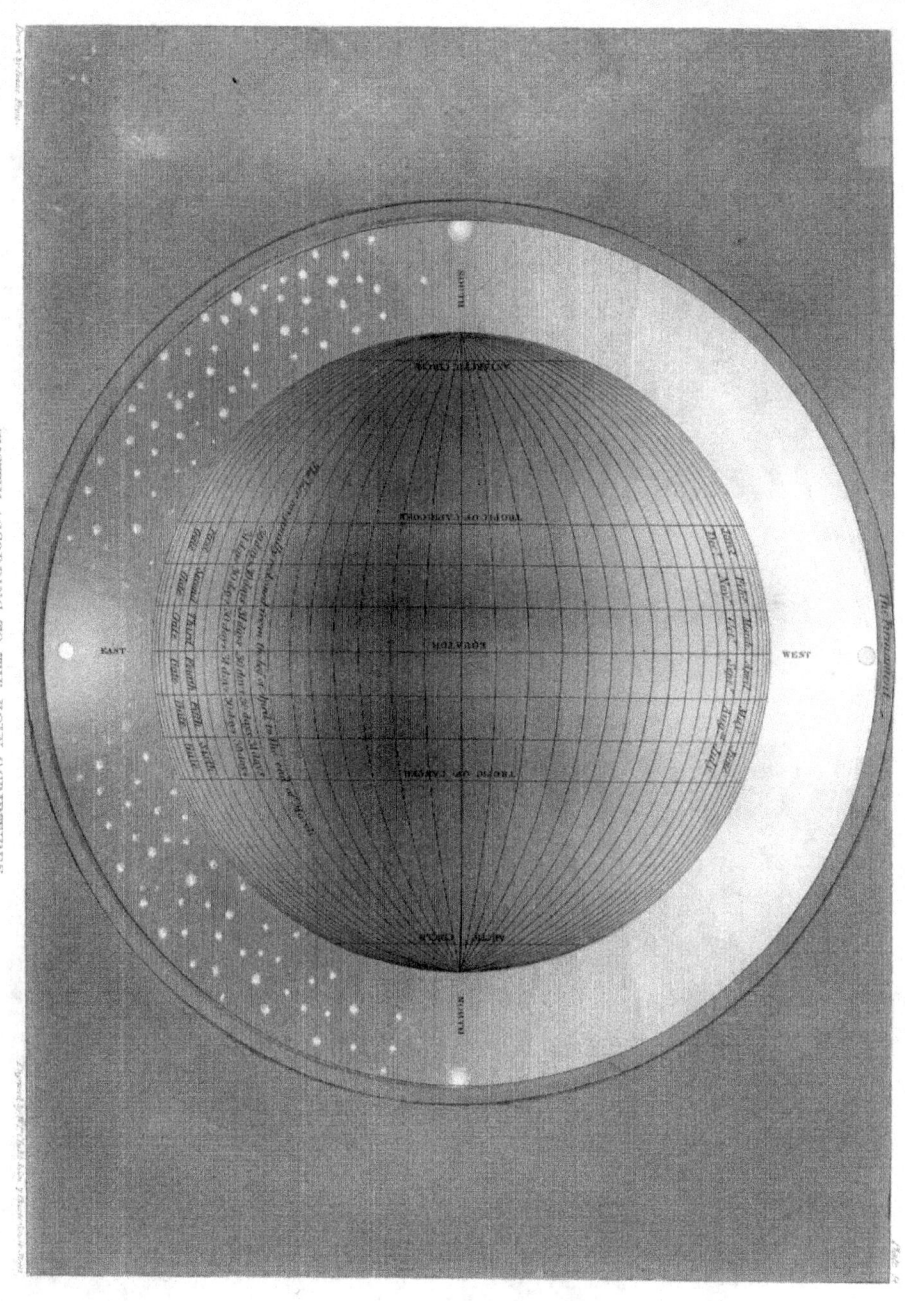

Plate 10

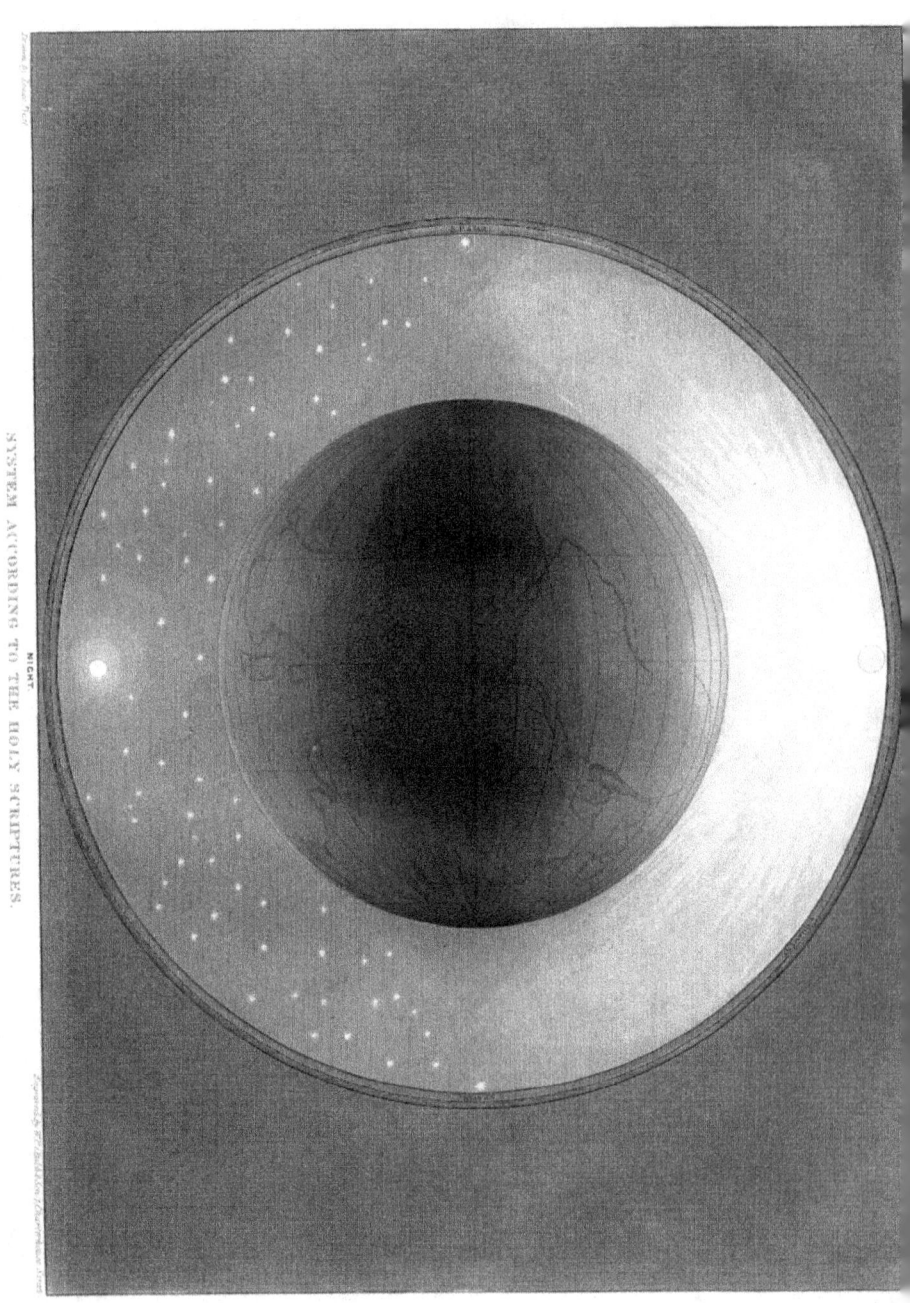

SYSTEM ACCORDING TO THE HOLY SCRIPTURES.

LODOWICK MUGGLETON.

by

J Hain Friswell

BOOKS CONSULTED.

A Remonstrance from the Eternal God; declaring several Spiritual Transactions unto the Parliament and Commonwealth of England, &c, &.c. By John Reeve and Lodowick Muggleton. 1651.

The New Witnesses proved Old Heretics. By William Penn, 4to. London, 1672.

A True Representation of the Absurd and Mischievous Principles of the Sect commonly known by the name of Muggletonians. London, 1694.

LODOWICK MUGGLETON.

FONTENELLE in his "Dialogues of the Dead"—a reproduction of a familiar subject which Landor's "Imaginary Conversation" has rendered more familiar still—brings the shade of Montaigne, that instant dismissed from the earth, to meet with that of Socrates, lonely and unaccompanied, in Hades. The gossiping essayist is delighted to see one from whom he has so often quoted, and begs the philosopher to tell him of the grand age in which he lived, and of the great men by whom he was surrounded—of Plato and Phocion, Pericles and Alcibiades, " to whom," says Montaigne, " the men of his own days formed so pitiable a contrast." To which Socrates—in a method by no means Socratic—replies, that Montaigne is altogether mistaken, that the age in which he lived was by no means grand, that people then did not by any means make the fuss over him which they do now, that distance and time, both grand enchanters, had magnified its virtues and buried its faults; and that, finally, the ages do not degenerate, the world being always about the same compound of fools and wise men.

This, which is not particularly new, is not particularly true. Ages do differ considerably, especially in outward forms, whether the proportion of wise men and fools be about the same or not. We differ so much, for instance, from the age of John Bunyan, Milton, and the more earnest thinkers of their day, that it is quite difficult to realize the men of their stamp. In the comedies of Beaumont and Fletcher, of Jonson, Massinger, and Shakerly Marmion, we find an extinct species of bully, soothsayer, spendthrift, puritan, or swaggerer, as interesting to the student of character as a bone of an icthyosaurus is to Mr. Water-house Hawkins. The fact is, that ages do change and characters die out. Perhaps Sam Weller and Becky Sharp may appear as strange to our descendants as do the "Copper Captain" and the "Roaring Girl" to us—in whom we can, indeed, trace scarcely one modern female trait, except that the young lady "dranke tobacco," and that the leaders of fashion imitated her, out of politeness no doubt, when entertained a few years ago on board the Pacha's yacht.

But strangest of all strange characters was the fanatic and Puritanic professor of religion, with whom Butler has made us somewhat familiar. It no doubt suited the cavaliers to represent these people as always hypocrites; but they were, in fact, as thoroughly in earnest as any body of men in the world: and one proof of this is that they carried the world with them. Everybody joined in the religious cry:—

> The oyster-women lock'd their fish up,
> And trudg'd away to cry no bishop;
> The mousetrap men laid savealls by,
> And 'gainst evil counsellors did cry.
> Some cry'd the Covenant instead
> Of pudding-pies and gingerbread;
> Botchers left old clothes in the lurch,
> And fell to turn and patch the Church.

Carried away and carrying others away as violently as any in this crowd of prophets—as earnest, and at the time more successful than their opponents, George Fox and William Penn—were two obscure men, John Reeve and Lodowick Muggleton, who achieved the honour of becoming the founders of a sect of Christians which has but recently expired, after a duration of two hundred years. As every false prophet must have his first aider and abettor—as Mahomet had his Abubeker, and Joseph Smith his brother Hiram, so John Reeve had his fervent disciple, Lodowick Muggleton, a mad tailor, whom he joined with him in his peculiar ministry, and pronounced to be his "mouth." About the year 1651 these two came prominently before the English people, already disturbed enough by so-called prophets, and for some time favoured the people every year or so with Epistles and Gospels which bear certainly a very distant resemblance to the Apostolic and Evangelic writings. The first of these is entitled: "A REMONSTRANCE from the ETERNAL GOD; declaring several spiritual transactions unto the PARLIAMENT and Commonwealth of England, unto His Excellency the Lord General CROMWELL, the Council of STATE, the Council of War, &c. &c. By John Reeve and Lodowick Muggleton, the two Last Witnesses and true Prophets imprisoned for the Testimony of Jesus Christ in Old Bridewell."

Mad as have been many of the indwellers of Old Bride-well, it never held a madder pair. It. appears that in the year 1651 there were many Richmonds in the field in the shape of prophets. To the first of these, one John Tanee, who had affirmed that there was "no Personal God," John Reeve and his "mouth" went, by virtue of a commission which they had received from the Omnipotent, and with well-chosen and hard texts so puzzled and belaboured him that he was fain to be still. Still they gave him no quarter, declaring that he and the Ranters were "the cursed children of the Dragon-Devil Cain, sporting themselves in all fleshly filthiness, as the people of Sodom and Gomorrah did, that they may justly be damned in themselves in the great day of the Lord. And so much for all ungodly Ranters and John Tanee their king." This is hard measure surely for the despised people called Ranters, of whom it will be remembered John Bunyan, pious and godly, was once one. Ranter—from the Dutch *randen, randien, delilare,* says Richardson—is one who tears a passion to tatters, to very rags, and was at that time almost a new name. Richardson's earliest citations are from Cowley and Bishop Hall's Satires; but certainly we do not hear that the Ranters were by any means a vicious people. It seems, however, to have been the peculiar province of Reeve and Muggleton to "deal damnation round the land," for the next prophet whom they damned was John Robbins, then in the New Prison; and him they approached for the express purpose of pronouncing a sentence of eternal death against. And here we learn that the word Prophet, used after this time by Milton as meaning a preacher, had assumed a far more important meaning. "For this person," says Reeve, "many people honoured as a God, for they fell on their faces before him at his feet, and called him their Lord and their God; likewise he was pray'd unto, as unto a God. Moreover he gave them a law, commanding them not to mention the name of any other God but him (his) only."

This madman might have been deemed by far too mad to yield to the two "commissionated prophets," as he had not yielded to the magistrates. Yet, after hearing the sentence, he bowed his head saying, "It is finished, the Lord's will be done;" and "so much for John Robbins." After this the two prophets were moved to deliver a general damning warning to all clergymen and ministers, forbidding them to preach unless commissioned by the two. As the Clergymen, Ranters, Shakers, Independents, and Quakers, did not pay the least attention to these warnings, Reeve and Muggleton proceeded to further acts, and were straight "seized, apprehended, and committed to Newgate for our faith, by the Lord Mayor;" upon which they at once damned the Lord Mayor and the " London Jewry " (the Mansion House was then in the Old Jewry), especially one Alderman Andrews. This occurred on October 15, 1653; and being thus made martyrs, there was a great outpouring of that peculiar grace which made many believe in Reeve and "his Mouth," Muggleton.

Their next production is "A General Epistle from the Holy Spirit," dated from "Great Trinity Lane, at a Chandler's Shop, over against one Mr. Millis, a Brown Baker, near Bow Lane End, London;" and in it they plainly assume to be the two last witnesses spoken of in the Revelation. They were, undoubtedly, well read in the Bible; and, like John Bunyan, they took care to stick closely by it, never being without a text to quote in their support. An epistle of the Prophet Reeve which follows, opens up somewhat more of their peculiar doctrines, which are, however, very undefined and foggy. The soul of man, they assert, is inseparably united to the body, with which it dies and will rise again. The sin against the Holy Ghost is the rejection of the truth as preached by Muggleton and Reeve. God has the real body of a man, and it is blasphemous to assert that he is an impersonal God or

Spirit. The Trinity is only a variety of names for God, who Himself came down to earth and suffered death, during which time Elias was His representative in heaven.

The founders of a sect very little less erroneous than their own were the most violent opponents of the new prophets. The State having, notwithstanding their flattery of Oliver Cromwell, whom they represented as "Mortal Hebrew Jew" to whom all were to bow down, and whose acts in putting to death the king and assuming the Protectorate they approved, quietly put them in prison, and left them there unnoticed, punishing them, indeed, by whippings for their cursings and blasphemies, but doing no more. William Penn and George Fox, who claimed for themselves a Divine revelation, set upon them with their pens, and would indeed, have taken more carnal weapons to them if they could. These works continued for nearly twenty years, William Penn leading the way in a tract called "The New Witnesses proved Old Heretics" (4to. 1672), and another hand closing it by "A True Representation of the Absurd and Mischievous Principles of a Sect commonly called the Muggletonians" (4to. London, 1694). Three years after this date, Muggleton, who had long survived his companion, died in great sanctity at the patriarchal age of eighty-eight.

Perhaps, as little causes determine great events, it is only to his peculiar surname that Lodowick owes the honour of naming the sect—perhaps it was because he was the more energetic and the longer liver of the two. His other opponents, for there were many, for the honour of being the two last witnesses of the 11th chapter of Revelation, made no mark on the world. Who now hears of Bull and Varnum, of John Tanee and John Robbins? The people appear to have accepted, on good faith, the assertions of John Reeve and his Mouth, and, in the midst of dumb instructors, to have listened to any rash madman who choose to cry out loud enough. As Oliver Cromwell had been pronounced a "Mortal and Spiritual Jew, a natural Lion of the tribe of Judah, according to the flesh," to whom Muggleton was "commissionated" to give advice—which, to be fair, was very good of its kind—so also the people were told, "You that are spiritual may know that the Roman Gentiles spoken of by John, are those people by men called Cavileers, whose princely Race sprang from the loins of King Herod, that bloody persecutor of the Lord of Glory, and so streamed into the line of the tyrannical Roman Empire, or Popedom." Whether this satisfied candid inquirers we are not able to say. Some, indeed, suggested that the Caviliers were Devil-born, and that Laud was Old Nick himself, just as others made Oliver and his Parliament derive all their spirit from the same diabolical source.

A writer in one of the encyclopedias, who tells us that a complete set of the works of Reeve and Muggleton was published by some of their modern followers in 1832 (it is far from complete), adds that these men held very singular and not very intelligible doctrines concerning angels and devils. According to them "the soul of man is united inseparably with the body, with which it dies, and will rise again." This doctrine may be a mere expansion of the belief in the Church of England, which declares in its creed the resurrection of the body—an apostolic article of belief. The question therefore of what became of the soul during the interval between death and judgment was not unreasonably solved by Muggleton, supposing that it lay torpid and rose again to reanimate the body and to receive its due punishment or its gracious reward. As the doctrine of purgatory, to which perhaps our High Church people presently may tend, was, and is by the Thirty-nine Articles declared to be a fond superstition and damnable error, having no warrantry in Scripture, where indeed there is not the shadow of the shade of a sentence (the book of the Maccabees being out of court) to be quoted in its favour. Muggleton's supposition that the soul subsides or is withdrawn from the body for a time, is not without reason. Not one of us knows anything about it; the question asked Lazarus[1] is still left unanswered; there lives no record of reply. Doctor Johnson arguing upon Kit Smart's madness, said that one charge against him was that he asked people to pray with him in the street, and said the doctor, "I'd as lief pray with Kit Smart as with anybody else." So we may as lief believe with Lodowick Muggleton as to the indivisibility of the body and soul. Not so with his anthropomorphism.

On the whole, Lodowick, if a blasphemous heretic, as William Penn called him, was infinitely purer and less mischievous than such prophets as Joseph Smith, Orson Pratt, and the rest of the Mormons. There is and there ever has been in the human mind a credulous disposition to believe in men of strong will who have the madness or boldness to declare that the heavens have been opened to them, and the decrees of God made plain. Muggleton and Reeve declared, indeed, that they were the last audible prophets from the Court of God; but every age since their time has seen its dozens of like prophets, of whom the world happily takes no heed, save when breaking the

---

[1] " Where wert thou, brother, those four days?"
   There lives no record of reply,
   Which telling what it is to die,
Had surely added praise to praise.

Behold a man raised up by Christ!
   The rest remaineth unreveal'd;
   He told it not; or something seal'd
The lips of that evangelist.

            TENNYSON, In Memoriam, xxxi.

Queen's peace they render themselves amenable to the laws of that society which they pretend to purify.

Muggleton, whilst he spread many errors, combated others. He was greatly opposed to those who believed only in King Jesus and his "Personal Reign" here on earth. "It is," he says, "rank folly to believe that men can read the designs of the Lord, and point out the day, the year, or the century in which the Lord's reign shall begin." But being himself "commissionated," he is permitted to know the names of the two last witnesses, and the time of their call. These were of course "Self and Co.;" and one part of their proof was that the witnesses were not to be clothed like citizens, Lord Mayors, and Aldermen, in silk and plush, but in sackcloth. Also, they were to be put to death; and we greatly mistake the temper of the mad self-styled prophets if the very fact of their being permitted to die quietly in their beds was not the unkindest cut which they could receive from an un-grateful and an unbelieving world.

The most curious work which they have left for the benefit of the spiritual discerning reader is called, "A Divine Looking-glass, or the Third and Last Testament of Our Lord, &c, whose personal Residence is seated on his Throne of Glory in another World." We omit many repetitions of the sacred names in giving these titles, for the two last Prophets were as fond of calling them out as is a Mussulman Fakir. In this last Testament the authors solve many scriptural riddles. They tell us of the form and nature of God from all eternity. They answer "the highest Querico concerning the eternal state of mankind." They assert that there is "no reason in God," and of what substances earth and water were from eternity. They tell us, but in so loose a manner that we are no wiser than before, of what form and nature angels were, and how they were created, and who Antichrist is; and they are especially learned about "the Serpent that tempted Eve," who, they assert, was a very beautiful and graceful young angel in the form of man, who certainly did not offer to our common mother "a mere apple from a wooden tree," but, in fact, seduced her from her allegiance to Adam, and thus became actually the Father of Cain, and through him of all the wicked people or sons of the devil upon earth. But unfortunately we have heard all this before. "I should never have done," says Bayle, "were I to relate all the fictions that are to be found in books concerning Eve and the Serpent;" and, indeed, from Josephus to Cajetan, Lanjado and Nicholas de Lyra, there have been some pretty theories broached, none more so than those by the over curious in the first and second centuries of the Church. "We are not to believe, therefore," sneers Bayle, "all the fine compliments which Alcimus Avitus reports to have passed on both sides; for according to the narrative of Moses, this great affair was ended in a few words."

The remainder of the last Testament of these two prophets is filled with a great deal of what Mr. Carlyle terms "clotted nonsense." The authors flounder from Trinitarianism to Unitarianism, and in and out of each; they condemn the unlawfulness of cutting off the head magistrate, and yet praise Cromwell; they propagate more errors than they preach against; they are ever ready with a "damnation to all eternity" for their opponents; and in short, they act like the wild, mad, hot Gospellers they were. Their books have a saddening effect on us. They prove how easily a little incoherent but vivid assertion without proof will attract the faith of man, without even an appeal to his cupidity or to his baser passions, such as have been made by other false prophets from Mohammed to Joe Smith the Mormon. Muggleton and Reeve are singularly free from any such base appeals, nor do they make any exorbitant promises to their spiritually discerning brethren—never being, to use their own trope, at variance with what they thought to be true, "any more than William Lily and his learned brethren, in the astrologian figure, dare say the sun and moon were with themselves." Perhaps it is to this want of mixture of the worst traits of human folly in their scheme that they owe the decay of their sect. So late as 1832 some of their followers reprinted in three volumes the Epistles and Gospels according to Muggleton; but in the Census of 1851, their names had disappeared from the classification of sects and faith in the prophet Muggleton was not found upon the earth.

THE ORIGIN OF THE MUGGLETONIANS.

BY ALEXANDER GORDON, M.A.

MY object in writing this paper is to furnish an authentic sketch of the Origin of the Muggletonians, a people so obscure that I may even call them unknown. Say to ninety-nine persons out of a hundred that So-and-so is a Unitarian, and you immediately suggest doubts more or less unfavourable to the salvation of So-and-so's soul. But say, instead, that So-and-so is a Muggletonian, and you raise no theological idea whatever; you simply excite a natural amusement that any one can be found who is odd enough to identify himself with so uncommon a name. Some time ago I had occasion to examine some papers at the Public Record Office connected with this subject, and on mentioning to one of the officials the purpose of my search, "Muggletonians!" said he, "I thought the leading authority was 'Pickwick'! "[1]

Indeed the name has served the turn of wits, from the period of the Restoration downwards. I might refer to Tom Brown's droll and scandalous invention of the marriage of Dr. Titus Oates to one Mrs. Margaret Wells, a Muggletonian widow;[2] I might quote Allan Ramsay's good-humoured rhymes, in which, giving a "short swatch" of his creed, he thus proclaims himself —

"Well then, I'm nowther Whig nor Tory,
Nor credit give to Purgatory:
* * * * * * *

---

[1] "Muggleton is an ancient and loyal borough, mingling a zealous advocacy of Christian principles with a devoted attachment to commercial rights." —Posthumous Papers of the Pickwick Club, chap. vii.

[2] "Since the saviour of the nation has join'd his saving faculty with a damning talent (for you are to understand his lady is a Muggletonian, and those people pretend to have the power of damnation), we may now expect to see a molly race of half-saviours and half-damners." — The Widow's Wedding: or a true Account of Dr. Oates' Marriage with a Muggletonian Widow in Bread street, Landon, August the 18th, 1693. In a Letter to a Gentleman in the Country. Tom Brown's Works, 9th edition, 1760, vol. iv, pp. 142-6. A curious plate, accompanying this edition, represents the Devil in one corner, engaged in tying the knot.

Nor Asgilite, nor Bess Clarksonian,
Nor Mountaineer, nor Mugletonian;"[1]

and, at a later date, I might mention that singular piece of scurrilous versification, in the shape of an anonymous lampoon upon Whitfield, which owes half its raciness to the fact that it professes to proceed from a Muggletonian pen.[2]

Nor have more serious authors been kinder to the memory of the founders of this out-of-the-way sect, and the principles they professed. Even well informed persons are in the habit of mixing up Muggletonians and Fifth Monarchy Men[3], as if the two were identical. When we find so genial and so acute a critic as Robert Alfred Vaughan[4] sanctioning a similar confusion, we need not wonder that writers less precise fall into the mistake. Lord Macaulay, as a matter of course, avoids this error; but the one sentence in which he deigns to address himself to our subject is full of contemptuous unfairness. It runs thus: "A mad tailor, named Lodowick Muggleton, wandered from pothouse to pothouse, tippling ale, and denouncing eternal torments against all those who refused to believe, on his testimony, that the Supreme Being was only six feet high, and that the sun was just four miles from the earth."[5]

No one seems to have taken in band to write the life of the man here alluded to, if we except the unknown author of a malicious

---

[1] Vide Epistle to Mr. James Arbuckle of Belfast, January, 1719; in the Glasgow Edition of Ramsay's Poems, 1770, pp. 149-153. In a note, p. 152, we find, "Mugletonian: a kind of quakers, so called from one Mugleton. See Leslie's snake in the grass."

[2] The following is the fall title-page of this unseemly production: —
The Amourous Humours, and Audacious Adventures, of one WH††††††††D By a Muggletonian.

"Jew, Turk and Christian differ but in CREED;
In ways of wickedness they 're all agreed:
None upwards clear the Road; they part and cavil:
And all jog on, unerring, to the Devil."—Lansd.

London; printed for the Author, and sold by M. Watson, next the King's Arms Tavern, Chancery Lane; at the corner of Cock Court, facing the Old Bailey, Ludgate Hill, and at the Pamphlet Shops of London and Westminster. [Price 6d.] N.D. 8vo, pp. 29.

[3] See Letter, by J. H. D [ixon], Inquirer, 3rd Jan., 1863.

[4] "The Muggletonians, Fifth Monarchy Men, and Ranters of those days were the exceptional mire and dirt cast up by the vexed times, but assuredly not the representatives of English mysticism."—Hours with the Mystics, 1856, vol. ii., p. 255.

[5] History of England, 1848, vol. i., p. 164.

pamphlet, brought out in 1677, on the occasion of Muggleton's being placed in the pillory.[1] This piece has evidently been made use of by the compiler of the brief notice of Muggleton in Chambers' "Book of Days."[2] It is, however, quite untrustworthy.

More recently Mr. Hain Friswell has included a paper on Lodowick Muggleton in his "Readings from Rare Books." This paper is of little or no value. Misled by the absence of the name from the Census returns of 1851, it speaks of the Muggletonians as being by this time extinct.[3] They are, I believe, about as numerous now as ever they were; and the writings of their recognised founders, which are constantly kept in print, are neither scarce nor dear, but may be had without any difficulty, on applying to the proper quarter.[4]

The rise of the Muggletonians is a very significant fact of that general surging up of the undercurrents of English religious life, which characterised the middle of the seventeenth century. The abnormal forms of English religion at that date have for the most part been sketched by our Church historians in a style both faint and loose, without firmness of outline, and without love for the work. Casual readers are certainly not aware what great and what varied forces of zeal and of activity were at work two hundred years ago, among what we may term the outlandish sects. People who took up Mr. Hepworth Dixon's recent volumes on "New America" were both startled and shocked at the multiplicity and strangeness of the religious communities which he describes as existing now in full vigour across the Atlantic, contemporaneously with our ripest civilisation. But exactly the same phenomena are apparent to the student of men and manners who will visit the obscure corners and travel on the by-paths of the religious history of the Commonwealth. I do not know that England contained then a community of

---

[1] A modest Account of the wicked Life of that grand Impostor, Lodowick Muggleton: Wherein are related all the remarkable Actions he did, and all the strange Accidents that have befallen him, ever since his first Coming to London, to this Twenty-fifth of January, 1676. Also a Particular of those Reasons which first drew him to these damnable Principles: With several pleasant Stories concerning him, proving his Commission to be but counterfeit, and himself a Cheat, from divers Expressions which have fallen from his own Mouth. Licensed according to Order. Printed at London, for B. H., in 1676 [1677], 4to, pp. 6. Reprinted, Harleian Miscellany, 1744, vol. i., p. 593.

[2] Book of Days, 1864, Vol. i., p. 362. The date (March 12) ender which this notice appears, is an error.

[3] Varia; Readings from Rare Books, 1866, pp. 241, 250.

[4] Mr. William Cates, 4, Gloucester Cottages, Loughborough Park, Brixton, S., will supply any of them to purchasers.

Polygamists, or that America contains now a community of Muggletonians; but if these be exceptions, they are about the only exceptions to the completeness of the parallel. Outside the more orderly Churches, whose history is tolerably well known,—the Catholics, Episcopalians, Presbyterians, Independents, and Baptists,—a host of minor sectaries sprang up and flourished before or about the year 1650. Of these some went by a name derived from the founder of their school, as the Brownists the Bidellians, the Behmenists, the Coppinists, the Salmonists, the Traskites, the Tryonists. Others were designated by their cardinal doctrine, as the Sabbatarians, or Seventh-Day Baptists; the Millennarians, or Fifth Monarchy Men; the Virgin Life People. Some chose their own distinctive title, as the Seekers or Waiters, the Family of Love, the Philadelphians. Others, again, such as the Dippers, the Ranters, the Shakers, the Heavenly Father Men, bore a nickname imposed by the ever ready wit of the populace. Some of these were rather Societies than Sects; and, like the early Methodists or the early Swedenborgians, went to church or conventicle at the usual hours of worship, and met for their own purposes at other times. But the tendency of Commonwealth freedom was to sectarianise these societies; just as afterwards the tendency of Restoration uniformity was to extinguish them.

To this motley assemblage of Sects, George Fox added, in the year 1649, the Society of Friends, soon to become better known by the soubriquet of "Quaker," due to the harsh humour of Mr. Gervas Bennet, justice of the peace at Derby, whom George Fox, under examination before him in 1650, had bid "Tremble at the word of the Lord!"[1] Not long after, in 1652, John Reeve and Lodowicke Muggleton came forward with a new doctrine, and the uncouth term Muggletonian began to be pronounced.[2] It is not, like the word Quaker, considered a nickname,[3] unless perhaps by younger members of the present body; and the substitutes for it, such as "Believers in the Third Record," or "Believers in the Commission of the Spirit," are too longwinded and inexpressive for general adoption, even by Muggletonians themselves.

One circumstance which leads us to class together Quakers and Muggletonians is the remarkable fate which has made them almost

---

[1] History of the People called Quakers, by William Sewell, 2nd edition, 1725. p. 25.

[2] The first recorded use of the word I have found is in an abusive speech by Chief Justice Rainsford, at the Old Bailey, 17th January, 1677. "You see he has got a set of thorn, and makes them call themselves Muggletonians, after his cursed name."—True Account of the Trial and Sufferings of Lodowick Muggleton, by [Nathaniel] Powell, edition of 1808, p. 6.

[3] See Letter, by William Ridsdale, Inquirer, 21st March, 1863.

the only representatives, in modern times, of that abnormal religious life of England, which produced so many singular phenomena in the heart of the seventeenth century. Not that all those sects, of which I have enumerated some, have quite faded out, so as to "leave not a rack behind." Some have developed beyond their first incipient stages. Some have been absorbed in stronger and more consistent bodies. Some have sobered down into good Christian common sense. The Seventh Day Baptists can yet show you the ghost of a Saturday congregation in the East of London; and in America are said to thrive. Plenty of orthodox persons may be found, I believe, at this day, who hold the distinctive doctrine of the Millennaries, that Christ will soon come to reign on earth for the space of a thousand years; though the old fury, which was occasionally roused in the Fifth Monarchy Men, has never inspired their modern representatives. Still, for practical purposes, the well known and everywhere respected Society of Friends, and the extremely obscure body of Muggletonians may be treated as the sole survivors of the commonwealth sects. Seekers, like pious John Saltmarsh, have left behind them no successors; Ranters, like John Robins, or the misguided and poetical Abiezer Coppe, have passed from human ken; Behmenists, like Humphrey Blunden or Durand Hotham, or that learned and reverend visionary Dr. John Pordage, and Philadelphians, after the fashion of Jane Lead and Dr. Francis Lee, we look for in vain to-day; but George Fox and Lodowicke Muggleton still find zealous and trusting disciples.[1]

Another circumstance, of more moment, causes us to name these two names together. They are the intellectual opposites of each other. The mutual repulsion of the schools of thought which they severally represented, contributed not a little to define each. The opponents of both made much of the points of apparent similarity between them. Charles Leslie, the Nonjuror,[2] and that apostate Quaker with the savoury name, Francis Bugg,[3] sought to discredit the claims of Fox,

---

[1] Of Churches and Sects, or Societies, in England, Alexander Ross, in his View of All Religions in the World, etc., 1653, mentions sixteen. George Fox enumerates fifteen sects, with which he had held reasonings in 1601 (Journal, edition of 1852, Vol. i. p.395). And in the Post-Boy robb'd of his Mail, etc., second edition, 1706, pp. 422-432, there is a description (by John Dunton?) of the tenets of twenty-four English Sects and Churches as existing in 1692.

[2] The Snake in the Grass, or Satan transformed into an Angel of Light, [by Charles Leslie,] 1696, pp. lxxv.-lxxviii., 9-10, etc. See also the second part of the Defence of the Snake in the Grass, Leslie, Theolog. Works, 1721, vol. 2, p. 357, for a curious comparison of the two men as to their personal appearance.

[3] The Pilgrim', Progress from Quakerism to Christianity, by Fr. Bugg, second edition, 1700, pp. 17-20,

by holding up Muggleton to him as a mirror in which he might see his own face reflected. On the other hand, the adherents of each made matters of life and death, of salvation or damnation, out of the points of dissimilarity which separated them.

In their day, it is true, it would scarce have been possible for a man to cleave to the one, without in some measure despising the other. Contemplating them at the distance of two hundred years, I can please myself with the indulgence of a. liking which is broad enough to take in the two. At least I know I love George Fox, while I cherish a sneaking kindness for Lodowicke Muggleton, and stand somewhat in awe of them both. No greater contrast of character can well be imagined than exists between these rival founders of sects. Muggleton is arrogant, dogmatic, and perfectly free from enthusiasm; George Fox, gentle and persuasive, but with an underglow of fiery flame which leaps forth sometimes, and burns up all before it. Muggleton is shrewd in his knowledge of men and of business, and far from disdaining the enjoyment of a full meal, a glass of ale, and a pipe of tobacco;[1] George Fox, in worldly matters unversed, is a child for simplicity, spare and abstemious by choice in his diet and ways.[2] Both are resolute and honourable men. No greater contrast of faith can easily be thought of than theirs. For while Muggleton comes before us declaring that God lives in regal state " above the stars," and interferes not with things below; while he believes religiously that prayer is a mark of weakness, a remnant of the corrupt nature, and that outward worship of any kind is a folly and a mistake; George Fox, on the other hand, is a man who dwells with God as an ever-present Spirit, who prays as no man had ever prayed before,[3] and institutes that most impressive and spiritual of all Church-worships, the silent meeting of Friends.

Yet, to come to points of coincidence, both these men were bold enough to assert that a new era in religion had begun, the era of the Spirit; that forms were of no value, ordinations and consecrations null and void; the life the evidence of the truth; and salvation the effect of a

---

[1] See Acts of the Witnesses of the Spirit, 2nd edition, 1764, p. 50. v. 12, p. 57, v. 11; Spiritual Epistles, 2nd edition, 1820, p. 497; Penn's New Witnesses proved Old Heretics, 1672, p. 38. This last not very friendly account was evidently in Lord Macaulay's mind when he penned the sentence already quoted; but Macaulay, as is his wont, adds a strong colour of his own. None of his contemporaries charge Muggleton with insobriety.

[2] See Journal of G. Fox, ut supra., vol. i., p. 50, and Penn's Preface, p. 35 "Civil beyond all breeding in his behaviour; very temperate, eating little and sleeping less, though a bulky person."

[3] The most awful, living reverent frame I ever felt or beheld, I must say, was his in prayer." So writes the placid and lawyerlike Penn. Preface, p. 32.

spiritual principle--a seed, as they both called it — quickened invisibly by God, in entire independence of outward professions and creeds. These opinions, and the like, were indeed part of a common stock of notions floating, as it were, in the air; and appropriated by each rising sect after its own fashion, as indications of its revolt against the tyranny of established Churches and the dead level of traditionary creeds. So too, the refusal to bear arms, and the objection to take oaths, were points of conscience not peculiar at that day to the Quakers and Muggletonians, but shared by them with many seekers after truth, who attained no permanent organisation, and have left scarce any traces of their influence on our religious history.

These things they held in common, and these things might possibly have drawn them together, had not a powerful influence kept them apart. The England of that day was not ignorant either of the name or of the charm of a German thinker, by whose mystical philosophy Muggleton, for a moment captivated, was quickly and permanently repelled. This was Jacob Boehme, or (if I may still use that old English corruption of his name, by which he was known to Sparrow and Elliston, to William Law and Francis Okely) JACOB BEHMEN.[1]

At the beginning of the seventeenth century, there dwelt in the small town of Gorlitz a hardworking respectable mechanic; a man of no learning, of no striking presence, with a bright gray eye, and a bent, worn frame; who lived harmless and retired with his wife and his four sons, and made and mended shoes for a livelihood; but who had imaginations beyond his craft, who saw deep into the mysteries of things, whose heart swelled within him till it threatened to burst the harness and trappings of orthodoxies, and sects, and schools. For a time the fire smouldered in his thought and did not break forth; for a long while the vision and the insight remained undisclosed to the world; but, going into the fields one morning at daybreak (ten years after the first luminous revelation had dazzled and startled him), the radiance of a more than earthly glory met and overpowered his soul; and with slow and quivering words, with rude and uncouth turns of phrase, he sat down at length to write. "Morgen Rothe im Auffgang" (Morning Red in the Orient)[2] was his first book. A more strange and subtle series of books than those which this humble cobbler of shoes

---

[1] Jacob Boehme was born in 1575, and died in 1624. His surname is also given in German writings as Boehm and Boehmen; and in its English form appears as Beam, Berne, Behme, Bebemen, Boman, Beamon, Bemoud, Bemand, Behmont, etc,

[2] Called afterwards Aurora, at the suggestion of his friend Dr. Balthasar Walter. Behmen himself published nothing, except the Way to Christ, in 1622; but his writings were copied and circulated in manuscript. The history of their appearance in print after his death is curious.

produced in the dozen of years which intervened between 1612 and his death in 1624, never perhaps flowed from mortal pen. These were books, whose object was to set forth the utter worthlessness of books; arguments which were to expose the fallacy of blind human reason; treatises in which a devout communicant and hearer of sermons would refine away the sacraments into mere acts of the inward life, would countenance no preacher but the Holy Ghost, and would assert that by salvation, or the soul's health, is meant the effect of no dogma, and the result of no purchase, but only the felt presence of Christ living in human souls.

This shoemaker of Gorlitz, little as he is known and read by us at the present day, has had many English followers, admirers, interpreters; but upon one Englishman his spiritual mantle seems unconsciously to have fallen. The year which saw Behmen die, witnessed the birth of Fox; as if Providence were willing to provide immediately a successor to the spirit which was passing away. Both sprang from the people, both were shoemakers by trade, both were of singularly innocent and guileless character, both had visions and revelations in early youth and in maturer age, both had laid open to them, in addition to the deep things of the spiritual life of man, the mysteries and occult qualities of nature, the virtues of plants, metals, minerals;[1] in short, from both the wail of the world was lifted, and they saw in man, in the universe, and in the Bible, things which not only the holy and the wise but even the angels desire to look into; and in the fruit of this knowledge both wrote, not as they themselves were minded, but as the unerring Spirit moved. There are passages in the Journal of George Fox which read exactly like passages from the Letters of Jacob Behmen; and though, in the case of Fox himself, it is clear that the resemblance is due not to any reading, but to a read community of spiritual gifts, yet the early Quakers, as we know from various sources, pondered and cherished Behmen's writings. The Quaker spirit and the spirit of Behmen were one,[2] and against that spirit Muggleton warred with all his heart.[3] How he came to do so, we

---

[1] This is often forgotten in regard to Fox; but see his Journal, ut supra, vol. 66. "I was at a stand in my mind whether I should practise physic for the good of mankind, seeing the nature and virtues of things were so opened to me by the Lord."

[2] See the Looking Glass for George For, 2nd edition, 1756, p. 10. "Jacob Behmont's books were the chief books that the Quakers bought, for there is the principle or foundation of their religion; for they cannot go beyond that, but there they build. This I know by William Smith's letters to me; and you George Foe are far below William Smith in the knowledge of Jacob Behment's writings."

[3] I did wear ribbons on purpose that I might not he taken or thought to be a Quaker, for I do hate the Quakers' principles." Spiritual Epistles, ut supra, p. 242.

shall better understand when we have traced the course of his early history, which is best read in his own quaint, racy, and picturesque account. In transferring the narrative from the "Acts of the Witnesses of the Spirit" to these pages, I shall take the liberty of condensing, and occasionally of transposing, and shall be able to add from other sources some illustrative matter.

LODOWICKE MUGGLETON, then, was born in Walnut Tree Yard, off Bishopsgate Street, London, at the end of July, 1609.[1] The family to which he belonged had its ancestral home at Wilbarston, near Market Harborough; indeed the original stock of the Muggletons exists there still, and must have been native to Wilbarston for upwards of three centuries. "Our forefathers," he writes, in 1678, to his cousin, Roger Muggleton of Wilbarston," were all plain men, yet downright honest men; men of no great repute in the world, nor of base report, as ever I could hear." His father, John Muggleton, was a smith and "farrier, or horse doctor, ... in great respect with the Post Master in King James' time." Of three children born to him by Mary his wife, "I," says Lodowicke, "was the youngest, and my mother loved me. But after my mother died,[2] I being but young [only three years old] my father took another wife; so I .... was exposed to live with strangers in the country, at a distance from all my kindred. I was a stranger to my father's house after my mother was dead.[3]

"When I was grown to fifteen or sixteen years of age, I was put apprentice to one John Quick, a tailor ... a quiet, peaceable man, not cruel to servants, which liked [pleased] me very well, for my nature was always against cruelty, I could never endure it neither in myself nor in others. ... I took my trade well, and pleased my master better than any of his other servants ... hating drunkenness and lust in the

---

[1] The Register of Christenings at St. Botolph's, Bishopsgate, for 1609, contains this entry, "Lodowicke the sonne of Johne Muggleton bapt. Ye 30 of Julye." His Christian name is usually spelled Lodowick; sometimes, by a misprint, Lodwick; or, through ignorance, Ludevick. He himself seems always to have signed Lodowicke. Perhaps it was a family surname. The burial of a John Lodowicke appears in the Register of St. Botolph's in 1612.

[2] The Register of Burials at St.Botolph's for 1612 contains the entry:— "[Aged] 35, Marys daughter Muggletone bury ye 30 of June."

[3] In J. Payne Collier's Memoirs of Edward Alleyn, Shakespeare Society Publications, 1841, pp. 133-135, there are two letters addressed to Alleyu by Stephen Gosson, Rector of St. Botolph's (author of the Schoole of Abuse) which refer to the admission, in October, 1616, of John Muggleton, a poor person, upon the point of threescore years, to Alleyn's Hospital (God's Gift College, at Dulwich), and his removal therefrom for some unexplained cause in August, 1617.

time of my youth. When my time of service was pretty far expired, I heard great talk amongst the vulgar ... of a people called Puritans; some of these Puritans came to talk with my master, though he was no religious man. ... Methought I had a love for those people called Puritans, and ... liked in myself their discourse upon the Scriptures, and pleading for a holy keeping of the Sabbath-day, which my master did not do, nor I his servant. ... In that great sickness after King James died, I was smitten with the Plague,[1] but I recovered quickly, and have not had half a day's sickness since. ... I never bestowed sixpence in physic in my life. ... My time of service grew near out, and my nature had a great desire to be rich in this world, that I might no more be servant to any man; and I thought the trade of a tailor would not gain much riches, I having little to begin with.[2] So I went to work in a broker's shop in Houndsditch, who made clothes to sell, and did lend money upon pawns ... a kind of distracted, harebrained man, his name was Richardson. The broker's wife had one daughter, and after I had been there awhile, the mother seeing that I ... knew how to manage, ... was willing to give her daughter to me to wife; and I loved the maid well. ... So the maid and I were made sure by promise ... and I was resolved to have the maid to wife, and to keep a broker's shop, and to lend money upon pawns, and grow rich as others did. ... But in the twenty-second year of my life, not being quite out of my apprenticeship ... I went to work as a journeyman ... with William Reeve, John Reeve's brother. He was a very zealous Puritan at that time, and many of that religion ... disputed with me about the lawfulness of lending money upon pawns, because they pleaded it was usury and extortion. ... I used all the arguments of reason I could for it, because I had a great desire to be rich, and ... I was engaged to this maid, and her mother would not let me have her to wife except I would keep a broker's shop and lend money. ... But these Puritan people ... pressed the Scriptures hard upon me; which exceedingly perplexed my mind, reasoning in myself that if I did lend money upon usury and extortion I should be damned; and if I would not, then I should not have the maid to wife. So that the love of the maid, and the fear of the loss of my soul did struggle within me. ... After much struggling in my mind I came to this resolution, that rather than I would lose my soul I would lose the maid. ... Thus I forsook the world and a wife. ... She is yet alive, and is worth seven hundred pounds a year."[3]

His account of the "working of his thoughts" at this time is exceedingly curious and full. In due course he became " earnest in the

---

[1] It began at the end of March, was at its height in the middle of June, and lasted till November, 1623; it swept away 35,417 persons.
[2] He says, in his Answer to William Penn, 2nd edition, 1751-3, p. 129. "I never received sixpence portion of my father," and speaks of having had to assist his father instead of to receive from him.
[3] Acts of the Witnesses, ut supra, pp. 6-11.

Puritan religion and practice ... was well versed ... in the letter of the Scriptures, had a good gift of prayer, and was very strong in disputes." "Neither did I hear any preach in those days but the Puritan ministers, whose hair was cut short; for if a man with long hair had gone into the pulpit to preach, I would have gone out of the church again, though he might preach better than the other." Long after his entire change of opinion, he bears testimony to the strength of Puritan principles;" there is no better faith in the world to this day (1677) in the generality of professors of religion." But in spite of all his zeal, he trembled every day under the dread of hell, and "for fear God had made him a reprobate before he was born."[1]

His domestic life scarcely seems to have contributed to the healthier action of his mind. He married twice during this his Puritan stage, each time to "a virgin of about nineteen."[2] Of his wife Sarah (whom he married about 1635, and who died in 1638 or 1639) we know nothing, except that she was the mother of the two daughters who survived him; but of his second wife, Mary, (whom he married in 1642 and who died in 1648) he tells us in one of his letters, that she "was a comely woman to see to, yet of a melancholy, dropsical nature and humour," given to much melancholy and discontent of mind, especially "if things did not go well in this world, as no man can assure his wife all things shall always." When her only surviving child, a scrofulous boy, died in 1653, "I was glad," says he, "(though I used means to help him, but all in vain) knowing that all the children I had by her did partake of her melancholy and dropsical nature."[3]

The outbreak of the civil war proved a crisis in his religious history. "The Puritans," he says, "were all for the Parliament, and most of my society and acquaintance in religion did fall away from that way we did use, and declined in love one towards another, and every one got a new judgment, and new acquaintance, and a new discipline. Some of them turned to Presbytery ... some turned Independents ... others fell to be Ranters, and some fell to be mere Atheists. Our Puritan people were so divided and scattered in our religion that I knew not which to take to, or which to cleave to. I was altogether at a loss. All the zeal we formerly had was quite worn out, and join with any of these new disciplines I could not, except I would play the hypocrite for a livelihood, which my heart always hated. ... So I gave over all public prayer, and bearing and discourse about religion, and lived an honest and just natural life; and I found more peace here than in all my religion. .. I considered that innocency of heart and a just, upright spirit was good in itself, if there was no God to reward it; and that unrighteousness and lust was wickedness in itself if there were no

---

[1] Ibid., pp. 11-15.
[2] Acts of the Witnesses, ut supra, p. 15.
[3] Spiritual Epistles, ut supra, p. 414, in a letter addressed to Mrs. Hampson, dated 11 June, 1674.

God to punish it ... and if there were anything, either of happiness or misery after death, I left it to God ... to do what He would with me. But I was in good hope at that time that there was nothing after death."[1] This lasted till he was about forty years old, viz., to the year 1650.

In this year London was rife with the intelligence of several "Prophets and Prophetesses, that were about the streets, and declared the Day of the Lord, and many other wonderful things, as from the Lord." Chief among these enthusiasts were two men, by the magnitude of whose pretensions Muggleton was evidently impressed, and whose names figure often in his and his coadjutor's writings as the types of all spiritual usurpation. These were John Robins and Thomas Tany.

JOHN ROBINS is a fair specimen of the wildest of the Ranter tribe. He was identified by his followers with God Almighty, was known in popular parlance as the "Ranters' god" and the "Shakers' god," and though, under examination, he denied the blasphemy,[2] it is clear that in private he was far from discouraging it, but allowed a species of divine worship to be addressed to him.[3] His follower, Thomas Tidford, did not scruple to affirm "that John Robins was God the Father, and the Father of our Lord Jesus Christ;" and in accordance with this empty deification, Joan (or Mary) Robins, his wife, indulged a similar fancy to that which, within the last hundred years, filled the disordered imaginations of Ann Lee and Joanna Southcott. In addition to a fluent utterance and a vast knowledge of the Scriptures, Robins possessed, according to the belief of his followers, the faculty of working many marvels. He even claimed the power of raising men from the dead, and had actually raised up thus, according to his own statement, that same Cain that killed Abel, Benjamin, the son of Jacob, the prophet Jeremiah, that same Judas that betrayed Christ, and now they were all redeemed to be happy. "I have had nine or ten of them at my house at a time," says Muggleton, "of those that were said to be raised from the dead. For I do not speak this from a hearsay from others, but from a perfect knowledge which I have seen and heard from themselves."[4] He put forth a wild scheme for gathering, out of England and elsewhere, an hundred and forty-four thousand men and women, whom he and Joshua Garment, his right hand man,

---

[1] Acts of the Witnesses, ut supra, p. 16, and again p. 19.
[2] See The Declaration of Alin Robins, the False Prophet, otherwise called the Shakers' God, etc., London, 1651, 4 to, pp. 6.
[3] See, in addition to Muggleton's personal testimony, Ranters of Both Sexes, wherein John Robins doth declare himself to be the Great God of Heaven, etc. by John Taylor, London, 1651, 4 to, pp. 6. Also A List of some of the Grand Blasphemers and Blasphemies, which was given in to the Committee for Religion, London, 1654, broad sheet.
[4] Acts of the Witnesses, ut supra, pp. 20-21.

his Moses, would lead to Jerusalem to the Mount of Olives, there to make them happy. He would divide again for them the Red Sea, and they should cross the gulf dryshod. He would feed them with manna from heaven; and, as a preparation for this celestial food, he trained his followers to live on nothing more substantial than "windy things, apples and other fruit," (a diet under which several of them starved) and to drink nothing but water. As for ale, that was prohibited, "because it is not of God's making."[1] These were but a few of his extravagances.

With this outrageous fanatic and his followers Muggleton was for a time in close intimacy; not that he ever joined them, but, as he says, "I was quiet and still, and heard what was said and done, and spake against nothing that was said or done."[2]

THOMAS TANY was an enthusiast of a somewhat similar stamp, though it does not appear that he ever reached the summit of Robins' claims. In Robins there was more of method, in Tany more of madness. Originally he had been settled in business as a goldsmith, in the Strand; but the distractions of the times, and the fascination of Jacob Behmen's books had evidently turned his head, and he came before the public in a new character. In a "Proclamation" which he published on the 25th April, 1650, dated "from the Three Golden Lions, without Temple Bar," he says, "I am a Jew of the tribe of Reuben; but unknown to me till the Lord spake unto me by voice; whose voice I heard, but saw no appearance, and He changed my name from Thomas to Theaurau John,[3] since the 23rd of November, 1649." Under this strange appellation he wrote several books, which were issued by the wellknown publisher of mystical works, Giles Calvert, at the Black Spread Eagle, at the West end of Paul's. In these books all the peculiarities which perplex the students of Behmen are so ridiculously exaggerated, as to render the pages of Tany little better than sublime nonsense. His writing stutters and stammers just as, we are told, did his tongue. He is a Behmen gone mad, yet with bright flashes of intelligence gleaming out now and then from beneath the load of ashes and rubbish.[4] Besides his pantheistic writings, his head

---

[1] Declaration, ut supra, p. 5.

[2] Acts of the Witnesses, ut supra, p. 22.

[3] Hence Reeve and Muggleton invariably refer to him as John Tany. His surname, which appears as Tany in the Proclamation, and in the List of Grand Blasphemers, 1654, ut supra., is also spelled by himself Tanni, Tanniour, Taniah, and Totni, and by others, Tane, Tanee, Tanny, Tannye, Taney, Tauney, and Tawney. Evidently it is the French tané (now tanné), our tawny.

[4] I am acquainted with two of these books; his Theousori Apokolipikal, or God's Light declared in Mysteries, etc., London, 1651, 4 to, pp. 78, with Preface, and his Disputive Challenge to the Universities of Oxford and Cambridge, 8vo, pp. 8, N.D. His first work

was full of schemes for the restoration of the Jews. He, too, was to conduct a mixed multitude to the Promised Land, and, as the Lord's High Priest, was to enact again the Law of Moses; therefore he circumcised himself according to that Law.[1] His mission was to follow John Robins with bow and spear. As the lineal descendant of "Charles of Castille, who was son-in-law unto Charles the Great," he claimed the throne of France, nay, the thrones of seven nations. Like John Robins, he came for a season within the clutches of the law. He suffered six months' imprisonment in Newgate, and this probably lost him his business. He changed his residence from the Strand to the City, and at length left London altogether, and went to live at Eltham He was accused of openly burning the Bible at Lambeth, calling it the "Great Idol of England." Among those who took pity upon him was Dr. Pordage, the wellknown Behnaenist and Philadelphian, at whose house he was now and then entertained for a week or a fortnight at a time.[2]

It is clear that the pantheism which lay at the basis of the fanaticism of both Robins and Tany had caught hold, for a time, of Muggleton's mind. The perusal of Jacob Behmen's works strengthened it in him. Many years afterwards he thus wrote concerning Behmen: "His philosophical light was above all men that doth profess religion, until this Commission of the Spirit came forth; which hath brought Jacob Bemon's light and many other high lights down very low within these ten years."[3] Once more he fell into a deep melancholy, from which he was at length delivered by just that same experience of inward revelation which formed the turning point in the religious lives of Behmen and Fox. He is able to give a precise date to the commencement of this inward revelation, even to the exact hour of the day. The windows of heaven were opened to him. He says, "I was in the Paradise of heaven, within man upon earth; neither could I desire any better heaven."[4] He took down the Scriptures, which he had laid aside some years before, and found they were now all plain to his understanding; he wondered no longer at any of the rapturous expressions of prophets or apostles. A single touch more, a slight kindling of enthusiasm, and he might have become a Behmenist or a Quaker. But it is observable that all the while this state lasted he was

---

was a treatise entitled Aurora in Tranlagorum, etc., London, 1651, 4to, pp. 60, and Introduction. Nothing but an actual facsimile would give any idea of the oddness of his title pages. For a summary of his heresies, see Ross, Pansebeia,ut supra. 377-379.

[1] Acts of the Witnesses, at supra, p. 20.

[2] See Christopher Fowler's Daemonian Meridianum, etc., 4to, London, 1655, part i., pp. 53, 60.

[3] Spiritual Epistles, ut supra, pp. 45, 16. The letter is addressed to his friend Mrs. Ellen Sudbury, and bears date 28 Nov. 1661.

[4] Acts of the Witnesses, ut supra, p. 32.

never moved either to write, as Behmen, or to preach, as Fox. He was so well satisfied and happy that he was resolved now to be quiet and still, and to get as good a living as he could in this world, knowing that all things would be well with him hereafter. "But when I thought to be most secure and most private, in a little time after it made me the most public; I not thinking that this revelation was a preparation for God to choose me to be a Commissioner of the Spirit, to declare the mystery of the true God, and the interpretation of the Scriptures ... whereby I was made the most public man in the world in spiritual things."[1]

This revelation continued with him from April, 1651, to January, 1652. "And in the same year John Reeve came often to my house." Compared with his cousin Lodowicke, who was the real builder up of the Muggletonian faith, from whom it rightly takes its name, John Reeve, its prime source, holds but a shadowy place.

Joan REEVE was a Wiltshire man, of a family which had fallen to decay. His father, Walter Reeve, gentleman, is described as "clerk to a deputy of Ireland," an office which I do not understand. His two sons, William and John, were both apprenticed in London to the tailor's trade; and John, who was born in 1608, was already out of his apprenticeship when Lodowicke Muggleton became acquainted with him. As to the precise connection between their families, which made the two men cousins, I have no information.[2]

Reeve's early religious history, I dare say, ran parallel with that of his cousin. Like Muggleton, he was a man of no learning, "no Latin scholar"; nor was he even a great reader, as Muggleton claims to have been.[3] Like his brother William, he doubtless began by being a Puritan; he was certainly, like that same brother, afterwards bitten by the Ranter spirit. William Reeve, we know, lost himself entirely in this direction, became a mere sot, and lived on the charity of others. During the Ranter stage of his experience John Reeve became, under the guidance of John Robins, a Universalist. "John Robins' knowledge and language overpowered John Reeve," as Muggleton testifies.[4]

John Reeve emerges from obscurity at the period of Muggleton's illumination, and we find him constantly at his cousin's house in Great Trinity Lane, extremely earnest to have the same revelation as Muggleton had. "His desires were so great that he was troublesome unto me; for I could not follow my business quietly for his asking me questions. If I went out of one room into another, he would follow me,

---

[1] Ibid., p. 35.

[2] In Acts of the Witnesses, ut supra, p. 45, it is said of the husband of one Dorcas Boose, "He was some kin by marriage to John Reeve and me both."

[3] Divine Looking Glass, 3rd edition, 1719, preface; Whole Book of Revelation., 3rd edition, 1808, p. v.

[4] Acts of the Witnesses, ut supra, p. 39.

to talk to me; so that I was weary of his company. Yet I was loath to tell him so, because I knew he did it out of innocency of his heart, and love to the things which I spoke."[1] However, one morning, about the middle of January, 1652, Reeve came in with a very joyful voice, exclaiming, "Cousin Lodowicke! Now I know what revelation of Scripture is as well as thee!" The cousins conversed, and compared their experiences. The result, in Reeve's case, was as full and glad a sense of peace as had already taken possession of the soul of Muggleton. He gives utterance to his feelings in language which is a mere echo of his cousin's words. "Cousin Lodowicke! Now I am satisfied in my mind, and know what revelation is; I am resolved now to meddle no more with religion, nor go forth after any upon that account [referring to his having gone after John Robins on that account], but to get as good a livelihood as I can in this world, and let God alone with what shall be hereafter." "Thus," adds Muggleton, "when he thought to be most quiet, and not to meddle with any about religion — and so did I also then — a little while after we were made the greatest meddlers in religion of all men in the world, because our faces were against all men's religion in the world, of what sect or opinion soever, as will appear hereafter by our writings and speakings. John Reeve nor I little thought, at that time, that this revelation we had given us did prepare us for a greater Work than for the peace of our own minds; but it proved that God prepared us for a Commission, and that he did intend to chose us two to be his last Prophets and Witnesses of the Spirit, as will be seen."[2]

This "little while after" was but the space of two weeks. For the account of what took place at the close of that period, I must abridge John Reeve's own testimony, as given in the "Transcendant Spiritual Treatise." On the 3rd of February, 1652,[3] "the Lord Jesus, the only wise God, whose glorious person is resident above or beyond the stars, ... by voice of words spake unto me, John Reeve, saying, 'I have given thee understanding of my mind in the Scriptures, above all men in the world.' The next words the Lord spake unto me were these, 'Look into thy own body, there shalt thou see the kingdom of heaven and the kingdom of hell.' ... Again ... I have chosen thee my last messenger for a great Work unto this bloody, unbelieving world; and I

---

[1] Acts of the Witnesses, ut supra, p. 36
[2] Ibid., pp. 38-39.
[3] As this event is invariably referred to by Muggletonian authorities as taking place in 1651, it is necessary to observe that Reeve and Muggleton need the ecclesiastical mode of reckoning, which was commonly employed in London, and which began the year on the 25th March (see Spiritual Epistles, tit supra, p. 492). Hence the date of the commission may be variously given as 1651, old style, or 1651, or 1652, which is our modern reckoning. The same correction is needed for many of the dates in Muggleton's correspondence, etc.

have given thee Lodowicke Muggleton to be thy mouth.' ... Again, I have put the two-edged sword of my Spirit into thy mouth, that who[m]ever I pronounce blessed through thy mouth is blessed to eternity, and who[m]ever I pronounce cursed through thy mouth is cursed to eternity.' When I heard these words, my spirit desired the Lord that I might not be His dreadful messenger. For indeed I thought upon the delivery of so sad an unexpected message unto men, I should immediately have been torn to pieces. Again the Lord spake If thou dost not obey my voice, and go wherever I send thee to deliver my message, thy body shall be thy hell, and thy spirit shall be the devil that shall torment thee to eternity.' Then, for a moment, I saw this hell within me; which caused me to answer the Lord these words, saying, 'Lord, I will go wherever thou sendest me, only be with me.' These were the Lord's words spoken unto me the first morning, and my answer unto my God; I being as perfectly awaked when He spake unto me, the Lord is my witness, as I was at the writing hereof."[1]

That morning, when, as usual, John Reeve ran to his cousin's house, "I asked him," says Muggleton, "what was the matter; for he looked like one that had risen out of the grave (he being a fresh coloured man the day before); and the tears ran down his cheeks apace. So he told me the same words as are written in his first book, and said unto me that God had given him a Commission; and that He had given Lodowicke Muggleton to be his mouth; and said at the same time was brought to his mind that saying that Aaron was given to be Moses' mouth. What my message was, he could not tell; 'but,' said he, 'if God do not speak unto me the next morning, I will come no more at thee.' Which I was in good hopes he would not, for I was willing to be quiet."[2]

Next morning, however, came a message (again "by voice of words,") bidding Reeve and Muggleton go together and deliver an admonition to " John " Tany; which they did, with some unction. Tany disregarded the admonition; whereupon Reeve, in obedience to his Commission, wrote the sentence of eternal damnation against him. Poor Tany soon after employed his distracted wits in making tents for the twelve tribes. At length he built a little boat to carry him to Jerusalem, wherein trusting himself to sail across to Holland, in company with one Captain James, for the purpose of gathering the Jews there, the frail vessel was wrecked, and he and his companion were drowned. "So all his power came to nothing."[3]

On the third morning came, in the same way, a message of still more peremptory character to be delivered to John Robins, at that time a prisoner in New Bridewell. Without even that chance of a respite which is implied in a premonitory warning, John Robins was

---

[1] A Transcendant Spiritual Treatise, etc., edition of 1756, pp. 4-5.
[2] Acts of the Witnesses, ut supra, p. 41.
[3] Ibid., pp. 42-45.

enrolled among the damned. "That body of thine, which was thy heaven, must be thy hell; and that proud spirit of thine, which said [it] was God, must be thy devil; the one shall be as fire and the other as brimstone burning together to all eternity. This is the message of the Lord unto thee." Robins, on hearing the curse uttered, "pulled his hands off the grates, and said, 'It is finished; the Lord's will be done.' These were all the words he spake" Two months after this he wrote a letter of recantation, addressed to Lord General Cromwell, and so obtained his release from prison. "He said, afterwards he should come forth with a greater power; but he never came forth more with any power at all to his dying day."[1]

The two men, against whom the curse of God was thus pronounced, were regarded by Reeve and Muggleton as typical of the upstart errors of the time in matters of religion. Tany was the representative of the Ranters' and Quakers' principles. Robins was the representative of all false Christs, false prophets and prophetesses, of whom there were many in that day; he was the Antichrist, or Man of Sin, mentioned in Scripture; there should come none after him with such high and delusive claims, to the world's end. The sentence passed on these men, and the consequent fall of their power, cleared the way for the Commission of the Spirit, and hence is very frequently referred to in the writings of the pair of cousins.

Reeve and Muggleton now came forward in their character as Prophets. Building upon an obscure intimation in the eleventh chapter of the Apocalypse, they proclaimed themselves the two Witnesses of the Spirit, the Lord's Last Messengers, the Commissionated Forerunners of the visible appearing of the Lord Jesus Christ, the only true God. Their office was twofold; first, as declarators of life and death eternal to individuals; and secondly, as expositors of a new system of faith and religion to mankind.

On carefully looking through their works, I find the names of forty-six persons who were individually assured (either by word or by letter) of their eternal blessedness, and of one hundred and three, who were similarly assured of their eternal misery. Both lists are very curious. The white list begins with the names of Muggleton's own children, Sarah and Elizabeth, and a boy not named, who were blessed by John Reeve on the eventful morning of the 3rd February, 1652; it ends in 1691 with the name of Sarah Delamaine, daughter of Alexander Delamaine the elder, to whose care is due the accumulation and transcription of that large and valuable collection of Reeve and Muggleton's correspondence, afterwards published as "A Volume of Spiritual Epistles." In the black list, which goes no further than 1677, occur the names of the principal men among the early Quakers, e.g., Fox, Whitehead, Penn, Penington; indeed more than half of those on the condemned list are Quakers.

---

[1] Acts of the Witnesses, ut supra, pp. 47-48.

The names recorded do not nearly cover the whole number of those who received the Muggletonian sentence, either at the hands of the Prophets themselves or of their immediate followers. This was not a sentence given at random. Reeve and Muggleton did not affirm that they had arbitrary power to bless or curse whom they would; but if any one committed the sin against the Holy Ghost, which sin the Scripture makes unpardonable, and which they believed to consist in denying the validity of any Commission sent by God, then the Prophet had authority to declare, and was bound to declare that person eternally lost. "Whoever," write the Two Witnesses, in the second year of their Commission, "is left, great or small, to speak evil of this Commission which God hath put unto us, by calling it blasphemy, delusion, a devil, or lie; in so doing they have sinned against the Holy Ghost, and must perish, soul and body, from the presence of our God, elect men and angels to all eternity; for God hath chosen us two only, and hath put the two-edged sword of the Spirit into our mouths as beforesaid, that whom we are made to pronounce blessed, are blessed to eternity, and whom we are made to pronounce cursed, are cursed to eternity."[1] By the application of this plain principle the exercise of so tremendous an authority is carefully distinguished from caprice. It rather vindicates for itself the character of a lex talionis, or tooth-for-tooth principle; and it is true that no language could well be stronger than that which, in the testimonies of Josiah Coale, William Penn, and many other Friends, was hurled against Muggleton.[2] "As for your saying," he writes to Richard Farnworth, "that I have reviled, cursed, and damned the beloved people of God, meaning you Quakers; to that I say, I never did curse any of them till such time as they did judge or despise my commission first; for I never do judge first."[3] However forbearant the Prophet may have been before passing his sentence of damnation, he certainly rejoiced in it, when given, with a stout robust appetite, worthy of Tertullian. "Whitehead said he did hear one that I had damned say, that I had said I was as glad I had given judgment and sentence of damnation upon him as if one had given me forty shillings. This I did acknowledge to be true."[4] "Oh how happy," he bursts forth, in a letter to Colonel Robert Phaire, "are we that shall sup with the great God, i e., in the assurance we have that God hath ordained wicked persecuting kings, and high captains, and judges, and mighty men more than the sand of the sea shore which cannot be numbered, to be damned to eternity. These I know shall be cast into a

---

[1] Spiritual Epistles, ut supra, p. 5.
[2] E.g., "Muggleton, and his obstinate brats, shall howl in the lake that burns with brimstone and fire for ever and evermore." —Penn's New Witnesses, ut supra, p. 42.
[3] Neck of the Quakers Broken, 2nd edition, 1756, p. 67.
[4] Spiritual Epistles, ut supra, p. 241. Omitted in Acts of the Witnesses, p. 117.

lake of fire, burning with brimstone to all eternity; and we, the fowls of heaven, shall eat or feed upon the miseries of these mighty men, as in a supper with the great God."[1]

As a set off against this full-blooded rapture of vengeance inspired by the sense of personal wrong, let it be remembered that it never was any part of the Muggletonian faith that none but Muggletonians can be saved. It is true that the Doctrine of the Third Commission is the touchstone of a man's spiritual condition, so that none who wilfully and knowingly reject it can be saved, and none who truly embrace it can be lost; but the real cause of salvation or of damnation lies far deeper than any intellectual act. There is a radical difference of race between the saved and the damned.

The religious philosophy of Reeve and Muggleton hinges on their cardinal doctrine of the Two Seeds, which give rise to two distinct races of beings whose attributes have come to be blended in human kind. At the root of their faith are Two Prime Mysteries; the mystery of God becoming flesh, and the mystery of the Devil becoming flesh. In Eve the Devil, a fallen Angel, once the noblest of that race whose nature is pure Reason, dissolved himself into seed; melted himself down, so as to lose personality; and Cain was born, a man-devil. Cain and his descendants are the Devil made flesh; a totally distinct race from Abel, and his brethren and their descendants, who, through Adam, inherit the pure life of God: for "the soul of Adam was of the very nature of the spirit of God." When the sons of God intermarried with the daughters of men, for the first time these two races mingled, and a mixed brood has been the result ever since. Every man is a kind of hybrid; and according as he has in him more of the seed of God, or of the seed of the Devil, is life or damnation his portion hereafter, "Damnation would be impossible," says Reeve, "if all sprang from one root."[2]

These two seeds, or "two sparks of fire," in man, as they may be called,[3] are readily distinguished by the instructed eye, as Reason and Faith. Reason is the seed or nature of the Devil; Faith the seed or nature of God. Reason is a searching, curious, speculative, hungering, supplicating impulse, ever feeding on mere notions and imaginations, except where, as in the case of the Angels, it is allowed to feed on the-overflowings of the wisdom of God; Faith is a calm, peaceful, assured and blissful principle, which may or may not, according to a man's opportunities, be accompanied and strengthened by right opinions on matters of religion.[4]

---

[1] A Steam from the Tree of Life, etc., 175S, p. 28. See also much more to the same purpose, Spiritual Epistles, pp. 580-561.

[2] Divine Looking Glass, ut supra, p. 11.

[3] Joyful News from Heaven, etc., 2nd edition, 1751-3, p. 13.

[4] "... ... ... Could we eliminate only
    This vile hungering impulse, this demon within us of craving,

There is thus no Devil except the persons of the damned. Similarly, there is no God but the person of the man Christ Jesus. For in the Virgin, God, who from all eternity was a spiritual being in the shape of a man, dissolved himself into seed, (every spiritual being is capable of this dissolution into seed,) and thus did not simply become incarnate, but was literally converted into the flesh of Jesus. Hence God died when Christ died. So completely were the attributes of Godhead in abeyance, while Jesus lived on earth, that Moses and Elias (with whom Enoch is sometimes associated) remained above as representatives of God, "trustees," as an early Muggletonian puts it, of the divine power.[1] By them was John the Baptist commissioned; to them Christ prayed; through them was the universe governed.

Accordingly the references to God's personality are of the most precise and physical kind, exceeding even the rigid Scripturalism of John Milton,[2] or the refined realism of Swedenborg. Indeed I know not where to find a parallel to the Muggletonian boldness on this subject, unless in the quarter from which the following rude lines come:-

The God that others worship is not the God for me;
He has no parts nor body, and cannot hear nor see;
But I've a God that reigns above—
A God of power, and of love—
A God of revelation—Oh, that's the God for me!
    Oh, that's the God for me!
    Oh, that's the God for me!

"A Church without a Prophet is not the Church for me,
It has no head to lead it; in it I would not be:
But I've a Church not made by man,
Cut from the mountain without hand;
A Church with gifts and blessings—Oh, that's the Church for me.
    Oh, that's," etc.[3]

On grounds of social order Muggletonians would sternly repudiate the smallest sympathy with Latter Day Saints; but this only makes the coincidence all the more remarkable.

Life were beatitude, living a perfect divine satisfaction."
—A. H. Clough, Amours de Voyage, canto iii.

[1] "He spake the decree, and left the virtue of his word in the hands of trustees in the heavens above."—The Harmony of the Three Commissions, or None but Christ, by Thomas Tomkinson, 2nd edition, Deal, 1822, p. 109.

[2] De Doclrina Christiana, lib. i., cap. 2, published 1825.

[3] Sacred Hymns, and Spiritual Songs, for the Church of Jesus Christ of Latter Day Saints, 12th edition, Liverpool, 1863, p. 349.

The main items of Muggletonian faith are summed up in what are called the Six Principles, an expansion of the Two Prime Mysteries. We may condense them thus:

1. There is no God but the glorified man Christ Jesus.
2. There is no Devil but the unclean Reason of men.
3. Heaven is an infinite abode of light, above and beyond the stars.
4. The place of Hell will be this earth, when sun and moon and stars are extinguished.
5. Angels are the only beings of pure Reason.
6. The soul dies with the body, and will be raised with it.

While thus they gave to many doctrines an aspect which will strike most educated minds as being strangely crass and crude, — an aspect which will forcibly recal to the student of Church history many characteristics of the Bogomilian heresy, as it appeared in Bulgaria during the eleventh and twelfth centuries, — it is nevertheless certain that the Muggletonians were in advance of the religious world of their day in some other points.

In particular, they advocated the most absolute toleration and liberty of opinion; did space permit, some noble passages might be quoted from their writings in assertion and defence of the lawfulness of free speech and action in matters of conscience and religion. Nor with the Muggletonians did liberty mean licence. Their system is pervaded throughout by a truly English common sense and love of law and order. It exhibits, on its intellectual side, a strong recoil from the unenglish mysticism of Behmen; and in its sound, sober, ethical character it establishes a solid protest against the equally unenglish laxity and extravagance into which Ranters and Familists, and even Quakers, sometimes insensibly glided, and sometimes avowedly fell.

What strikes one more perhaps than anything else, in examining this system, is its singular union of opinions which seem diametrically opposed to each other. It is one of the most purely spiritual, and at the same time one of the most rigidly dogmatic faiths on record. It deals largely with the most mysterious parts of nature and theology; yet it is always matter-of-fact, and eager to get rid of superstitions. Its followers contend with the utmost fervour for the use and virtue of the Spirit of the Scripture, in contradistinction to the nullity of the bare letter; yet to this day they believe and maintain, on the authority of the letter of Scripture, that the sun rolls round the earth in a day's journey, and that the whole Newtonian system of Astronomy is a series of wanton blunders. An unfriendly critic of the Muggletonian faith might complain that there is a stupid and almost wooden reality about its doctrines; but no one, I imagine, could come soul to soul with John Reeve and not confess the purity and tenderness of mind which may dwell in its piety.

In this slight sketch I have by no means exhausted the details of the Muggletonian system, or entered upon the history of the Muggletonian Sect. I have simply attempted to fulfil the promise of giving some account of the circumstances which led to its origination. The literature and philosophy of the Muggletonians may be thought perhaps to deserve further enquiry and study; and I may take a future opportunity of presenting to the members of the Literary and Philosophical Society the result of enlarged investigations into the writings and fortunes of this singular people.

There are many interesting personages connected with them besides the two founders of the faith. Laurence Claxton, who began life as a Clergyman of the Church of England, Thomas Tomkinson, the Staffordshire yeoman, John Saddington, and James Birch, the leader of the Birchites, are worth, at least, a passing notice.

At present I will anticipate what I may recur to hereafter, only by recording that John Reeve died, after long sickness, in 1658. "Frances," said he to one of the three sisters who watched at his bedside, "close up mine eyes, lest mine enemies say, I died a staring prophet."

Lodowicke Muggleton, a man of harder mould, lived longer, and weathered many storms. Not till his eighty-ninth year was he gathered to his fathers, on the 14th March, 1698.

His tomb in Bethlehem New Churchyard is said to have once borne the following inscription; but the tomb and the grave-yard in which it stood have long since been swept away, and a railway station now rises, in the heart of London, close to where his bones were laid:

"Whilst mausoleums and large inscriptions give
Might, splendour; and past death make potents live;
It is enough briefly to write thy name:
Succeeding times by that shall read thy fame.
Thy deeds, thy Acts around the globe resound;
No foreign soil where MUGGLETON'S not found."

ANCIENT AND MODERN MUGGLETONIANS.

By ALEXANDER GORDON, M.A.

ON the evening of the 14th of February last, while the members of this learned society were enjoying the bounties of providence at the Alexandra Hotel, the writer of the following paper was hospitably entertained by the Muggletonians of London, at their chief annual festival. During the week which followed, he was kindly permitted to examine and arrange the curious store of manuscripts in the possession of this singular community. Having thus so recently imbibed from Muggletonian sources, both classical and convivial, he may, perhaps, be allowed to plead the fact as his excuse for once more thrusting the present subject under the notice of the Literary and Philosophical Society of Liverpool.

At the outset it is necessary to state, that the much greater accumulation of materials than was anticipated has compelled the omission of whole sections of the subject. There is no room here for any discussion of the principles of Muggletonian philosophy and theology. This part of the inquiry will, accordingly, be left precisely in the condition in which it was left on a former occasion. It would scarcely be possible to enter satisfactorily into any such discussion, without trespassing into a region marked "dangerous" by a very salutary law of this Society.

Let it be assumed, then, that the Society is in possession of the Six Cardinal Principles of Muggletonianism, viz.,

1. That God and the Man Christ Jesus are synonymous expressions.
2. That the Devil and Human Reason are synonymous expressions.
3. That the Soul dies and rises again with the Body.
4. That Heaven is a place above the Stars.
5. That, at present, Hell is nowhere, but that this Earth, darkened after the last Judgment, will be Hell.
6. That the Angels are the only beings of Pure Reason.

Let it also be assumed that the Society will recollect by what reaction from the pantheistic spirit which Muggleton detected in Jacob Behmen, in the Ranters, and in the Quakers, these Six Principles were evolved and shaped. And now let us proceed to resume the thread of the historical narrative.

The result of further researches has been very much to confirm the impression that the main interest of Muggletonian history, both theological and biographical, is to be found at its outset, and is concentrated in the personal career of the honest London tailor, whose name is identified with the system which his cousin Reeve claimed to have received by immediate revelation from heaven.

We have traced already the early history of these two men, and brought them to the point of their joint appearance in the world of London as prophets of the Lord; "Witnesses of the Spirit," as they most commonly call themselves. This was in the spring of 1652. In the ferment of conflicting religious opinions which then agitated the mind of London, the new prophets were sure of a hearing, at least for a time. The crowd that had listened to John Robins, and wondered at Thomas Tany, quickly gathered round Reeve and Muggleton. "There came," says the latter, "a many people to discourse with us, and asked questions about many things in matters of religion, and we answered them to all questions whatsoever could arise out of the heart of men. Some few were satisfied and believed; and many despised."[1]

To place their position in a more definite form before their admirers, John Reeve, assisted by his cousin, wrote an account of his illumination, and of the leading principles of his doctrine, which he termed A transcendent Spirituall Treatise. It was printed, but not published, for fear of the ordinance against blasphemy; indeed it would have been impossible to obtain a license for its publication. The crowded title-page bears upon its face, among other matters, this advertisement — "If any of the Elect desire to speak with us concerning anything written in this Treatise, they may heave of us in Great Trinity Lane, at a Chandlers shop against one Mr. Millis, a brown Baker, neer the lower end of Bowlane." The address here given is that of Muggleton's private residence. This work is usually referred to by the title of the Commission Book, and is regarded as containing the credentials of the writers. On the truth of its statements they base their authority. "Many people," we are told, "were more offended at the doctrine therein, than at the Commission"[2] itself, i.e., at the power of declaring men saved or damned according to their faith. It was not to be supposed, considering the temper of those days, that the two Commissioners should be allowed to proceed on their way without some annoyance and persecution. Persons who had been "sentenced," hooted after John Reeve in the streets, "There goes the Prophet that damns people!" Little boys pursued him through Paul's Churchyard with the cry "Prophet! Prophet!" and threw gravel and stones at him, till he took refuge within the sacred walls. One Mrs. Turner, whose husband it seems was willing to go with the Prophet, being "exceeding wroth, and fearful that her husband would be brought into trouble by it, said, if John Reeve came again to her husband, that she would run

---

[1] Acts of the Witnesses of the Spirit, 2nd edition, 1764, p. 48.
[2] Ibid., p. 49.

a spit in his guts." A certain Mr. Penson, in the course of a discussion with Lodowicke Muggleton, broke out at length, "'Wilt thou say I am damned to eternity?' Yea,' said I, 'thou art.' Then he rose up, and with both his fists smote upon my head."[1]

These were minor vexations. The serious troubles of the Witnesses did not begin till their enemies contrived to bring them within reach of the law. At first it seemed difficult to do so. As Lodowicke Muggleton sagaciously observed, on more than one occasion, "they could not tell what to do in it, seeing there was no law against any man for saying a man is damned."[2] A charge of witchcraft was suggested, but nothing came of it. And meanwhile the two cousins were making converts, and converts of some position. Among these were one Jeremiah Mount, a young gentleman of means (of whom one would like to know more— there are some letters of his in the Public Record Office which seem to imply that he got into political trouble in 1663); Captain Clark, a friend of Mount's; Captain Stasy, in the Parliamentary service; and Richard Leader, a rich New England merchant, "and a great traveller into many parts of the world; he was a religious man, but had somewhat declined the outward forms of worship, because he could find no rest there; so he applied his heart more to philosophy and the knowledge of nature than religion, for he thought he had seen the utmost of religion, and that there was nothing in it."[3]

At length, in September 1653, a clergyman named Goslin, a "Cambridge scholar," as he is termed, an excise-man named Ebb, a shopkeeper named Chandler, and two soldiers whose names are not given, having procured a copy of the Transcendent Spiritual Treatise, and being armed with other evidence, joined together to obtain a warrant against Reeve and Muggleton, in the Lord Mayor's court, on a charge of blasphemy in denying the Holy Trinity. After a month's durance in Newgate Jail, they were brought to trial, before the Lord Mayor, Sir John Fowke, found guilty, and committed to the Old Bridewell for a term of six months. They give but a doleful account of their prison fare. Of Newgate, for example, they say, "the boards were our bed, we had no sheets, only a poor flock bed upon the ground, and one thin blanket at top; and we paid seven groats a-week for this lodging, and thought ourselves very well used in a prison, which thing we were never acquainted with before. But we were more perplexed with the prisoners within than with the imprisonment itself." A very ludicrous and graphic account is given of violence and mischief which prevailed within Newgate walls. When Muggleton went to the gates to speak with any, the boys would snatch off his hat, and "pawn it for half a dozen of drink." Three wild highwaymen actually tried to hang poor John Reeve, with a rope tied to the beam of his cell. Nor was

---

[1] Acts of the Witnesses, ut supra, pp. 49, 43, 50.
[2] Ibid., p. 85.
[3] Ibid., p. 58.

their importunity much more reasonable than their malice; one poor prisoner, when he got very drunk, would kneel down on his knees and say, "For Jesus Christ's sake, John Reeve, bless me, for I am a wicked sinner." Nothing like order was maintained in this miserable hateful den till the keeper employed "four condemned and convicted men" to act as underkeepers, and to help him to "shut up the prisoners every night."[1] In spite of the ill-treatment they suffered, our friends did not lie idle in their prison: they wrote and printed Letters and Remonstrances, addressed to the Lord General Cromwell, to the Lord Mayor, and to the clergy in and about London. After leaving Bridewell, in April 1654, John Reeve composed "that spiritual and heavenly treatise, entitled A Divine Looking-glass, and he got it printed in the year 1656. Jeremiah Mount was at the greatest part of that charge. But the printer, being knavish and covetous, quite spoiled it in the press; he huddled it up so close together, for want of more paper, that nobody had any delight to read it through; so that it never yielded the money it cost printing."[2]

This was nearly John Reeve's last work. His life had a plaintive close. He went to pay a visit in 1656 to some friends at Maidstone; but here, in consequence of his passing sentence of damnation on certain persons who despised his Commission, they got a constable to apprehend him; but having timely notice of it he left in haste, and "overheated his blood with travelling to the water side, which was sixteen miles, and he went upon the water at Gravesend when he was all in a sweat, and cooled himself too soon. So he surfeited his blood, and drove him into a consumption, which killed him. He lived almost two years afterwards, but in a sick, wasting condition."[3] Some of his letters, written at this time, contain touching references to his poverty and ill-health. Unable to work at his trade, he was dependent on the contributions of his friends, who, he complains, "make no enquiry after me, whether I am dead or alive. I still continue very sick and weak, so that of necessity I must either mend or end in a little space."[4] His wife was also an ailing creature, and died before him, on the 29th March 1656.[5] When she was gone, he had his dwelling with three sisters, Mrs. Frances, Mrs. Roberts, and Mrs. Boner, who kept a

---

[1] Acts of the Witnesses, ut supra, pp. 73, 75.
[2] Acts of the Witnesses, ut supra. p. 78.
[3] Ibid., p. 79.
[4] Supplement to the Book of Letters, 1831 pp. 1, 2.
[5] This date, 1656, may be strongly suspected to be an error, and should doubtless be corrected to 1658. Reeve had a daughter, for we are told (Sp. Ep., p. 114) that "John Reeve's wife and his daughter did get most part of his living. One Ann Adams, who afterwards married William Cakebread of Orwell, is spoken of as 'his handmaid to guide him to friends' houses.'" (Ibid., p. 530.)

sempstress' shop in Bishopsgate Street, near Hog-lane End; and in their house he died, "about the latter end of July 1658, in the seventh year of the Commission, and in the forty-ninth year of his life."[1] He was interred in Bethlehem Churchyard, an extinct burying ground, the site of which is to be looked for in Liverpool Street, opposite the Broad Street Station of the North London Railway.

His health probably never had been robust, and this gave a plaintive tone to his religion, very different, even on points in which their opinions altogether coincided, from the vigorous self-assertive spirit of his coadjutor and cousin. A remarkable illustration of this divergence of temper, or rather of nature, may be formed by comparing the relations they severally held to a distinguished religious writer of their time, with whom each came into controversy at different periods. John Reeve had seen and read a volume entitled Divine Essays, written in 1654 by Isaac Penington, the younger, before he joined the Society of Friends. He entered into correspondence with Penington in 1658, on the subject of this book, and addressed an Epistle to the Earl of Pembroke on the same topic. Reeve's language throughout is modest, tender, anxious, and conciliatory; to Penington he says, "though this everlasting Light have not clearly manifested itself in thy soul at present; yet because thou mayest enjoy it in due time when the Holy Spirit presents the super-excellency of it unto thy spirit, therefore suffer me to write a little of the effects of it in my own soul;" and to the Earl of Pembroke he writes, "I would not willingly wear out your patience with superfluity of words: Oh! bear with me a little, I humbly beseech you, and conceive it to be from the love of the Divine Voice of God himself, our Lord Jesus Christ, in sending me unto you and all of your sweet and tender spirit."[2]

Many years after, in 1668, Isaac Penington, who had by this time been nearly twenty years a member of the Society of Friends, published Observations on some Passages of Lodowick Muggleton, a pamphlet to which Muggleton replied, in an Answer to Isaac Pennington, Esq., couched in an exactly opposite style to that which Reeve had adopted. "I do remember," he says, " several letters of yours to John Reeve, and of his unto you; some are yet to be seen; and this I say, your language was then very high, only it was groundless; and I suppose you had no faith in what you writ yourself; if you had, sure you would not have left that high language, and have fallen to the silly Quakers' principles, where there is neither head nor foot, bottom nor top." His criticism of Penington's Observations is full of asperity, and he presents his own doctrine in its severest and hardest form, so that one is quite prepared to find the Answer closing with the sentence of

---

[1] Acts of the Witnesses, ut supra, p. 78.
[2] Sacred Remains, 2nd Edition, 1752, pp. 44, 51.

damnation. He adds (and doubtless with truth), "I give not judgment on you out of any malice or hatred, but had rather you had been quiet and still, as you have been many years, since you wrote to John Reeve; if you had not written to me against me and my revelation, I should have let you alone, for I never did judge any man or woman till they did judge me first." Yet Penington's tone was so far from being harsh, that he had expressly said, at the close of his Observations, " Now as for him (notwithstanding all he hath done against the Lord, and against his people), so far am I from wishing any harm unto him, that I could wish with all my heart that it were possible for him to come to a true sense of the true light of God's Holy Spirit." It is very characteristic of the two Witnesses, that Reeve met and accosted such a man with a pleading persuasion, whereas Muggleton strode over him with an imperious dogmatism.

Notwithstanding his sickness, John Reeve had written, in his last hours, a book called Joyful News from Heaven, or The Soul's Mortality proved—strange work, it may be thought, for the deathbed of a man who was certainly religious. By mortality, however, as applied to the soul, Reeve was far from intending absolute extinction without possibility of revival; he meant what has sometimes been called the sleep of the soul. He held that soul and body perish together, and will, at the end of time, together rise; a doctrine entertained apparently by some of the Early Fathers of the Church; a doctrine at any rate by no means uncommon in this country; for, not to speak of such heretical communities as the Soulsleepers in the seventeenth century, the Unitarians of the school of Priestley in the eighteenth, and the Freethinking Christians in the nineteenth,[1] or such wayward thinkers as Richard Overton, Henry Layton, and William Coward, M.D., it may be sufficient to point out as advocates of the doctrine the well known names of John Milton, Thomas Hobbes, Henry Dodwell, Archdeacon Blackburne, Edmund Law, Bishop of Carlisle, and the late Bishop Hampden, of Hereford. Nay, it is not without significance, that of the original Forty-two Articles of Religion, published by royal proclamation in 1552, Article XL., against those who said "that the souls of such as depart hence do sleep, being without all sense, feeling or perceiving, until the day of judgment; or affirm that the souls die with their bodies, and at the last day shall be raised up with the same," was expunged by Convocation in 1562, which thus refused to condemn the opinion.

Reeve spoke of this doctrine by the name of the mortality of the soul; an appellation which prima facie gives a false impression. He might almost as reasonably have called it the immortality of the body; since what he actually believed was that soul and body are found only

---

[1] A small Scotch sect, called the Christadelphians, or Brethren of Christ, who have a meeting-place in Edinburgh, hold this view.

in union, and disappear and reappear together. Of their reappearance he had no manner of doubt, though, strictly speaking, the body that rises is not the identical body that dies. When the death-sleep is over, "the soul quickens," and a spiritual body arises, shaped like the first. On awaking, death will seem but the sleep of a quarter of an hour, or the interval of a moment.

After John Reeve was dead, Lodowicke Muggleton had a clear field for the assertion of his own undivided claim to the prophetic function, and he was not slow to make use of it. It is curious to notice how, even during their joint lives, the more powerful nature of Lodowicke had gained its own way in the shaping of the system which Reeve's Commission had originated.[1] "You say," he writes to Walter Buchanan, in 1671, "I contradict John Reeve. To this I say I have power to do so, and I had power so to do when he was alive, and did contradict him in something when he was alive; and John Reeve wrote somewhat that was error to me, and error in itself, which I did oppose him in to his face, and he could not deny it. And yet, notwithstanding, John Reeve was infallible, and did write by an unerring spirit. This will seem a riddle, except it be unfolded thus. As to the doctrinal part contained in our writings, the Six Principles were written by an unerring infallible spirit in John Reeve, and the interpretation of Scripture written by him was infallible; but John Reeve's experience and apprehension of God's taking immediate notice of every man was an error . . . as I did prove to his face."[2]

This difference of opinion, in which Reeve gave way to Muggleton, was a singular result of their strange boldness in conceiving of God as strictly humaniform, even as to shape and size. Said Reeve, in his epistle to the Earl of Pembroke, "The Creator is no such vast bodiless spirit as you have described him to be . . . he is a glorified body of flesh and bone in the likeness of a man; and the compass and substance of his glorious substance is no bigger than a man is, and the essence of it is but in one place at once. Only take notice of this, that his little eyes are so transcendently bright and glorious, that at one look or view they pierce through heaven and earth, angels and men; and at once, or one word speaking through his heavenly mouth, it entereth (if it be his pleasure) into all the spirits of men or angels."[3] Reeve therefore held, in a form appropriate to his peculiar theology, the common doctrine that God exercises an immediate oversight on all human actions. Muggleton, on the other hand, affirmed that God takes notice of human actions only in virtue of "his law, written in every man's heart, both saint and devil, and no otherwise." Further, he affirms that "whoever doth not act well, by that law written in his

---

[1] Penn asserts (New Witnesses, p. 62), that Muggleton told him he thought Reeve "hot brained and distempered in his head."
[2] Stream from the Tree of Life, 1758, p. 13.
[3] Sacred Remains, ut supra, p. 56.

heart, and doth not stand in awe of that, and fear to offend that law of conscience as if God himself did stand by, all his well-doing is but eye-service, and respected of God no more than the cutting off a dog's neck." "Neither," he adds, "do I refrain from evil for fear of God's Person seeing me, and because he seeing me will punish me; but I refrain from evil because the law written in my heart seeth all my doings, so that God need not trouble himself to watch over every man's actions himself, for he hath placed his Law a watchman in every man and woman, to give notice of all their doings, whether good or evil."[1] Reeve unreservedly deferred to his cousin's judgment on this point, yet it must, I imagine, have gone severely against the grain with him.

The doctrine that God takes no immediate notice has proved a test of othodoxy and a fertile source of division among the Muggletonians from that time to this. It has created that which forms the greatest outward distinction between them and other sects—the entire abandonment of prayer as a spiritual access to God; and indeed the abolition of formal worship of any kind. Reeve himself was by no means disposed in all cases to charge the practice of prayer with weakness or profanity. "I do not," he says, "in the least deny the use of the tongue in prayer, and praises also, so that a man be undoubtedly moved thereto by the true light of the righteous Judge of quick and dead; but glittering words, flowing from natural parts only, in merciless men, are an abomination to our God and his tender love in our newborn people."[2] Indeed there are on record some short prayers of his, and of Muggleton's too, dispersed through their works. Nor was there in the first instance any injunction laid upon Muggletonians to abstain from frequenting the usual places of public worship. "I never did," says Muggleton, "forbid any believer of this Commission of the Spirit to go to church; neither did John Reeve in his time; they all went to church, or to meetings. But [in his Interpretation of the Book of Revelations, 1665,] I had occasion to write concerning worship, and, the believers reading it, their eyes were opened to see it was idolatry to worship as the nation doth, so that many of them refrained from it. Some could not refrain because of persecution; but those that did refrain had much peace in themselves, and were better beloved with me than the other; they that did go to worship had shame and trouble and doubting in themselves, and I let them bear their sin and never reproved them for it."[3] At the present day strict principle induces Muggletonians to forego any attendance upon public worship, even at such occasional services as a funeral or a marriage. And in the few isolated instances in which Muggletonians indulge in the private

---

[1] Stream from the Tree of Life, ut supra, pp. 2, 3
[2] Sacred Remains, ut supra, p. 46.
[3] Acts of the Witnesses, ut supra, p. 147.

use of prayer, the habit is regarded by their fellow believers as an inconsistent eccentricity, the sign of an immature, and so far imperfect faith.

It is odd enough, therefore, to find a caustic and amusing writer, one of whose clever books has just been reproduced, selecting the Muggletonians as extreme advocates of an exactly opposite opinion, viz., the doctrine of a particular providence. Somewhat clumsily says the Tin Trumpet: "Fanatics, whose inordinate conceit prompts them to believe that the Deity must be more engrossed with the affairs of an obscure Muggletonian in Ebenezer Alley, Shoreclitch, than with the general and immutable laws of the universe, presumptuously wrest every unexpected occurrence in which themselves are concerned into a particular Providence, more especially if it be an escape from any kind of danger." And again: "Even a Muggletonian would hesitate at calling this a providential intoxication." Yet a third time: "We submit this accident to the joint and serious consideration of the Muggletonians and Phrenologists."[1]

Though Muggleton managed to secure his own way in the community of which he was now the sole head, it was not without opposition that he did so. His first rival arose very shortly after John Reeve's death.

At the beginning of February, 1658, the Rev. LAURENCE CLAXTON appeared in London. This Laurence Claxton describes himself as a beneficed clergyman of the Church of England, holding a small living of £100 per annum. He was now forty years of age, and had a family of five children dependent on him. Although a parish priest, he seems to have been one of that numerous class who in those days were on the look out for a religion, Seekers or Waiters, as they modestly called themselves. He had been attracted by the pantheistic teaching of the Ranters, and was in the habit of preaching in this strain himself. He came to London, because he had been informed that the two Witnesses, mentioned in Revelations xi., were now to be seen and spoken with; and he was anxious to hear what they could say for themselves. John Reeve lent him one of his books; and this made a deep impression on him. "For the space of three weeks," he says, "I could not be at quiet, sleeping nor waking, going nor riding." He decided at last, after much painful uncertainty, that he must quit his "trade of preaching," resign his benefice, and trust to providence for a livelihood for himself and his little ones. At the instant when he had formed this decision these words came into his thoughts —

---

[1] The Tin Trumpet, published 1836, republished 1869, pp. 7, 8. Horace Smith evidently makes use of the name in entire ignorance of its history, simply for its odd sound; just as Douglas Jerrold in Nell a Wynne, or the Prologue (1833), makes Mrs. Snowdrop say—" Nothing now will serve her but to go upon the stage. 'Tis n't my fault; I'm sure I put the pious Mr. Muggleton under her pillow every night."

"Remember me, how here, in this world where now thou livest, I was a poor despised Saviour, though now a rich immortal God; and therefore take no care, I will provide for thee and thine." At the same time, he adds, the Lord freely forgave him all that was past, present, and to come.[1]

Henceforth Claxton thoroughly threw in his lot with the fortunes of the Muggletonians. After John Reeve's death he asked leave to write in vindication and justification of the Commission of the Spirit. Muggleton gave his consent, and he accordingly wrote four books, one after another, which had a great run among his friends of the Commission, and succeeded in gaining many adherents to the cause he had at heart. Of these books the present writer has seen three in print and one in manuscript. They are written with some power, and, as one might expect, with more polish than was at the command of his associates. What seems specially to have attracted his imagination, and principally engaged his pen was the Muggletonian doctrine of the Devil, as being no invisible malign agent, but, since the fall of Eve, existing only as the unclean Reason in Man. He is merry on the applications of this doctrine. Derisively alluding to the popular portrait of a hoofed and horned King of Darkness, —the only "devil," says he, "that ever was, is, or shall be, is for the most part as comely a creature as walks in London streets; and hath as neat a foot and a hand as any lady in the land!"[2] And the title of the first book he wrote was, Look about you, for the Devil that you fear is in you.

Claxton might have continued to render great service to Muggleton, had not his confidence in his own abilities proved fatal to his submissively working under his chief. "He grew so proud as to say that nobody could write in the vindication of this Commission, now that John Reeve was dead, but he; and to that purpose he wrote another book, intituled "The Lost Sheep Found, 1660."[3] When

---

[1] See Introductory Epistle to The Right Devil Discovered, &c., by Laur. Claxton, 1659.

[2] Right Devil, ut supra, p. 22. Compare the following question and answer from Fielding's Eurydice (1735):

"Mr. Spindle, Well, but what sort of a fellow is the old gentleman, the devil, hey?

"Capt. Weazle. Is he? Why, a very pretty sort of a gentleman, a very fine gentleman; but, my dear, you have seen him five hundred times already. The moment I saw him here, I remembered to have seen him shuffle cards at White's and George's, to have met him often on the Exchange, and in the Alley, and never missed him in or about Westminster Hall. I will introduce you to him,"

[3] Sir Walter Scott had seen this Lost Sheep, which the present writer has not yet found. He treats it, however, as the production of a Familist; evidently confusing the Muggletonians with the Grindletonians, an earlier sect. See Note E. to Woodstock,

Muggleton read this book, at the instance of several believers who complained of Claxton's lording it over them in it, he discovered that his new assistant was exalting himself as the only true Bishop (note the recovered accent of the priest, the only true Bishop) and faithful messenger of Jesus Christ; and that he was describing Muggleton as merely John Reeve's mouthpiece and no more. Whereupon Muggleton at once and for ever interdicted Laurence Claxton from writing in defence of the Commission. This was in 1660.[1] For a year Claxton stood out in opposition; but obtaining no followers, and finding Muggleton's power too strong for him, he humbled himself and acknowledged his fault. Muggleton accordingly forgave him, and took him again into his favour; cautiously tying him down, however, to write no more. His end is thus narrated, by the man whom he had vainly opposed. "It came to pass, when the fire destroyed the city of London, he, to get a livelihood, did engage to help persons of quality to borrow money, to build their houses again. But the persons that had the money did run away, and left Claxton in the lurch; the debt was £100. So he was arrested and put in Ludgate Gaol for this money. He lay there a whole year, and died there, But he gave a very good testimony of his faith in the true God, and in this Commission of the Spirit, and of that full assurance of eternal happiness ho should enjoy to eternity."[2]

Matters went on pretty smoothly with our Prophet for about ten years after Claxton's recantation. He wrote books, disputed with all comers, paid visits to his friends in various parts of the country. Among other places, he visited Nottingham in 1663, at the expense of a "Society of Behmenists, mixed with Quakers," who invited him thither at the instance of his friend Ellen Sudbury, wife of Richard Sudbury, an ironmonger of Nottingham. It was on one of his journeys that he got into difficulties at Chesterfield, where his valued friend and correspondent, Mrs. Dorothy Carter, a widow, and the aunt of Ellen Sudbury, kept a small school. He was apprehended and committed to Derby Gaol, at the instance of the Rev. John Coope, the vicar of Chesterfield, on the old charge of denying the Holy Trinity. The horse on which he rode was also seized on behalf of the Lord of the Manor, and he was more troubled for the horse than for himself,

---

[1] Muggleton spoke of Claxton as a Gehazi, and attributes his change of tone in part to his having "consulted with that venomous serpent," his wife, Frances, who seems never to have shared her husband's belief in the Witnesses, and had been sentenced by John Reeve. Muggleton bade the believers in Maidstone allow Claxton "no more maintenance weekly, as you have done formerly;" still he continued to recommend his earlier writings, and furnished them to believers as late as 1684.

[2] Acts of the Witnesses, ut supra, p. 82.

"because his friend, John Brunt, was surety for the horse, else pay four pounds." The Earl of Newcastle, however, who was Lord of the Manor, on hearing of the circumstances, "was angry," and said, " Will you take away a man's horse before he be convicted and condemned? I charge you," said he, "that the horse be put to grass, and let the owner pay for his meat." Coope, the prosecutor, was surprised at the sense and courage which Muggleton displayed on examination; and said to the aldermen, when the prisoner was removed, "that this man was the soberest, wisest man of a fanatic that ever he talked with;" he had fancied him a sort of Quaker. However, Muggleton lay in Derby Gaol nine days, and then was released on bail to meet his trial at the next assizes. Probably then the prosecution was allowed to drop, for he complains of nothing except the nine days' imprisonment and the fees of the prison, and the grief which his detention caused to his newly married wife.

This imprisonment in Derby Gaol is worth noting, inasmuch as it was the occasion of an interview between Lodowicke Muggleton and that same Gervase Bennet (or Benet) whose sarcasm gave rise to the fixing of the name "Quakers" upon the "Society of Friends of Truth," or followers of George Fox. It does not appear that we have any other account of Judge Bennet which gives any insight into the character of the man. Muggleton describes him as "more atheistical" than his brother magistrates, "being of the Sadducee spirit," and says that on his wisdom and knowledge they all depended. He speaks of him too as "a moderate man, who asked his questions moderately." For four hours they talked together on points of theology. They had agreed to refer the topics of their discussion to the arbitrament of Holy Scripture, in the handling of which Muggleton showed his wonted shrewdness. Bennet was nonplused, to the great delight of the magistrates, the sheriff's men, and the jailor, who were present at the interview, and rejoiced in the defeat of one who had so often vanquished them in argument. They could not restrain their glee, but frequently interrupted the colloquy. "Mr. Bennet, we think you have met with one that is too hard for you now!" "Now, Mr. Bennet, you have met with your match!" Bennet showed great good humour in the disputation; he evidently was very much taken with his stout opponent, and acknowledged that he approved of what Muggleton had spoken better than of anything that ever he heard in his life, and could not gainsay it; but said, moreover, he could not venture his salvation on any man's words. On one point they were agreed, to begin with. Bennet had "been a long time of the opinion that the soul of man is mortal, and doth die."[1] This picture of the man, candid, materialistic, literal, fond of disputation, and of all things abhorring fanaticism, answers exactly to the character which Fox's Journal

---

[1] Acts of the Witnesses, ut supra, pp. 93-102.

leads us to form of him, and supplies an interesting historical confirmation of its truth.

Earlier in the same year in which he suffered imprisonment at Derby, Muggleton had married for the third time. His wife, Mary Martin, was the daughter of John Martin, a tanner, at East Mailing, in Kent. "I had been," says he, "a widower sixteen years before I took this maid to wife; she was twenty-five years of age when I married her, and I was about fifty-three years old when I took her to wife. She was of a good, meek, innocent and just nature, besides the strong faith and zeal she had in this Commission of the Spirit; so that she was very suitable, both in spiritual and temporal qualifications, unto my nature."[1] Indeed this last marriage of his seems to have been a very happy one. His wife brought him a little property, and devoted herself to his interests till the day of his death; often by her quickness of wit standing between him and danger; and tending his latter years with the most patient care. She survived him twenty years.

Derby Gaol was not the last prison into which Muggleton found his way. His books were seized in London in 1670; but he escaped the malice of his persecutors, and remained in hiding for a time. Nor would he have appeared again, probably, in a court of law, had not the death, in 1675, of a well-to-do friend of his, Deborah Brunt, widow of John Brunt (one of the first believers, and a good friend to the Witnesses during their imprisonment in 1653), left him in the position of her executor. He brought an action of trespass against Sir John James, in respect of some house property, formerly belonging to Mrs. Brunt, in the Postern, London Wall. This led to a lawsuit, in the course of which he was obliged to make his appearance in the Spiritual Court, only to be once more apprehended on the charge of blasphemy.

This was at the lowest ebb of his fortunes. For, during his enforced absence from home, certain of his followers had revolted; and, under four notable ringleaders (a scrivener, a flaxman, a brewer, and—what Muggleton hated of all things—a Scotchman), had declared that Nine Assertions made by the prophet, which they specified in writing, were contrary both to common sense and to the principles of John Reeve. The Assertions are certainly strong enough; however, Muggleton defended them through thick and thin. As to common sense, what was that but reason; and reason was the Devil. And as to John Reeve, why faith in a living prophet's word was surely better than quotation of a dead one's writing.

---

[1] Ibid., p. 86. The marriage took place in 1663, at some time previous to 14th Nov. 1663. (See Letter to Dorothy Carter, of that date.) It was solemnised "according to the law of England." It is presumed that it did not take place at Church, as no entry of it is to be heard of in any likely Parish Register.

It showed the power of the man's character that, although circumstances forbade him to meet the rebels openly, yet his denunciation of them by letter was enough to put an end to the division. The four leaders were expelled; one only of them being allowed afterwards to return to the fold. As for the Scotchman, Walter Buchanan, he received his sentence of damnation, expressed in language which was sufficiently warm. "You have showed yourself a right Scotchman, a dissembling, false-hearted man, of the Scottish nature. And it would be a rare thing to meet with a true-hearted Scotchman or woman, that is upright in heart either to God or man; for I have been in this Commission almost twenty years, and I never knew but two, a Scotchman and a Scotchwoman, that made a profession of this faith; and they both proved false-hearted both to God and man."[1]

However, the internal conflict among his followers must have added greatly to the bitterness of a persecution, which in itself was sufficiently severe. After long delay, Muggleton was tried, before judges Atkins and Rainsford, at the Old Bailey, on Wednesday, the 17th January, 1677. Sir Robert Atkins was lenient to him on the trial; but Sir Richard Rainsford, Chief Justice of the King's Bench (who had recently succeeded Sir Matthew Hole), pelted him with gross abuse from the bench; and when it is added that sentence was given by the notorious George Jefferies, then Recorder of London, it may be presumed that it did not err on the side of leniency.

The trial can hardly be termed a fair one. The evidence against him was indeed derived from his own books, which had been seized at his house by the wardens of the Stationers' Company.[2] Still there was some difficulty in shaping the case so as to procure a verdict against him; because anything not published within the last three years came within the Act of Indemnity of 1674; and Muggleton had sent nothing to the press since 1669. Unfortunately, however, to evade the difficulty of publishing a heretical book in England, he had formerly allowed one of his books against the Quakers to appear with the imprint "Amsterdam, printed in the year of our Lord God 1663, and are to be had in Great Trinity Lane, over against the Lyon and the

---

[1] Stream from, the Tree of Life, ut supa, p. 10.

[2] Some of the actual books seized are still extant. One is in the Lambeth Library, and bears on the back of the title the inscription, "Aug: 30th, 1676. Seazed att Muggleton's house in the Posterne by Samuel Marne & Richard Clarke, Wardens." Another is in St. Paul's Library, and has on the fly leaf the words "30th August, 1676. Seized at Lodowick Magglton's house by Samll. Mearne & Richard Clark, Wardens." This copy belonged to Bishop Compton, and was presented to St. Paul's Library, with the rest of the Bishop's benefaction, in July, 1715.

Lamb." The "Amsterdam" was palpably a ruse;[1] might not the volume have also been antedated, so as to put it under the protection of the Act? This was the argument adopted by his prosecutors, and it was successful. The indictment set forth that "he, the said Lodowicke Muggleton, on the 30th of August, in the 23rd year of His Majesty's reign, in St. Giles' Parish without Cripplegate, London, by force and arms, did unlawfully, wickedly, maliciously, scandalously, blasphemously, seditiously, schismatically, and heretically, write, print, and sell, utter and publish, a certain malicious, scandalous, blasphemous, seditious, and heretical book, entitled The Neck of the Quakers Broken." Being found guilty, he was condemned to pay a fine of £500, and to stand upon the pillory in three of the most eminent places of the city, the Exchange, Temple Bar, and Smithfield, on three several days; his books to be burned with fire before his face. The pillory he accordingly suffered, and was much knocked about in it, "his grey hairs gilded with dirt and rotten eggs," according to a contemporary account. The fine he could not pay, and was accordingly sent to prison; but having remained there six months, he was released after paying £100, and finding two sureties for his good behaviour during life, on the 19th July, 1677; a day of joy to his people, and a red letter day in their calendar.

If any one were anxious to vindicate the salutary effect of persecution, as a means of keeping obstinate people in order, he might fairly refer us to the case of Lodowicke Muggleton, as an instance in point. There can be no doubt that the Last Witness was cowed by his appearance in the pillory. He was an old man, or at least not a young one, being sixty-eight years of age, and though he survived his rough usage twenty years, it deserves remark that he never again ventured, at all events in writing, to pass the merciless sentence of damnation upon an opponent. Certainly this is a very significant fact. He had learned a lesson. No more for him of "the modest punishment of a wooden ruff." He was not willing to expose himself again to the jeers and violence of the mob. They had spilled his blood, and it would cry out in vengeance against them, he said; but for all that, he took care not to come in the way of the authorities again. With this event therefore his public life ends; henceforth we know him only in his correspondence, which forms a large collection. He wrote his autobiography for posthumous publication, bringing it up to the date of his release from prison; and nothing shows more plainly how the degradation of his cruel punishment had eaten into his soul, than the awful denunciations against judges, jury, wardens, lawyers,— in short, against all who had taken part in his prosecution, — which fill the later pages of his autobiography. The terrible

---

[1] It was not an uncommon evasion. For instance, the first edition of Richard Overton's Man's Mortalitie bears the imprint, "Amsterdam, Printed by John Canoe, Anno Dom. 1644."

vehemence 'and deep searching thirst for vengeance' of his complaint and supplication to God against his enemies is so real and vivid as to make one shudder.

It would appear that he lived hereafter a quiet easy life; dispensing his blessings to his followers; joining in their social meetings; twice a-year commemorating the two great events of the giving of the Commission to John Reeve in February 1652, and his own release from custody, in July 1677; looked up to as an unerring oracle in things spiritual, an excellent guide and adviser in things temporal too. In his later letters, a large space is taken up with counsel and suggestion on matters of this material kind. It is difficult to resist the temptation of extracting one of these, unique in its kind, which, as a study of character, is simply delicious.

A Copy of a Letter written by the Prophet Lodowicke Muggleton to the Widow Mrs. Elizabeth Marsden, [formerly Elizabeth Smith, and servant to Dorothy Carter,] of Chesterfield, bearing date from London, April 18th, 1685.

" Dear friend in the true faith, Elizabeth Marsden.

Having an opportunity at this time to inform you, that there is a design in agitation that will be for your good, (and your children's good also, as long as your natural life in this world, if you please to accept of it,) I thought it convenient and necessary to give you timely notice of it, that you may not be surprised, but may have time to consider of it. The business is this; there is a friend of ours that is a widower, that is of this faith, that is a shopkeeper and of a genteel trade, (namely, a salesman and a tailor both, that selleth all new apparel,) and he hearing that you are a shopkeeper (though of another trade) and of this faith, and of a good natural temper, doth conceive you would make a good wife to live here at London, if you shall think good.

The man's name is John Croxen; he liveth at the corner house at Houndsditch; it is the best house for trade in all the street, being a corner house. His trade doth bring in at least two or three hundred pounds a year. And as for his person, I suppose you will not dislike it; and for his age it is very suitable unto yours, de is about four or five and forty years old is the most, (and I suppose you are seven or eight and thirty years old, which is very suitable.) And this is one of this faith we own, and we know him to be as good a natured man to a wife as any I know in the world. I know you may live in as much splendour and credit as any merchant's wife in London doth, if you have him to your husband. You shall have a maid servant, and men servants to be at your command. My wife's brother's son is apprentice with him, and hath served now, at Midsummer, five years of his time; which if I had not known him to be a good natured man, (and a good trade,) he should never have been put apprentice to him.

All the rich believers here in London do very well approve of his having of you to wife, and of your having of him to your hasband; and would be glad to have you live at London; that you may be numbered among the rich in this world—as well as being numbered with the rich in faith, rich in the world to come, as I know you will. Besides I cannot conceive how you can raise yourself, or prefer yourself or your two children, if you should match with any man there in the country. Though it were with a man of a hundred a year, yet your person will be made a mere drudge, and your children mere slaves. Neither is there any of this faith there in that country (as I know of) that is worth any thing considerable; and for you to match with one that is contrary, it will cause shipwreck to be made of the peace of your mind, which is of more value than the whole world.

Now I shall tell you how the state of this man's condition is; that if you cannot bear with it you shall have your liberty to choose or refuse, and save him a journey. This John Croxen hath had two wives, and hath at this time five children, all alive. Two by the first wife, before I knew him; and those two are both out of the way—the daughter getteth her living, being a good needle-woman, or at service; or might be married, but her father doth not like the man that she would have, because he hath no trade, (for a trade is the surest thing to get bread in this England, if a, man be a good husband;) the other is a boy that is apprentice to a silk weaver, which hath served great part of his time, so that he will be no trouble nor charge to his father nor his wife. And by this last wife he hath three daughters; the eldest is (I think) a matter of twelve or thirteen years old, and she is put apprentice to a friend of ours for five years, to be a shop-keeper. So that there are but two young daughters that are at home with him; the one of them is about eight years old, and the other (I think) about four years old. These two must be at-home—yet no great trouble to his wife, because the maid can make them ready and send them to school. For if you should be his wife you would do more good ten times, in locking to the shop and selling of garments, and to know the prices, and learn the trade; that in case he should die before you, you may drive the trade yourself. Thus I have given you an account of the whole matter.

Now he and William Chaire, a batchelor, do intend after Whitsuntide to make a journey into those parts, to see you and other friends in Staffordshire. Mr. Croxen cometh only to you, upon that account as to make you his wife, if you like the man when you see him. And William Chaire he cometh on purpose to Elizabeth Burton, to make her his wife if she will accept of him: he had a great love for her when she was here in London.

But now, dear friend, the case is thus; you must send me word whether you are resolved to keep yourself a widow always, or whether

you are resolved to live there where you are always, or whether you are minded to change your condition you are now in, or whether you will suffer him to come to see you. And if you do not like him when you have seen him, you shall have liberty in your mind to refuse him; for I would not persuade you to anything against your own mind, nor advise you to anything that were not for your good. Therefore I would desire you to send your answer unto me as soon as you can conveniently (and as short as you can) to these particulars, in the latter part of this letter. Likewise, I desire you not to let any of our friends in those parts see this letter, neither would I have you to mention it to any one, till after you have given me your answer. And if you do incline in your mind to hearken to the conditions contained in this letter, then keep it to yourself, and let none know of it; until Mr. Croxen and William Chaire doth come to see you and the rest of our friends, which will be after Whitsuntide. So, with my love and my wife's love remembered unto yourself, I take leave, and remain
    Your friend in the true faith,
      LODOWICKE MUGGLETON.
London, the 18th day
 of April, 1685.

Direct your letter unto me, thus, For Mr. Delamain, upon Bread Street Hill, at the sign of the "Three Tobacco Pipes," in London.[1]

This curious letter affords no bad index of Muggleton's character on its practical side. He combined with his large and dogmatic claim to a specialty of religious teaching considerable acuteness and experience in the management of affairs. In his own calling he was industrious, and apparently successful, until his peculiar religious position began to interfere with his temporal advancement; but neither before nor after that period, though acutely sensible of the advantage of means and position, did he show on his own behalf any greed of gain. Very early in life he relinquished the fair opportunity of a prosperous marriage, because his conscience would not allow him to sanction the making of money by usury; some years later he lost "a great stroke of work" at his trade, because he could no longer follow the Puritans in church fellowship; he prides himself on his independence, asserts that while he had "spent many a pound for the Commission's sake," he " did not live of the Gospel, as the Apostles did, without working," and claiming to be "more true in that particular than over any Apostle was, or ever any Quaker was."[2] When he gave up business he could fearlessly affirm: "I owe the world nothing; I never wronged any in the world the value of sixpence in my life, to my knowledge."[3] His calling was one against which jokes have been

---

[1] Supplement, ut supra, pp. 44-17.
[2] Spiritual Epistles, 2nd Edition, 1820, p. 113.
[3] Ibid., p. 474.

directed, ever since mankind first profited by the productions of its skill, yet he continued to take an honest pride in it. "What were the prophets of old, many of them, but herdsmen? and the apostles but fishermen? Very mean employments; yet God hath honoured them with great honour, and hath made poor men kings, prophets, and apostles. And why should it seem strange to the world, that God should choose two tailors . . . to be His two last Prophets and Witnesses of the Spirit in this last age of the world? A tailor is more honourable with kings, and princes, and noblemen of this world than herdsmen and fishermen."[1]

He was proud, too, of the old Northamptonshire stock from which he came, and of the great London in which he was born. With a pardonable feeling of the John Bull kind, he describes himself as "a free-born Englishman, and a freeman of London by birth, and never was out of England in all my life." A great dread of the perils of the ocean not only forbade him "to concern himself with any ship or sea affairs, if it were ever so much for his profit," but kept him from ever quitting English ground. "I have," he writes to a friend in Ireland," such an antipathy in my nature, that if I might have ten thousand pounds I would not come through that sea gulf to see you; though I have travelled several thousand miles in England in my time by land."[2] Indeed he can find no simile strong enough to realise his imagination of the horrors of the sea passage, than that great gulf which cut off communication between Dives in hell (Ireland) and Lazarus in heaven. His amusing hatred of England's ancient northern foe has already been referred to.[3] Of foreign nations or of foreign affairs he never seems, judging from his letters, to have taken much notice. When one of his friends thought to better his fortunes by emigration to Virginia, "I wonder," wrote he, "what is in men's minds, to run amongst the heathens who are without God in the world. My nature is so contrary to go out of the land of Canaan, of England, amongst the heathen, that I had rather live in prison here all days of my life."[4] Nay, even of home politics he seems to have been quite unconscious, except when the legal enactments of his time pressed indirectly upon him or his followers. He lived through the most exciting period of English history; he honoured and reverenced Oliver Cromwell as a true "Lion of the tribe of Judah"; yet his correspondence, so far as it is preserved, contains not a single allusion to the restoration of the monarchy, nor does it even speak of events which must certainly have touched him nearly, the Great

---

[1] Spiritual Epistles, ut supra, p. 440.
[2] Supplement, ut supra, p. 54
[3] The prejudice extended to his followers, and was not overcome till the time of John Peat, a Scotchman by birth, and a leading Muggletonian, between 1750 and 1774.
[4] Spiritual Epistles, ut supra, p. 405

Plague and Fire of London. Public matters had no interest for him; he was equally happy under a monarchy, a commonwealth, or a dictatorship. He only asked to be let alone. Yet though in this respect he was one of the quietest and most easily governed of subjects, he was by no means the man to sit down tamely under oppression. Every constitutional means that could be taken for the maintenance of his own liberties he would take; and he had somehow possessed himself of a very accurate knowledge of the limits and the requirements of the law. His constant endeavour on his own part, and his constant recommendation to his followers, was never to come into conflict with the law of the land, or give spiritual enemies a legal handle against them. He never would have them resist the arm of the law, but besought them to pay the stipulated fine at once, when brought into trouble through refusing to take the oath of allegiance or to attend at church. "It is only a money business." "It is better to give them their fess now while it is but little, so you can keep the mind free from oaths and worship." "It is better to part with silver than to part with peace of conscience."[1] Such was his sound advice, and such, it may be added, was his own constant practice. He paid fines repeatedly, because, having been chosen to serve on various parish offices, such as scavenger, questman, or constable, he refused to qualify for them by taking the oath of allegiance.

The refusal to take an oath was a common scruple with tender consciences at that day; and along with it generally went the belief that it was unlawful to make war, or to bear arms. Muggleton was not so rigid and absolute in his objection to the former as the Society of Friends have always been. Where an oath was a mere legal form and order in a court of justice, he permitted it to be taken. The only oaths utterly forbidden to him were "swearing to unrighteous things," and swearing vainly in common discourse.[2] He made but one exception, however, to the unlawfulness of war, and it is a characteristic one. He allowed a disciple of his, Thomas Nosworthy, a settler in Antigua, to bear arms "for the defence and preservation of the temporal life, and the estates of the people, against the heathen, and any other enemies that seek to invade that island." The case was different "in those strange islands, amongst the heathen," to what it was "here in England, Ireland, and Scotland, who profess all one faith; though very few have true faith. . . . Therefore, as the old proverb saith, 'If you will live at Rome, you must do as Rome doth.'"[3] Here we see something of his contempt, not only for aliens, but also for those who left their native land for the chances of success on foreign soil.

---

[1] Spiritual Epistles ut supra, pp. 112, 107, 181.

[2] p. 59.—He was opposed to capital punishment, even for murder. Div. Looking-glass, chap. xiv.

[3] Spiritual Epistles, ut supra., p. 469

The profession of a soldier was not the only one which Muggleton regarded as unlawful. He condemns each one of the three learned professions, not sparing any. When he was consulted on the choice of a profession by a young disciple, John Cowlye, who had received his education at the University of Cambridge, Muggleton "convinced him of the unlawfulness of all three, for any saint or God's elect to undertake." We should hardly expect him, considering what was his religious position, to have a good word for the clerical vocation. He pronounces their ministry all false, "from the first Pope to the last Quaker," even one as well as the other. "As for the doctors of physic, they are the greatest cheats, upon a natural account, that are in the world. They cheat people of their money and of their health; and it would be good if there were never a doctor of physic in the world; people would live longer, and live better in health. For God never appointed any doctor of physic, but he appointed nature to preserve nature." "And as for the lawyers, they keep the keys of the knowledge of the law, and will neither enter into truth and honesty themselves, nor suffer others to enter in that would." Hardly is there a man to be found but is "deceived either by the physician, lawyer, or priest. Nay they deceive one another, for the priest is deceived by the doctor of physic, and the doctor of physic is deceived by the priest . . . . And as for the lawyer, he cheats the doctor and the priest both . . . . and they do the like by him . . . . so that they get pretty even one with another. But all people besides, that deal with them, are sure to be deceived and to lose by them." After such an exposition as this (which is much fuller and more fearful in the original account, where it goes into questions of the world to come), we need not wonder that "when the young man heard these things, he left all preferment that way, for truth's sake, and became a steadfast and true believer; and he, being a scholar, was mighty able to oppose the learned."[1]

Among the scruples which Muggleton derived from his puritan training was an abhorrence of card-playing, which he classed with drunkenness,[2] and other vices of a reprobate life. Yet he was not averse to amusement on its own account, or to the enjoyment of life in a sober and chaste way. Against the vice of uncleanness he was especially severe, and in his own person he seems to have been, not simply strict in outward conduct, but pure of mind. True, his language is plain enough, and now and then runs into coarseness, especially in invective; when provoked, as he admits, he could sometimes speak "unsavoury" words. He was a puritan in the severity with which he reprobated whatever approached to vice or to injustice. In his sober common sense view of things, and in his genuine love of toleration and hatred of all kinds of religious persecution, he was

---

[1] Acts of the Witnesses, ut supra, pp. 112, 114. Whole Book of Revelation, ut supra, pp. 239, 244.

[2] Acts of the Witnesses, ut supra, p. 125.

something more than a puritan. "I always loved the persecuted better than I did the persecutor," he writes to George Fox; "and I always had compassion upon the afflicted for conscience-sake, though I knew they suffered for a mere lie, as all you Quakers do. Yet I say, whoever doth persecute you for conscience in meeting and worshipping an unknown God (as you Quakers do), I say those men that do persecute you willingly, will be every man of them damned to eternity."[1]

From some of the prevalent superstitions and delusions of his age he was singularly free. Witchcraft was still, in his time, widely believed in and feared. He treated it as a sinful surrender on the part of witches and possessed persons to the power of their own disordered imaginations; and wrote a treatise (which he himself valued very highly), called the Witch of Endor, expressly to apply this explanation to the Scriptural accounts of witchcraft. He laughs at the popular notion that witches have power over "infants, which are not capable of fear; for fear and belief are the inlet to all witchcraft."[2] In like manner he interpreted the phenomena of demoniacal possession as evidence only of disease. Distracted men, madmen, or fools are "possessed with devils, that is, with distempers of nature. These are devils that are produced through accidents of nature; some extraordinary grief, fright, or loss hath broke the brain, and so the seat of reason is quite out of order."[3] In harmony with this rationalistic explanation Muggleton seems inclined, not only to spiritualise certain of the miracles of our Lord, but even to regard the spiritual meaning as the only legitimate sense of some of them; e.g., of the casting of the demons into the bodies of swine.[4] His strong disinclination to the ready acceptance of mere marvels is aptly shown in a postscript to a letter, bearing date 19th June, 1669, and addressed to his friend Thomas Tomkinson, which to us, who have lately been favoured with the story of the Welsh fasting girl, will not be without interest. "I would desire," he writes, "when you send to me or Mr. Delamaine, if it be not too much trouble, [that you would tell me] whether that maid that fasted a whole year, as was reported, be alive yet, or no; because I heard at Chesterfield for certain that she was yet alive, and that it was a mere cheat to get money."[5]

Lodowicke Muggleton's end was a peaceful close to a long and, in some respects, an arduous life. The old man's latter days, spent amid the reverence of his followers, and watched over by the faithful affection of his wife, must have been happy. "Upon the first day of March 1697/8, the prophet was taken with an illness and weakness; upon which he said these words, 'Now hath God sent death unto me';

---

[1] Letter to George Fox, 2nd Edition, 1756, p. 88.
[2] Spiritual Epistles, ut supra, p. 412.
[3] Letter to George Fox, ut supra, p. 65.
[4] Stream from the Tree of Life, Edition of 1758, p, 59.
[5] Spiritual Epistles, ut supra, p. 291.

and presently after was helped to bed. And though he kept his bed, yet we could not perceive that he was sick, only weak; and he lay as if he slept; but in such quietness as if he was nothing concerned with either pain or sickness. So that it was mere age that took him away. The fourteenth day of March he departed this life, with as much peace and quietness as ever any man did, being about eighty-eight years of age; so that he had that blessing to come to his grave in a full age, like as a shock of corn cometh in at his season. Upon the sixteenth day his corpse was removed to Lorimer's Hall [close to his house in the Postern, where he died], and on the seventeenth day was from thence attended on with two hundred and forty-eight friends, with six of us appointed to carry the pall, each with gloves and hatbands, accompanying him to Bethlehem Churchyard: where he was buried by [beside] his fellow Witness, which was according to his own appointment."[1] The rhyming inscription on his tomb was quoted in a former paper. A copy of verses, entitled An Elegy on the Death of Mr. Lodowicke Muggleton, appeared shortly after his decease, and, though not written by a disciple, was printed as a broad-sheet at the request of his followers, in 1698, and has by them been at least twice reprinted, in 1754 and 1831.

In the portrait of Muggleton we may easily discern the traces of that combination of integrity, shrewdness, and determination, which formed his somewhat remarkable career. There exist three original likenesses of him. Of these the best executed is an oval oil painting of the head and bust, looking to the right, at present hanging in the Bird Gallery at the British Museum. It was presented anonymously to the Trustees of that institution, through Dr. Maty, the then Librarian, on the 26th October 1758. There is a memorandum in pencil accompanying the Report on the subject of the presentation, "aged 66, 1674." Another most interesting painting, is a full length (also looking to the right), by Muggleton's friend, William Wood, of Braintree, now in the possession of the Muggletonian body. It was formerly in the hands of Mr. Tweene at Ware, at whose death it was purchased by the late Mr. Isaac Frost. Of more value than either of these, perhaps, is the cast of the prophet's features taken after death. This also is in the possession of the Muggletonian body. Copies have been taken from it at different times; on the last occasion (early in the present year) the original was unfortunately broken, yet not so as to injure the face; it has been carefully put together again, but has not been improved by a new coat of thin black paint. It had been painted black at a former period. From this east a small copperplate engraving was executed at an early date. It bears the engraver's name, G. V. Caffeel, but has no date. The plate is in the possession of the Muggletonian body; it is

---

[1] Acts of the Witnesses, first Edition, 1699, end of Epistle Dedicatory by Thomas Tomkinson.

poorly engraved and nearly worn out; early copies of it are rare, as it seems to have been much in request among the believers. A small oil painting was made from it in May 1813, by Richard Piekersgill, himself a Muggletonian; of this several copies are in existence, one of them being preserved by the Muggletonian body. In 1829, at the expense of Joseph and Isaac Frost, a half length engraving was executed by J. Kennerley, from the full length portrait. This is usually found prefixed to the Divine Song-book, and is to be had separately. It does the original from which it is taken no sort of justice, and introduces accessories, allegorical and otherwise, which are peculiar to itself. This engraving has been photographed in carte-de-visite size. Muggleton's personal appearance furnished matter for jest to his and George Fox's opponent, Charles Leslie, who compares the two men in respect of their "long straight hair, like rat's tails;" and adds, "it hath been observed of great enthusiasts that their hair is generally slank, without any curl; which proceeds from a moisture of brain that inclines to folly. It was thus with Fox and Muggleton."[1] An early and good copy of Caffeel's engraving, prefixed to the copy of the first edition of the Acts of the Witnesses, in the Lambeth Library, has written below it these words, in a contemporary hand: "He had yellow hair and a ruddie complexion."

It is time to speak of some of the prominent followers of Muggleton. The "eldest son of the Commission of the Spirit", as he has been called, was JOHN SADDINGTON, a Leicestershire man, from Arnesby, who seems to have been afterwards engaged in business in London in the sugar trade. He was a fine handsome fellow, and is addressed, in a copy of contemporary verses, as "John Saddington the tall." He it was who, at the time of the rebellion against the Nine Assertions, did most to secure the attachment of the wavering believers to their absent chief. He is the author of two works in print, and of three or four which remain in manuscript.

But though not the "eldest son," yet certainly the chief advocate of the Commission was THOMAS TOMKINSON, of Sladehouse. This staunch defender of an unpopular faith came of an old family of Staffordshire yeomen, who for generations had held the farm of Sladehouse,[2] in the parish of Ilam, not far from Dovedale. About Easter of 1869, the present writer made a pilgrimage to the locality, and examined the registers of Ilam and Blore-Ray, in search of traces of the family. There are plenty of such traces to be found, but, owing

---

[1] Leslie's Theological Works, 1721, vol. ii. p. 357.

[2] This Sladehouse was the scene of the murder of Joseph Mycock by his younger brother Benjamin Mycock, on the 10th February, 1812. They were sons of a labourer at Grindon, and the elder brother, who was forty or fifty years of age, had married his former employer, Mrs. Sarah Maulton, of Sladehouse.

to the extreme frequency with which the christian names Thomas and Ann occur in various branches of the Tomkinson family, it is very difficult to extricate the lines of descent. Their pedigree goes up to a William Tomkinson, who died in 1559. Several members of the family appear to have been, for their station, men of some culture. There is a curious tablet in Blore church to the memory of Thomas Tomkinson, who died in 1640, respecting whom the local tradition is that he was a great scholar. Another ancient member of the family, a former tenant of Town End Farm, in Swinscoe, is celebrated as having been a man of huge stature; a qualification of which the rural mind was-probably a better judge than of scholastic attainment.

Our Thomas Tomkinson, born in 1631, the son of Richard and Ann Tomkinson, of Sladehouse, was a great reader from his youth, and his favourite subject was church history. He had himself "procured a library of Presbyterian books,"[1] and from his landlord, the Earl of Ardglass, at Throwley Hall, he "borrowed St. Augustine's City of God, and Dr. Hammond's Works." His mother "a zealous Puritan," was "a virtuous good woman, and greatly charitable." His father seems to have been but an incompetent person: at his wife's death, he made over his affairs to his son, and boarded with him as a lodger. Tomkinson heard nothing of the Commission of the Spirit till he was thirty years old, when he came across one of Claxton's books, the very title of which not only startled him, but more than half convinced him that there was truth in it. A year later he arrived in London, on May-day, 1662, expressly "to see and discourse with the surviving Prophet." He found him in Great Trinity Lane, at work at his trade, and enjoyed some conversation with him. At this time he was on the eve of matrimony, and on his return home he united himself to "a good virtuous maid." This step threw him back somewhat in his allegiance to Muggleton. His father was a decided enemy to the faith; his wife did not favour it, though she was, he says, "pretty moderate. So, to please an old father and a young wife, I went to church by fits." A man of his intelligence, however, soon made other converts, and a community of Mugletonians, over twenty in number, sprang up in the north-eastern corner of Staffordshire. They met occasionally at each others' houses, but still went sometimes to church. A quarrel in 1674, with the parson of his parish seems to have precipitated Tomkinson's hostility to the Establishment; and henceforth he went no more to church. In consequence of this he was vexed with writ after writ, accused of popery, and injured in his farm business. His great enemy was one Archdeacon Brown; while his great friend was a certain Archdeacon Cook, who had overheard him zealously contend with a Quaker, at the Dog Inn, in Lichfield, on behalf of the doctrine of the resurrection of Christ's body. He was excommunicated by his

---

[1] Truth's Triumph, pub. 1823, p. 258.

parson; but, through Archdeacon Cook's interest, and the payment of a fine, he received absolution of this sentence. On this fact he thus moralises. "On the Sunday following, he [the parson] published my absolution and remission of my sins; and so I was taken into the Church as a dear brother, through a little money and friendship. . . . And truly I thought it was cheap enough to escape their Hell and to gain their Heaven for twenty shillings charge."[1]

Some years after this he removed to London, and became one of the most zealous pillars of the Muggletonian community there. But few of his many written contributions to Muggletonian literature have found their way into print; one only, so far as I am aware, was published during his lifetime, The Muggletonians Principles Prevailing, by T. T. 1695, being an answer to Dr. John Williams' (anonymous) True Representation of the Absurd and Mischievous Principles of the Sect commonly known by the name of Muggletonians, 1694. Others of his numerous works were circulated in manuscript; and those which have been published are still much read and highly prized by his fellow believers. They are clearly and logically written, entertaining and powerful. Much cannot be said for their grammar or their orthography, which latter forms a system by itself. Nor is it possible to avoid noticing the singular and almost incredible blunders, which, however, were only the natural pitfalls in the literary path of a man who made himself a great reader, without the requisite education to correct and balance his reading. Nothing which it has ever been our good fortune to come across, in the way of literary blunders, can compare with the following remark of Tomkinson's upon Aristotle. He quotes as Aristotle's opinion, "that law that is most filled by reason must needs be most victorious and triumphant," and then adds, "Howbeit, Aristotle was something dampled in his judgment by reading Julius Scalinger, who said that the beginning of reason was not reason; Aristotle, admiring of this sentence, said, Certainly there is something before and better than reason, wherein reason itself had its rise."[2] The picture of the old Greek perusing the sage criticisms of his modern commentator, and being "something dampled in his judgment" thereby, until admiration ensued, is conceived in a truly delicious vein of exquisite anachronism.

Here it may be well to say something about the Muggletonian sacred books. They recognise, first of all, in common with all Christians, the Holy Scriptures of the Old and New Testaments. They exclude, however, the Apocrypha of the Old Testament from the

---

[1] These facts are taken from a MS. narrative, entitled The Christian Converte, or Christianytie Revived by that Christian Convert, Thomas Tomkinson, written in the year of our Lord God 1692. The copy above used seems to have been transcribed by Arden Bonell, circa 1740.

[2] Truth's Triumph, ut supra, p. 178.

canon, following here their puritan origin;[1] they exclude also the writings of Solomon, as being the utterances only of natural wisdom. "Solomon, indeed," says John Reeve, "was a very wise man, but I never read that he was a holy or prophetical man; therefore it does not appear to me that that he was a penman of Holy Writ."[2] In this way they get rid of the testimony of Ecclesiastes to the separate existence and destiny of the soul.

Second only to the received books of Scripture, the Muggletonians venerate that curious and ancient production called the Testament of the Twelve Patriarchs, an apocryphal work, older than Origen's time, and probably dating from the second century; but which they, like Bishop Robert Grosseteste of Lincoln (1175-1253), who introduced it into this country, refer to and quote as inspired. Grosseteste first heard of the book from John de Basingstokes; he at once sent to Athens for it, and himself translated it from the Greek to the Latin. It was first printed in 1577, englished by A. G. (Arthur Golding), and has been very frequently reprinted down to the present time, often with woodcuts, as a sort of chap book. Dibdin describes it as "one of the most popular manuals of the sixteenth and seventeenth centuries." Whiston held it to be of canonical authority.[3] The first mention of it by a Muggletonian writer, is to be found in a manuscript letter by Thomas Tomkinson, in 1674.[4]

A similar place to that occupied by the Testament of the Twelve Patriarchs, among the standard authorities of the Muggletonians, has been allotted to the Book of Enoch, ever since its appearance in English in 1821. This apocryphal book was, up to the time of St. Augustine, much prized by the Christian Fathers. It passed out of sight, however (with the exception of a few Greek fragments in the Chronographia of Syncellus), until in 1773 some manuscripts of the Ethiopic version were brought to Europe by Bruce, the Abyssinian traveller. One of these was deposited in the Bodleian Library, and from it the English version of Dr. Laurence (afterwards Archbishop of Cashel) was made, and published at Oxford in 1821. Laurence also published the Ethiopic text in 1838; and another Ethiopic text was

---

[1] The same circumstance led to a preference for the "Old Translation," or Geneva Bible, which was greatly strengthened by finding in it such renderings as "there is no man good but one, which is God," and "their soul dieth," &c.
[2] Joyful News, ut supra, p. 8.
[3] Notes and queries, second series, vol. vi., p. 3.
[4] It may be mentioned that there is now a very excellent and scholarly edition of the Greek text, with an introductory essay, attributing the origin of the work to the Nazarene body. See The Testaments of the XII. Patriarchs: An attempt to estimate their Historic and Dogmatic Worth. By Robert Sinker, M.A., 1869.

published at Leipsig in 1851, by Dr. A. Dillman. Two German translations have appeared since 1833, and the book continues to excite much interest and controversy among biblical and oriental scholars. It may occasion surprise that this book should so readily have been adopted as canonical by the Muggletonian body. It is even more remarkable, considering that no English version of any part of it existed in Muggleton's own time, that we should find the following passage in a letter of his in 1682. "The first man God chose, after the fall of Adam, was Enoch; and God did furnish him with revelation to write books........ He left this revelation to Noah, and Noah left it to Shem, and Shem left it to his sons, until it came to Abraham, Isaac, and Jacob. So that [this was] Enoch's revelation and declaration to the fathers of old; and all that did believe the books of Enoch, they were as a Parliament to enact it as a Statute-Law to their children from generation to generation for ever."[1] The late Mr. Isaac Frost was, it is believed, the means of introducing the book to his fellow Muggletonians; and he makes considerable use of it, in his painstaking and handsome work, Two Systems of Astronomy (1846), as confirming the Muggletonian, in opposition to the commonly received theory of the Universe.

Next in order come the writings of John Reeve and Lodowicke Muggleton, regarded, though not verbally inspired, as of equal or greater authority than Holy Scripture; at least so far as the enunciation of the Six Principles is concerned; because the "Commission of the Spirit hath deeper mysteries held forth in it than the other Commissions had."[2] Muggletonians speak commonly, therefore, not of Two Testaments, the Old and the New, but of Three; they enumerate Three Records; Three Commissions, each to be obeyed in its own time and place, and having force so long as God sustains it. The Commissions of the Water (that by Moses), and of the Blood (that by the Apostles), have made way for the Commission of the Spirit, which is thus at once the last and the highest. Any further development of revelation they believe to have been expressly excluded by the voice of God.

Muggletonians have no recognised formula of Creed. Adherence to the Six Principles is the sole criterion and requisite of membership to their Church. At different times, however, private believers have drawn up statements of their doctrinal belief. Thus in 1675, John Saddington elaborated XLVIII. Articles of True Faith, which were printed in 1830. In 1723, an anonymous believer drew up xxxvi. Articles of the Third Record; and in 1794, William Sedgwick

---

[1] Spiritual Epistles, ut supra, p. 516, and again p. 587. Muggleton no doubt derived his impressions of the book from the references to it in the Testament of the XII. Patriarchs.
[2] Stream from the Tree of Life, of supra, p. 32,

(apparently in consequence of the Birchite Schism) prepared xvi. Articles to express the true Muggletonian belief. Neither of these two formularies have been printed. A printed paraphrase of the Apostles' Creed in the Muggletonian sense, with Scripture references, which is signed James Tennant, is sometimes found pasted on the fly leaf of Muggletonian books. The earliest copy of this is printed in black letter, but it bears no date, nor is anything known respecting its author. There is also a curious rhyming Creed of twenty-eight lines, in manuscript, perhaps a hundred years old, which seems from its condition to have been suspended from a wall, or otherwise publicly exhibited.

It will not do to forget, in this connection, the collection of Divine Songs, or Songbook, as it is familiarly called, which supplies to them the place of a collection of hymns, and indeed is the only approach to a devotional manual. For while prayer is by them eschewed, songs of gratitude and thanksgiving are deemed lawful, though by no means incumbent upon any believer who may think them savouring too much of the exploded idea of worship. Collections of these Songs were circulated in manuscript from the earliest days of the sect, many of them having been written by the immediate followers of Muggleton. A great number of these manuscript collections are still preserved by the body; several of them being in the autograph of the composers. The first mention of a printed Songbook in the records of the body, is on the 16th February, 1794; many entries of the sale of the volume are to be met with up to 14th August, 1796. No copy of this book has fallen in the present writer's way; it seems, from a letter of James Frost, 29th March, 1812, that it was not executed at the expense of the body, but "made a present of to the church by a printer." The church, however, compiled in 1829 the collection at present in use. It consists of two hundred and twenty-eight Songs, all by Muggletonian authors, and a good number of them expressly written for the collection. The largest contributor is Boyer Glover, a London watch-and-clockmaker, who may be deemed the poet of the Muggletonians. His name first occurs in their records in 1771. He contributes forty-nine Songs. James Miller (who wrote between 1730 and 1750), follows with twenty-seven. There are one or two by John Nicholls, a musician, who "played on the Lord Mayor's Day and in the waits," who died, old and helpless, about 1745, and through whom the only fragment that exists in John Reeve's autograph came into the possession of the body. The earliest Song-writers seem to be Thomas Turner, John Ladd, William Wood, Elizabeth Goodwin, and Elizabeth Henn. Thomas Tomkinson also tried his hand at verse composition.

It is not very difficult to estimate the extent to which the Muggletonian doctrines have met with success. Their influence has been confined almost entirely to the small body which professes them; for their writings have seldom been published in the ordinary way; they have never invited converts, and have found no opportunity, and looked for none, of bringing their opinions before the notice of the world. Neither Reeve nor Muggleton were preachers; they disseminated their views in conversation and by letter: and this has ever been the habit of the body. Persons of influential position have rarely been attracted to their community, but the personal character of its members has always stood high; few in numbers, they are and have been an industrious, and, in the main, a well-to-do and thriving set of people. Muggleton's own times were the palmy days of the society, as respects the social standing of its members. He could point among his supporters to people of all classes, from Colonel Robert Phaire, the governor of Cork, to good, "sober, and conscientious" Mistress Dorothy Carter. Both of these had come to Muggleton from the Society of Friends, and from this body, as well as from their predecessors the Ranters and the Anabaptists, he received many, if not most, of the early adherents to his cause. In their case (as in Reeve's own), the change was a natural consequence of the exhaustion of their previous views, which threw them, by an inevitable reaction, into the opposite extreme.

In the absence of any express information, we must refer to such casual indications of the progress of the body as we may discover in their own writings, or in other places. Already, in 1654, two years after the revelation of John Reeve, some of their books had found their way to New England, when an order was made that every inhabitant who had in custody "any of the books of John Reeves and Lodowick Muggleton, 'who pretend to be the two last witnesses and prophets of Jesus Christ,' which books were said to be full of blasphemies, should bring or send them in to the next magistrate, within one month, on pain of ten pounds for each book remaining in any person's hands after that time."[1] By 1660, Muggleton himself testifies of his Commission, that "the sound of it hath gone through many parts of Christendom, as in this part of England, Scotland, Ireland, New England, Virginia, Barbadoes, and many other places I will not here mention. But the doctrine of the Commission of the Spirit hath been very little received in the world; but the most that have received it are here in London, and in Cambridgeshire, and in Kent."[2] In 1669, the Muggletonian views were thus introduced to the continent of Europe. "There is a great increase in the faith," writes Muggleton, "here at London, and in some countries. There have been with me of late two or three German men, that were banished out of Germany for not submitting to the worship set up by that power ...... The one of these is a doctor of physic, and another was a minister in Germany. The

---

[1] Hutchinson's History of the Colony of Massachuset's Bay, 2nd edition, 1765, p. 196. Hutchinson evidently supposes them to have been Quakers. The books probably came from Bristol, where there were believers in 1654. Sac. Rem. p. 59.
[2] Spiritual Epistles, ut supra, p. 36.

minister could not speak English as well as the doctor, but the doctor bought all the books, and hath written the Commission Book into the German language, and hath sent it among the Germans. So what the issue will be, time will bring forth; for there are many that would believe, did they but understand it in their own language."[1] In spite of this it remained true that a prophet is without honour in his own house. "This thirty-three years that I have been in this Commission," confesses Muggleton in 1685, "there hath not [been] one neighbour, or acquaintance, or kindred here in London (as I know of) that hath believed my report, save my own children."[2]

Still the Muggletonian views made way, and were handed down, from generation to generation, although obscurely. Out of London, the first society of believers appears to have been that which John Reeve visited in 1656, when he found some half score believers near Cambridge, poor men, "husbandmen and tradesmen, that labour for their bread."[3]

We have seen already that, about the year 1664, there were over twenty believers in Staffordshire. In September, 1667, it was reported, in "an account of the number of the conformists, nonconformists, &c.," that, "at Ashford [in Kent] and at other places, we find a new sort of heretics, after the name of Muggleton, a London tailor, in number thirty."[4] In the seventeenth edition of Edward Chamberlayne's Angliae Notitia, 1691, they are mentioned for the first time, and placed among the dwindling sects. In the eighteenth edition, 1694, we are told (p. 378), "the Muggletonians are scarce extant." The same words appear in succeeding editions till the twenty-first, in 1704, when all mention of this body is omitted. In William Maitland's History of London, 1739, there are enumerated (p. 517), among the places of worship (which, of course, is a mistake), two Muggletonian Meetings, one at Barnaby Street (south of St. Olave's, Southwark), and the other in Old Street Square (top of Aldersgate). This information is repeated in the Rev. John Entick's edition of Maitland, in 1756. A careful search of their records since 1770 would enable us to ascertain pretty accurately the names and numbers of the London Muggletonians from that time to this. There is a manuscript "Collection of the names of male friends residing in England, 14 August, 1803," which contains ninety-eight names, distributed over London, Kent, Hertfordshire, Norwich, Derbyshire, Bristol, Oxford, Walworth (and one in Ireland). The lists of subscribers' names prefixed to the Interpretation of the Revelation, 1808; to the Volume of Spiritual Epistles, 1820; to Truths Triumph, 1823; and to the Songbook, 1829, are useful in this connection.

---

[1] Spiritual Epistles, ut supra, p. 293.
[2] Spiritual Epistles, ut supra, p. 575.
[3] Supplement, ut supra, p. 2.
[4] The Genuine Remains of Dr. Thomas Barlow, late Lord Bishop of Lincoln, 1693, p. 313.

In 1863, one of their body estimated their numbers as follows :—
"There are, perhaps, two hundred and fifty, or three hundred, in London and its suburbs, a few in Kent, about sixty or eighty in Derbyshire, twelve or fifteen in Nottingham, and half a dozen in Mansfield; but as we believe that public worship is not now acceptable to the Deity, of course we have no places in which to meet for worship, and no record of our numbers, so it is very possible that there may be Muggletonians in other districts with whom I have never communicated. For example, those in Derbyshire were ignorant of the existence of any persons entertaining the same faith in London, until one of their number removed thither to seek employment, and, after residing there a short time, heard of the London brethren by mere accident."[1]

No regular and systematic records of their history have ever been kept by the Muggletonians. The manuscripts in the possession of their body, which do not seem to have been formally examined and collected before 1772, the time of the Birchite schism, and have not yet been catalogued, consist of I., a number of expository treatises, poems, songs, and other writings, illustrating the growth and character of their peculiar faith; II., a large collection of letters, some trivial enough, but many of them curious and interesting, extending, but in no connected series, from the origin of their community till the present day; III., a mass of bills and account books, beginning about 1770, and relating to the subscriptions for and sale of their printed books, and the expenses incurred at their social meetings. In 1804, the Community first became possessed of property, through the bequest of Catherine Peers, for the formation of a relief fund; and from that time to the present an exact account has been kept of its monetary affairs.

Among the manuscripts in Class I. are a few (including a transcript of great part of the Commission Book), in Muggleton's thick, tremulous, laboured hand-writing, which contrasts curiously with Reeve's fine, clear, minute penmanship. Thomas Tomkinson's stiff, upright, very legible characters (more like printing than writing), and his marvellous orthography, are largely represented in the collection. It seems almost a pity that the modern editors of the early Muggletonian literature should have felt themselves bound to adhere so rigidly as they have done to the grammar and punctuation, though not, except in case of proper names, to the spelling of the originals. The present writer has been obliged, in order to make his quotations intelligible to the general reader, to repunctuate freely, and now and then to smooth over a grammatical inequality, which impaired the sense as well as the elegance of the passage.[2]

---

[1] Letter by William Ridsdale, Inquirer, 21st March, 1963,
[2] It is not easy to hit the medium between an exact transcript for the curious eye, and too unsparing a revision. George Fox's Journal, for

There is no room here for an account of the numerous materials embraced in the letters which form Class II.; and in truth, to an outsider, an analysis of their contents would be exceedingly dry, at least where it was not exceedingly ludicrous. Appeals for help, addressed to the London Society, by or on behalf of poorer brethren in various parts of the country, were pretty frequent. One cannot but feel compassion for poor Edmond Feaver (whose tone had been high enough in his day of prosperity), when he writes from Kettering, 28th January, 1759, to John Austin Garrett, the chief person among the London believers, begging for charity with the touching plea, " I am Reduced to the Loest Degree my Coat, wastcoat and Britches are not all worth one shilling."

The various controversies which these letters reveal turn more or less on the original difference (already described) between Reeve and Muggleton as to the immediate notice of God. From an early time there seem to have been Reevites, (or Reeveonians) in contradistinction to Muggletonians. This may be what Muggleton means, when he speaks in 1663 about "those that disadhere unto John Reeve," most of whom however were then dead, and others fallen away from the steadfastness of faith.[1] Even the Rebellion against the Nine Assertions of Muggleton in 1671, partook in some degree of this party character. For, as Muggleton observes in his Answer, "it is the nature of Reason to believe dead prophets rather than living prophets. And it is the nature of Faith to believe live prophets rather than dead prophets."[2] A similar division of allegiance is hinted at in Thomas Tomkinson's Epistle Dedicatory to the Acts of the Witnesses, 1699, when he says, (p. vi.) "there can be no salvation to such as shall reject him or his writings, although they pretend to own John Reeve." It may be conjectured that the Sacred Remains, published in 1706, which consist exclusively of "treatises epistolary and public by the Lord's last immediate messenger, John Reeve," proceeded from this party.

There were some small internal controversies on other points, as in 1736, when Arden Bonell opposed a new doctrine of the Ascension of Beasts, or the resurrection of the lower animals. This curious discussion, together with some skirmishing on doctrinal points between Bonell and Phillip Lathorp, and again between Bonell and Joseph Horrell; and, a few years later, between John Meall and Edmond Feaver, constitutes nearly all our knowledge of Muggletonian history during the first half of the eighteenth century. No serious division occurred in the Muggletonian forces until that occasioned,

---

instance, has been greatly over-edited from the first. His autographs and his own publications are as uncouth, as those of Muggleton, or more so.

[1] Spiritual Epistles, ut supra, p. 129.
[2] The Acts of the Witnesses, ut supa, p. 150.

about 1772, by the defection of the Birchites. William Crabb, of Braintree, speaks in July 1773 of a "misunderstanding in the Church," and this misunderstanding soon reveals itself as connected with the doctrine of immediate notice and the leadership of James Birch.

This JAMES BIRCH, a Welshman by birth, was a watch motion maker, living near Aldersgate, London. There exists a rhythmical account, from his own pen, of his conversion to Muggletonian views, which occupies fifteen rude stanzas, of eight lines each, and is dated the 5th December, 1771. In the same year his name heads the subscription list to a work of John Brown, of Norwich, on the Devil's Downfall. By the next year his opinions seem to have carried him out of harmony with his fellow-believers. He rejected their doctrine, that those who hold the true faith enjoy at once an absolute assurance of salvation, and held that this assurance was often withheld till the hour of death. He believed also, in opposition to Muggleton's teaching, that God does exercise an immediate oversight in human affairs, and affords an immediate inspiration, without which his former revelations are of no avail. He acquired a certain following, who did not, however, as yet formally separate from the original community. By degrees, however, he applied this doctrine of immediate notice in his own favour, and founded a small separatist community of which he was the prophet, immediately directed by a divine call. One William Matthews, of Bristol, was his high priest. This assumption of a prophetic office, in 1778, lost him ten of his followers, who withdrew from him in consequence of it; they did not return to Muggletonian orthodoxy, but remained true to Birch's more sober views, under the leadership of Martha Collier. There were now three divisions among the Muggletonians: the original body or Church, represented by Benedict Shield in London, and Roger Gibson in New York; the Birchites, or Anti-church; and the Collierites, or Immediate-notice people. Birch was maintained in independence by the contributions of his followers, of whom in 1786 there were some thirty in London, and others in Wales, in the parts about Pembroke. Two strange fantastic hooks by Birch were printed about the end of last century, they are called the Book of Cherubical Reason, and the Book upon the Gospel and Regeneration. They are more incoherent than the writings of Thomas Tany, and read like the productions of a madman. Their author seems to have outlived his influence and most of his followers, and to have died soon after the beginning of this century, but when and where has not been ascertained. Whether at this moment there are any Birchites in existence, does not appear. Very likely there may be, for these small sects die hard; but it is scarcely probable that they continue to hold regular meetings. Their last known place of meeting was in the Barbican, and there are several persons living who remember having known Birchites. The influence of their opinions is deprecated in the following opening of a Song by James Frost, written in 1809, and included in the collection of 1829 :-

> "You faithful Muggletonians, who truly do believe
> The doctrine of Muggleton to be the same as Reeve;
> Let no wise anti-followers infuse into your ear,
> That a prayer Christ does hear from us mortals here below."

As the Muggletonians countenance no form of worship whatever, their gatherings are almost entirely of a festive character. They have two yearly gatherings, or Holidays, one of which at least dates from their prophet's time; for it was instituted 19th July, 1677, for the purpose of commemorating his release from prison on that day, and has been held annually ever since, though now, in consequence of the alteration in the calendar, it is kept on the 30th July. The account of contributions and expenses at one of the earliest of these meetings has been preserved, and is here given, as it is a curious specimen of a tavern bill nearly two hundred years ago.

At our meeteing at Holloway on the 19th of July 1682. At Mr. Hoolbrookes at the Greene Man, Present there

The Prophitt of God	
Mis Muggleton	
Mis Delanall	00 : 05 : 00
Mis Smith	00 : 05 : 00
Mis Webb	00 : 05 : 00
Mis Euans	00 : 05 : 00
Mr Cooper	00 : 05 : 00
Mis Cooper	00 : 05 : 00
Mr. Atkinson	00 : 05 : 00
Mis Atkinson	00 : 05 ; 00
Mr Gouldique	00 : 05 : 00
Mr Rich: Smith	00 : 05 : 00
Mr. Whitehead	00 : 05 : 00
Mr. Brocke	00 : 05 : 00
Mr. Symonds	00 : 05 : 00
Delamain Senr	00 : 05 : 00
Mis Delamain	00 : 05 : 00
Delamain Junr.	00 : 05 : 00
Mr. Burrell	00 : 05 : 00
Mis Henn	00 : 05 : 00
Mis Roe	00 : 05 : 00
Received	04 : 15 : 00

Monyes Paid away the 19th July 1682, at Mr. Hollbrookes at the Greene Man in Holloway

pd for 18 Pulletts at 14d a Pullett is	01 : 01 : 00
pd for 18 Sivell Oringes at	00 : 01 : 08
pd for 6 penny post Letters of advise	00 : 00 : 07
pd for the prophitt's Coach	00 : 03 : 06
pd a porter from London with the fowles	00 : 01 : 06
pd for 5 1/2 of Bacon at 7d1/2	00 : 03 : 04
pd for 5 large Collyflowers	00 : 01 : 00
pd for Bread and Beere	00 : 09 : 04
pd for Wine	01 : 06 : 00
pd for Dressing Meate and fowleing Linning	00 : 14 : 00
pd for 5 Tarts at 16d a Tart	00 : 06 : 08
pd for Butter and Cheese	00 : 01 : 06
pd to the Servants of the House	00 : 02 : 00
pd to ye man of the Bowleing Greene	00 : 01 : 00
ffor 1 Quartern of Tobacco	00 : 00 : 06
	04: 13 : 07

The other yearly Holiday is the anniversary of the giving of the Commission to John Reeve on the 3d, 4th, and 5th February, 1652, but now kept on the 14th, 15th, and 16th February. The two festivals are referred to as "the Holy Days" as early as 1763, and were probably so termed much before that time. These assemblies (especially the February one) bring together from various parts of the country as many of the believers as can contrive to be present.

In addition to these larger gatherings, more frequent meetings, monthly or weekly, have been arranged from time to time to suit local convenience. This custom dates also, there is little doubt, from the earliest time. "These Muggletonians," writes S. Rogers from Cambridge, in 1692, "meet at their prophet's (as they call him), where he expounds the Scriptures, and answers any question they put to him."[1] And "about the year 1770," we are told, "there was a small community of Muggletonians, who met every Sunday afternoon in a room one story high, built out in the garden of the Gun, a well known public house, in Islington, where they used to smoke and drink with a great Bible before them."[2] From the Gun, Islington, in 1770, we can trace their meetings, by help of tavern bills, to the Blue Boar, Aldersgate Street, 1787-1790, and 1796-1802; the Hampshire Hog, Peartree Street, Goswell Street, 1791-1795; the Nag's Head, Aldersgate Street, 1815; the Bull's Head, Jewin Crescent, 1818-1825; the Coach and Horses, St. John's Square, Clerkenwell, 1845, and probably to other similar places. All members of the community were expected to attend these meetings, and to contribute a small sum to the general entertainment; a trifling fine was imposed (in 1799) for non-attendance. Occasionally the fare was provided by special bounty; this was usually the custom on the death of any well-to-do member. Hence we read that, at the monthly meeting on the 2nd March, 1831, "two legs of mutton were had, they being left by Mrs. Sarah Gander, as a token of her spiritual love to the church, of which the following friends partook in commemoration." The only regulations that seem to have been passed for the conduct of these meetings were such as were designed to exclude discussions on "natural" matters, that is, any subjects except those, which concerned points of faith. A resolution to this effect was passed on 24th November, 1793, and "signed by the Church present," twenty-five in number. Again, on the 4th March, 1798, we find the following prudent regulation subscribed by forty-one members present. "For the peace and good order of the Church, it is agreed on by this Church that no natural affairs, neither public nor private, shall be brought up in this Church, so as to disturb the peace of it. And if any person or persons shall bring up any natural affairs, either public or private, so as to disturb the Church, and being called

---

[1] The Post-Boy Robb'd of his Mail, 2nd Edition, 1706, p. 423.
[2] Dictionary of All Religions, by Hannah Adams, [U.S.A.] Edited by T. Williams, N.D. [1823.] Art. Muggletonians.

to order by the Church shall not comply therewith,—the reckoning shall be paid, and the Church leave the room, and leave the disturbers of it to themselves; and if any money shall be above the reckoning, the said money to be put into the Closet and spent the next meeting." O sensible Church!

There was a book-closet belonging to the Society, for the safe custody of which, at the inn which formed their place of meeting, they paid a certain rent. Otherwise they had no local habitation as a Society, up to last year, 1869; now, however, a new era in their history has been begun, by their acquirement, for the first time, of a home which they can call their own. The place of meeting at present held on lease by the Muggletonians of London and the vicinity, is a small house, in New Street, off Bishopsgate Street Without. This New Street, which was considerably widened some years ago, is specially interesting to the community, inasmuch as they believe it to occupy the same site as Walnut Tree Yard, in which Lodowicke Muggleton was born in 1609; and it is possible they may be right. Their meeting room is on the first floor, and might, at a pinch, hold seventy people; on the floors above and below it are dressing and cloak rooms, and the apartments of the keeper. Beside the fire-place in the meeting room hangs the full length portrait of Muggleton by William Wood; and between the front windows is placed the following inscription:

THIS TABLET
WAS ERECTED ON THE 16th DAY OF MAY
1869
To commemorate the opening of the
NEW READING ROOM,
No. 7, New Street, Bishopgate. But more
especially to denote the place as formerly called
WALNUT TREE YARD,
WHERE THE LORD'S LAST WITNESS WAS BORN.
ALSO,
To record the names of a few of our
Christian Brethren, who, as believers in
THE THIRD COMMISSION
declared by
JOHN REEVE & LODOWICK MUGGLETON,
have greatly aided the Church, & partly
endowed the present building.

BENEFACTORS.
CATHERINE PEERS,
JOHN GANDAR,
JOSEPH GANDAR,
JOSEPH FROST,
ISAAC FROST.

TRUSTEES.

JAMES P. SMITH,	J. D. ASPLAND
WM. CATES,	ISAAC FROST, Jr.

Here, on the evenings of the 14th, 15th, 16th of February last, the believers assembled; never to the number of more than forty, nor more than twenty-five men at one time. Of those present only one-fourth, it was said, were born in the faith. Their business was to converse, take a meal together, and sing selections from the Divine Song Book. On the first evening the proceedings opened with tea, about five o'clock. About six, the Commission Song (" Arise, my soul, arise!") was sung, not by all the company, but by a lady who volunteered to do so. Then came in a large bowl of port wine negus, with slices of lemon floating upon its surface, and the believer whose seniority entitled him to take the lead in the proceedings (there was no chairman) gave, "Our usual toast—absent friends, and all the household of faith wherever they may be." The negus was conveyed into wine glasses by means of an antique silver ladle, the gift of a former believer (who bore the appropriate name of Mr. Thomas Spooner). When it had been handed round, more songs were heard; each person who chose volunteering to sing one. None of the airs were sacred, with the single exception of the evening-hymn tune, which had a very discordant sound as applied to a production of Boyer Glover's, beginning, "Oh ! wondrous, great, amazing, strange." In about an hour, beer was brought in, but few partook of it; and by half-past eight supper was ready. It was a plain, substantial meal; consisting of a round of beef, a ham, cheese, butter, bread, and beer. Throughout the evening, every one seemed heartily to enjoy himself and herself, with no lack of friendliness, but with complete decorum. No speeches were made, but between the songs conversation became pretty general. By ten o'clock all were on their way homeward.

It is not necessary to describe the programme of two subsequent evenings, which very closely resembled the opening one, except that the negus was omitted, and the time occupied was shorter. At the breaking up of the Holiday on Wednesday evening, a very short speech was made, or rather a few words were said, by one of the principal members. He referred to the fact that this was their 218th Anniversary, and the first occasion of its being held in a room of their own. He referred also to the fact that, for the first time in their history, a stranger had been permitted to attend their February Holiday, and paid the present writer the compliment of saying that he thought there had been no harm done, and that the experiment might safely be repeated.

One virtue, if it be a virtue, the modern Muggletonians seem to have nearly lost; the virtue, namely, of passing sentence of damnation upon their fellow creatures. In the prophet's days it was regarded almost as a duty, certainly as a mark of faith, and a means of strengthening faith, for private believers to pass this sentence in proper cases.[1] There were only two limitations to the exercise of the power; one was, that Muggleton himself reserved the privilege of taking off, or ratifying, as the case might be, the sentence which any of his followers had imposed;[2] and the other was, that "if a man give sentence, and afterwards doubts, that sentence returns on a man's own head, and the party so sentenced is freed from the power of his curse."[3] Accordingly there are well authenticated instances of the use of this power by Muggleton's favourite daughter Sarah, by his wife, by his friend Dorothy Carter, and by many other believers not specified by name. In the internal controversies of Muggletonians during the last century it was a weapon frequently resorted to as an ultimatum. That it is scarcely heard of now, is due partly to the peace and quiet presently enjoyed by the body, and partly to the influence of modern

---

[1] Spiritual Epistles, ut supra, p. 340.
[2] Acts of the Witnesses, ut supra, p. 144
[3] Spiritual Epistles, ut supra, p, 340.

ideas even upon this conservative little community. The same influence shows itself in an opinion, which is now tolerated, respecting the number of the lost. John Reeve, who was once a Universalist, going to the opposite extreme, expresses himself as "fully satisfied that there is a generality of men and women . . . . ordained to an estate of unbelief . . . . that they might everlastingly perish."[1] He charitably held, however, that all children without exception will be saved.[2] Muggleton, who in 1662 declared that "the greatest part of mankind" are the seed of the serpent, yet considered, in 1665, that half the world would be saved, counting children, and half would prove reprobate.[3] Notwithstanding this, the present writer has been informed, by a much respected member of the body, that in friendly talk upon the subject with a fellow believer of more conservative tendencies than himself, his friend held that very few would be saved, while he on the contrary believed that very few would be damned; and he expressly ascribed his own view to the influence of modern opinions upon the subject.

The present writer has indeed seen and conversed with a sensible Muggletonian, who yet was bold enough to pass the damnatory sentence upon an unfortunate Swedenborgian lecturer; but the majority of existing believers would probably never think of following this example. Among the last instances of the formal delivery of this sentence in writing, is that of the Author of Waverley, who was sentenced under that title by the late Robert Wallis, on the 18th July, 1826, on account of offensive expressions in the novel of Woodstock, which speak of "those Grindletonians or Muggletonians in whom is the perfection of every foul and blasphemous heresy, united with such an universal practice of hypocritical assentuation, as would deceive their master, even Satan himself."[4] The latest case of all is perhaps that of the notorious Richard Carlile, who in his coarse way had made much game of the little sect, telling them "though they have no priests, they stand in much need of a schoolmaster," and indulging in sundry unmannerly jests respecting members of the body in Nottingham. At that time Joseph and Isaac Frost were living, and they jointly passed the sentence on him by letter.[5]

---

[1] Stream from The Tree of Life, ut supra, p. 52.
[2] Divine Looking Glass, 3rd Edition 1719, p. 155.
[3] Interpretation of Eleventh Chapter of Revelation, p. 23. Spiritual Epistles, ut supra, p. 180.
[4] Woodstock, 1826, vol. 3, p. 205. Sir Walter evidently had in view, not Muggletonians, of whom he knew nothing, but Familists.
[5] See Carlile's publication, The Lion, ii. 13, and iii. 9.

The works of Reeve and Muggleton are the following, enumerated here in the order of their publication.

Transcendent Spiritual Treatise, 1652.
General Epistle from the Holy Spirit, 1653.
Remonstrance from the Eternal God, 1653.
Divine Looking Glass, 1656.
Joyful News from Heaven, 1658.
Interpretation of Revelation, cap. XI., 1662.
Neck of the Quakers' Broken, 1663.
Letter to Thomas Taylor, 1664.
Interpretation of Whole of Revelation, 1665.
Looking Glass for George Fox, 1668.
Witch of Endor, 1669.
Answer to William Penn, 1673.
Acts of the Witnesses, 1699. Written, 1677.
Sacred Remains, 1706. Written, 1652-1657.
Occasional Discourse, 1719. Written, 1668.
Answer to Isaac Pennington, 1719. Partly Printed, 1669.
Spiritual Epistles, 1755. Written, 1653-1691.
Stream from Tree of Life, 1758. Written, 1654-1682.
Supplement to Book of Letters, 1831. Written, 1656-1688.

Bibliotheca Anti-Quakeriana;

OR

A CATALOGUE OF BOOKS

ADVERSE TO THE SOCIETY OF FRIENDS,

ALPHABETICALLY ARRANGED;

WITH

Biographical Notices of the Authors,

TOGETHER WITH

THE ANSWERS WHICH HAVE BEEN GIVEN TO SOME OF

THEM BY FRIENDS AND OTHERS.

BY JOSEPH SMITH,

Author of "A DESCRIPTIVE CATALOGUE OF FRIENDS' BOOKS," in Two Vols.

London:

JOSEPH SMITH, 6, OXFORD STREET, WHITECHAPEL, E.

1873.

CLAXTON, Laurence, of *Cambridgeshire.—He* had been a Preacher amongst the Ranters, but coming to believe in the doctrines of John Reeve and Lodowick Muggleton, he became (soon after the decease of the former) a writer in vindication of their principles. After issuing 4 books Muggleton says, "he grew so proud, and Lording over the Believers, saying, *That no body could write in the vindication of this Commission, now* John Reeve *was dead, but he,* and to that purpose he wrote another book, wherein he had proudly exalted himself into John Reeve's Chair, exalting John Reeve and himself, but quite excluded me. Whereupon I put him down, for ever writing any more. He continued thus 4 years, until the year 1661, and in a while after humbled himself to me, and acknowledged his fault, and I forgave him, but ty'd him not to write any more."

When the Fire destroyed the *City of* London; he employed himself in helping persons of quality to borrow money to build their houses again, but the persons that had the money run away, so he was arrested, and put in *Ludgate Goal* where he died (1667?) after being imprisoned about a year."—*Muggleton's "Acts of the Witnesses, &c."* 4to. 1699. p. 80-82.

-----The Right DEVIL Discovered:

$$\left.\begin{array}{l}1\\2\\3\\4\\5\end{array}\right\} \text{In his} \left\{\begin{array}{l}\text{Descent.}\\\text{Form.}\\\text{Education.}\\\text{Qualification.}\\\text{Place and nature of Torment.}\end{array}\right.$$

With many other Divine Secrets, never as yet extant. Published for Confutation of the Learned, Instructing the Wise, and undeceiving of the Simple. Written by Laur. *Claxton.*

London : *Printed for the Author, and are to be sold by Francis Cossinet, at the Sign of the Anchor and Mariner in Tower-street.*
Small 8vo. 1659. $9_{1/2}$?

(Brit. Mus. 694. c. 26/9)

-----The QUAKERS DOWNFAL, with all other DISPENSATIONS their inside turn'd outward: Wherein you have it infallibly interpreted,

$$\left.\begin{array}{l}1.\\2.\\3.\end{array}\right\{\begin{array}{l}\text{What Scripture is, what not.}\\\text{By whom it was writ.}\\\text{For whom it was writ.}\end{array}$$

4. *The end wherefore it was writ.*

Also, A Brief NARRATION of the *Quakers Conference* with us the second of *July* 1659. wherein we made appear, That all their Sufferings in *New England,* or any other Nation, they suffer justly as evil doers, so that neither they, nor their Persecutors, so living and so dying, shall escape Damnation. With a clear Confutation of all ARMENIANS [called FREE-WILLERS] that deny God's Prerogative Power in matter of Damnation and Salvation. Written by *Laurence Claxton,* the alone, true, and faithful Messenger of Christ Jesus the Lord of Glory.
> London: Printed for the Authour, and are to be sold by Will. Learner at the Blackamoor, near Fleet-bridge

4to. 1659. 9

Note.—A Copy of this book may be found in the Friends' Library, at Devonshire House Meeting House, Houndsditch, also in the Library of Lambeth Palace, London.

HARWOOD, John, of *Yorkshire.*

— The Lying Prophet *Discovered and Reproved;* In an answer to several particulars in a book called *The Quakers Downfal,* said to be written by *Lawrence Claxton,* who blasphemously stiles himself the alone true and faithful Messenger of Christ Jesus; but his Spirit being tried by the fruits it hath brought forth, he is found to be a Messenger of Satan, &c.
> London: Printed for Thomas Simmons, at the Bull and Mouth near Aldersgate.

4to. 1659. 3

-----A Paradisical Dialogue between Faith and Reason.
   (In the Library of Lambeth Palace.) . . . . . 4to. Lon. 1660.

-----A Wonder of Wonders. . . . . 1660.

-----The Lost Sheep Found: or The Prodigal returned to his Fathers house, after many a sad and weary Journey through many Religious Countreys. Where now, notwithstanding all his former Transgressions, and breach of his Fathers commands he is received in an eternal Favor, & all the righteous & wicked Sons that he hath left behind, reserved for eternal misery; As all along every Church or dispensation may read in his Travels, their Portion after this Life. *Written by Laur. Claxton.*

4to. London: Printed for the Author. 1660. 8

MUGGLETON, Lodowick, was a Journeyman Tailor, who with his Companion JOHN REEVE, set up for *Prophets, in the* turbulent times of OLIVER CROMWELL. They gave out that they were THE TWO LAST WITNESSES spoken of in the

Revelations. The followers of Muggleton were strong opposers of the common notion of the Trinity, and seem to have entertained proper ideas of the Injustice, Impolicy and Odiousness of Persecution. This appears from a work, entitled, *The Muggletonian Principles prevailing,* published in 1695.—It is a reply to an Adversary. "When God gathers up his Jewels, many of those that have been judged *Heretics,* will rise *Saints,* and many of those that your Churches have canonized for Saints will rise *Devils!* For no *Persecutors of Conscience* will escape the stroke. If any man object *Paul's* persecuting the Church, they may know that *Paul* at that time acknowledged no Jesus at all; therefore when both sides acknowledge *a Jesus,* take heed how you persecute!"

Since writing the above paragraph, I have met with the following Inscription—taken from the Church-Yard,* Spinning-Wheel-Alley, Old Bethlem. *Mr. Ludovick Muggleton,* died Monday, March 14, 169 7/8, in the 88th year of his age.

> "Whilst Mausoleums and large Inscriptions give;
> Might, Splendor, and past death realm potents live,
> It is enough to briefly write thy name,
> Succeeding times by *that* will read thy fame;
> Thy deeds, thy acts, around the globe resound,
> No foreign soil where Muggleton's not found!

This is a singular instance of the extravagance of the followers of this now almost forgotten Prophet. I have been down to *the ground,* and no stone tells where *the Prophet* lies.—*Evans's Sketch of the Denominations of the Christian World,* 13th edition. 1814.

> Now the Terminus of the North London Railway, BROAD STREET STATION.

----- A Transcendent Spiritual Treatise upon several heavenly Doctrines, from the holy spirit of the man Jesus, the only true God, sent unto all his elect, as a token of his eternal love unto them, by the hand of his own Prophet, being his last Messenger, and Witness, and forerunner of the visible appearing of the distinct personal God in power and great glory, in the clouds of Heaven, with his ten thousands of personal Saints, to separate between the elect world, and the reprobate world, to all Eternity: Containing those several Heads set down in the next page following. John Reeve *and* Lodowick Muggleton, *the two* last *Witnesses and true Prophets of the man Jesus, the only Lord of Life and Glory, sent by his holy Spirit to seal the foreheads of the Elect, and the foreheads of the reprobate, with the eternal Seals of Life and Death, and suddenly after we have delivered this dreadful Message, this God the man Jesus, will visibly appear to bear witness whether he sent us or not: ye that are the blessed shall patiently wait for the truth of this thing.* If any of the Elect desire to speak with us concerning anything written in this Treatise, they may

Bibliotheca Anti-Quakeriana 179

hear of us in *Great Trinity Lane,* at a Chandlers shop, against one Mr. *Mills,* a Brown Baker, near the lower end of *Bow-Lane.*
    Printed for the Authors, and are to be sold by them at the place above-named.   4to. [1652.] 6

— The same. . . . . 8vo. *Re-printed in the Year,* 1711.   5 ¼

----- The same. . . . . . 4to. *Re-printed in the Year,* 1756.   6

----- The same. *Re-printed in the year* 1756: *and Re-printed by Subscription, in the year* 1822, *by W. Smith, King Street, Long Acre.* . . . . . 4to.

----- A General Epistle from the Holy Spirit unto all Prophets, Ministers, or Speakers in the World. Wherefore if any Man in the World shall be left to despise this writing from the greatest to the least by calling of it blasphemy, a devil delusion or a lie in so doing they have committed that unpardonable sin against the holy Spirit that sent us wherefore from the presence of the Lord Jesus, elect men and angels we pronounce them cursed and damned soul and body to all eternity. John Reeve and Lodowick Muggleton, the two last Spiritual Witnesses, and alone true Prophets of the Holy Spirit, by commission from the true God that ever shall write or speak unto unbelieving Magistrates, Ministers and People until the only Lord of Life and Glory, the Man Jesus personally appeareth in the air, with his mighty Angels, to bear witness to this testimony: even so come Lord Jesus. From Great Trinity Lane, at a Chandler's Shop, against one Mr. Millis a Brown Baker, near Bow Lane End, London, 1658, in the Second Year of our Commission by voice from heaven.
    4to.? 1658.

    Reprinted.—With, *"A Remonstrance, &c.* . . . 4to. 1719.

    Reprinted.— *R. Brown, Printer,* 26 *St.John Street, Clerkenwell.*   4to. [1881?]

----- A Letter presented unto Alderman Fouke, Lord Mayor of London, from the two Witnesses and Prisoners of Jesus Christ, in Newgate, as an eternal Witness unto him; with a Declaration unto the Recorder Steel, and the Lord Chief Justice Rowles, with the whole Bench and Jury; and in general, unto all Civil Magistrates and Juries in the World: John Reeve, and Lodowicke Muggleton, the two last Spiritual Witnesses, and true Prophets, and only Ministers of the everlasting Gospel, by Commission from the Holy Spirit of the true God, the Lord Jesus Christ, God and Man, in one Person, blessed to all eternity.
    1653.

----- Reprinted in "A Volume of Spiritual Epistles," 1755 and 1820.

----- A Remonstrance from the Eternal God declaring several Spiritual Transactions unto the Parliament and Commonwealth of England unto his excellency the Lord General Cromwell the Council of State the Council of War and to all that love the Second Appearing of the Lord Jesus the only God, and Everlasting Father blessed for ever. By John Reeve and Lodowicke Muggleton, The two last Witnesses and true Prophets, imprisoned for the testimony of Jesus Christ, in Old Bridewell. 1653.

----- The same,—Printed in *the Year,* 1653, and *Re-printed in the Year* 1719. . . . . 4to.

> Note.—The next following, "A General Epistle, &c." is reprinted with this edition. Remonstrance 2 } Sheets. General Epistle 1

----- The same,—London: *Printed in the Year* 1653. *Re-printed in* 1791. [1719 2] *and Re-printed in the year* 1831, *by R. Brown,* 26, *St. John Street, Clerkenwell.* . . . 4to.

----- The *same,—Printed in the Year* 1653, *and reprinted* in 1793. Small 8vo.

----- A DIVINE LOOKING-GLASS: or the third and last Testament of our LORD JESUS CHRIST, whose personal Residence is seated on his Throne of Eternal Glory in another World Being the Commission of the Spirit, agreeing with, and explaining of the two former Commissions of the Law and the Gospel, differing onely in point of Worship. Set forth for the Tryal of all sorts of supposed *Spiritual Lights* in the world, until the Ever-living true JESUS, the onely High and Mighty God personally appear in the Air, with his Saints and angels. By *John Reeve* and *Lodowick Muggleton,* Penmen hereof, and the last chosen Witnesses unto that Everblessed Body of Christ Jesus glorified, to be the only wise, very true God alone, Everlasting Father, and Creator of both Worlds, and all that were made them. 1656.

----- The same (being the 2nd edition)
> *Printed in the Year of our Lord* 1656, *and since reviewed by, and reprinted for Lodowick Muggleton, one of the said Witnesses, dwelling in great Trinity-Lane, in London, near the Sign of the Lyon and the Lamb, where this Book is to be had.* (With a Portrait) 4to. 1661. 27

(*Brit. Museum,* 4410. cc.]

----- The same,—*The Third Edition.*---
> *London ; Printed in the Year of our Lord* 1656, *and since Reprinted by Subscription in the Year,* 1719. 4to. 27 ½

----- The Fourth Edition.
    4to. *Printed in the Year of our Lord* 1656, *and reprinted (by Subscription) in the Year,* 1760. . . . . . 33 ¾

----- 𝔉𝔦𝔣𝔱𝔥 𝔢𝔡𝔦𝔱𝔦𝔬𝔫.-----
    London First printed in 1656; *revised by, and printed for Lodowick Muggleton, in* 1661; *Re-printed (by Subscription) in* 1846, *by Catchpool & Trent,* 5, *St. John's square, from the Second edition revised by the Prophet Lodowick Muggleton; and may be had of Joseph and Isaac Frost, St.John's square, Clerkenwell; Joseph Gandar* 18, *Northampton Park, Islington; and William Ridsdale, Lenton, near Nottingham; and of Booksellers. (Portrait)*

                                                                                         8vo. 1846. 12 ½

    An Occasional Discourse, &c., at the end.

(*Brit. Museum,* 1012. d. 14.)
    Note.—An Additional or 2nd Title was added to the 3rd. edn.viz.--

----- A Divine LOOKING GLASS: or, Heavenly Touch-Stone; Proceeding from the unerring Spirit of an Infinite Majesty, whose Personal Residence is Seated on his Throne of bright burning Crowns of Eternal Glory in another World. Purchased in this World from his Divine Self only, by Vertue of powring forth his unvaluable Life Blood unto Death, through the Transmuting of his incomprehensible Glory into a Body of Flesh, sent forth for a Tryal of all sorts of supposed Spiritual Lights in this Nation, etc., etc.
    Printed in the Year of our Lord, 1656. *And Reprinted by Subscription in the Year,* 1719.

----- Joyful News from Heaven or the last intelligence from our Glorified Jesus above the Stars wherein is infallibly recorded how that the Soul dieth in the Body, and lieth in the grave until the day God will raise it from death with a true description of the Kingdom of Heaven and of Hell. Also is discovered, I. What that is which sleeps in the Dust. II. The nature of its Rest. III. The manner of its Waking. IV. The mystery of the Dispute between Christ and the Woman of Samaria as touching the true Point of Worship clearly open'd. Wherein you have, drawn up, a Divine Charge against the Teachers of the Baptists. With all other Teachers publick and private for counterfeiting the Commissions of the Man Jesus being therein convicted of spiritual High Treason against Christ the Great Commissioner of Heaven and Earth. With a true Description of the Kingdom of glory, prepared only for the Seed of Adam that blessed Seed of Faith and true Relation of the Kingdom of Darkness prepared for the cursed Seed of Cain, World without end. Written by John Reeve and

Lodowick Muggleton, the Last Commissionated Witnesses and Prophets of that only High, Immortal, Glorious God, *Christ* Jesus.

                  1658.

----- The same.   .   .   .   . Small 8vo.   *Re-printed in the Year, 1706.* 5

  Re-printed. 4to. *No Printer's name, per, or date,*   [1761-8.] 7

----- A TRUE INTERPRETATION of the Eleventh Chapter of the *Revelation* of St. *John,* and other Texts in that Book; As also many other places of Scripture. Whereby is unfolded and plainly declared the whole councel of God concerning Himself, the Devil, and all Mankinde, from the Foundation of the World, to all Eternity. Never before revealed by any of the sons of men, until now. By Lodowick Muggleton, *one of the two last Commissionated Witnesses and Prophets of the Onely high, immortal, glorious God,* CHRIST JESUS.
  Printed in the Year of our Lord 1662, for the Author, dwelling in Great Trinity-lane in London, near the Sign of the Lyon and the Lamb.

                 4 to. 24 ½

(Brit. Museum, <u>1016.K.</u>/2)

----- This, with *The Sacred Remains,* and *The Soul's Mortality,* and *The Answer to* William Penn, Reprinted by Subscription in the Years 1751, 1752, and 1753.

               4to. [1758.] 27

----- The same.
  London.- *Printed for the Author in the Year* 1662. *Re-printed by Subscription in the Year* 1753. *And Re-by Subscription in the year* 1833, *by* R. Brown, *St. John Street, Clerkenwell.*

                4to.   27

----- The Neck of the QUAKERS Broken: or, Cut in sunder by the two-edged Sword of the Spirit which is put into my Mouth.
  First, in a Letter *to Edward Bourne,* a Quaker.
  Secondly, In Answer to a Letter to *Samuel Hooton and* W.S.
  Thirdly, In a Letter to *Richard Farnsworth,* Quaker.
  Fourthly, In an Answer to a printed Pamphlet of the said *Richard Farnsworth,* Entituled, *Truth Ascended:* or, *The Anointed and Sealed of the Lord defended* &c.
Written by Lodowick Muggleton, *one of the two last Prophets and Witnesses unto the High and Mighty God, the Man Christ Jesus in Glory.*
  Amsterdam: Printed in the Year of our Lord God, 1668. And are to be had in Great-Trinity-Lane, over against the Lyon and the Lamb.

                4to.   10

----- The same. . . . . 4to. *Re-printed in the Year,* 1756. 12 ¾

> Note.—It was for publishing this book that Muggleton was tried at the Old Bailey, in 1877, and being found guilty was sentenced to pay a fine of £500, and to stand upon the Pillory in three of the moat eminent places of the City, the Royal Exchange, Temple Bar and Smithfield on three several days. He however clears the Quakers of having any hand in this persecution.*
> The Imprint, "Amsterdam, &c." is without doubt a ruse, and the vol. was thought ante-dated, so as to put it under the protection of the Act of Indemnity of 1674.
> * See "The Spiritual Epistles," p.

----- A LETTER sent to THOMAS TAYLOR, Quaker, In the Year 1664. In *Answer* to many blasphemous Sayings of his in several pieces of Paper, and in the Margent of a Book. Amongst many of his wicked ignorant Sayings, I have given an *Answer* to some of the chief and main things of Concernment, for the Reader to know: The particular Heads are seven.—*By* Lodowick Muggleton.

> 4to. *Printed in the Year of our Lord,* 1665. 2

----- The same. . . . . . . *Re-printed in the Year,* 1756. 21

> Note. --this edition wee re-printed and added to "The Quakers' Neck broken," the pagination running on.

----- A TRUE INTERPRETATION of All the Chief TEXTS, and Mysterious SAYINGS and VISIONS opened, of the whole Book of the REVELATION of St. JOHN. Whereby is unfolded, and plainly declared those Wonderful deep Mysteries and Visions interpreted; concerning the *true God,* the *Alpha* and *Omega;* with variety of other Heavenly Secrets, which hath never been opened nor revealed to any man since the creation of the World to this day, until now. *By* Lodowick Muggleton, *one of the two last Commissionated Witnessesd Prophets of the onely high, immortal, glorious God,* CHRIST JESUS.

> *Printed in the Year of our Lord,* 1665, *for the Author Lodowick Muggleton, in Great Trinity-Lane London, near the Sign of the Lyon and Lamb.*
>
> 4to. 82

----- The same.
> *First printed for the Author in the Year* 1665, *and now re-printed by subscription,* 1746. 4to. 21

----- The same.
> 𝔏𝔬𝔫𝔡𝔬𝔫: *First printed for the Author in the Year* 1666; *Printed by Subscription in* 1746, *and Reprinted by subscription in* 1808. *Morris and Reeves Printers,* 83, *Red-Cross Street, Southwark.*
> 4to. 48

184   Academic Literary and Scientific Interest

----- A LOOKING-GLASS for GEORGE FOX THE QUAKER, and other QUAKERS; Wherein they may see themselves to be Right Devils. In ANSWER to *George Fox* his Book, called, *Some thing in Answer to* Lodowick Muggletons *Book, which he Calls* The QUAKERS Neck Broken. Wherein is set forth the Ignorance and blindness of the Quakers Doctrine of Christ within them; and that they cannot, nor doth not know the true meaning of the Scriptures, neither have they the Gift of Interpretation of Scripture. As will appear in those several Heads set down in the next Page following. Written by *Lodowick Muggleton,* one of the two last Prophets and Witnesses unto the High and Mighty God, the Man Christ Jesus in Glory.

4to. *Printed in the Year,* 1668. 12 ½

Note.—In the lines of page 88, for Russell's wife and another woman read Bridget Russell and Mrs. Poole.

----- The same. . . . .   4to. *Re-printed in the Year,* 1756. 18 ¾

----- A True INTERPRETATION Of the 𝔚𝔦𝔱𝔠𝔥 𝔬𝔣 𝔈𝔫𝔡𝔬𝔯. *Spoken of in* 1 Sam. XXXVIII. *begin at the* 11th *Verse.* Shewing, 1. How She and all other Witches do beget or produce that Familiar Spirit they deal with, and what a Familiar Spirit is, and how those Voices are procured, and Shapes appear unto them, whereby the Ignorant and Unbelieving People are deceived by them. 2. It is clearly made appear in this TREATISE, that no Spirit can be raised without its Body, neither can any Spirit assume any Body after Death; For if the Spirit doth walk, the Body must walk also. 8. An Interpretation of all those Scriptures, that doth seem as if Spirits might go out of Men's Bodies when they die, and subsist in some place or other without Bodies.—Lastly, Several other things needful for the mind of Man to know; which whoever doth understand, it will be great Satisfaction. *By* LODOWICK MUGGLETON, *Penman hereof, and the last chosen Witness unto that Ever-Blessed Body of Christ Jesus Glorified, to be only Wise, very true God alone, Everlasting Father, and Creator of both Worlds, and all that were made in them.*

4to. *London, Printed in the Year,* 1669. 7 ¼

Reprinted.—𝔗𝔥𝔢 𝔖𝔢𝔠𝔬𝔫𝔡 𝔈𝔡𝔦𝔱𝔦𝔬𝔫.

4to. *London, Printed by Subscription in the Year* 1724. 6 ¾

Reprinted.—The Third Edition.

London, Printed by Subscription in the Year 1724, *and Re-printed in* MDCCXCIII.   Small 8vo. [1793.] 3 7/8

The same.—The Fourth Edition.
>London: *Printed by Subscription in the Year* 1724, *Reprinted in* 1798. *And Re-printed in the Year* 1831, *by R. Brown*, 28, *St. John Street, Clerkenwell.*
               4to. 9

Note.—To the second edition of this book, there is added, beginning at page 45, the following, viz.—

----- *A Copy of a Letter written by the Prophet* Mugggleton, *to Mr.* Edward Fewterril *of* Chesterfield, *bearing Date from* London March 29, 1660." (Concerning Witchcraft.)

Reprinted, in, "A Stream from the Tree of Life, &c.," at page 80.
               4to. 1758.

----- THE ANSWER To WILLIAM PENN, Quaker, His Book, Entituled, *The New Witnesses proved old Hereticks.* WHEREIN He is proved to be an ignorant Spater-brained *Quaker,* who knows no more what the true God is, nor his secret Decrees, then one of his Coach-horses doth, nor so much; *For the Oxe knoweth his Owner, and the Ass his Master's Scrip,* but *Penn* doth not know his Maker, as is manifest by the Scriptures, which may inform the Reader, if he mind the Interpretation of Scripture in the Discourse following. I. That God was in the Forme, Image and likeness of Man's bodily Shape, as well as his Soul from Eternity. II. That the Substance of Earth and Matter was an eternal, dark, sensless Chaos, and that Earth and matter was eternal in the Original. III. That the Soul of Man is generated and begot by Man and Woman with the Body, and are inseparable. IV. That the Soul and Body of Man are both Mortal, and doth die and go to dust until the Resurrection. V. That to fulfill the Prophecy of *Esaias* God descended from Heaven into the Virgin's Womb, and transmuted his spiritual Body into a pure natural body, and become a Man-Child, even the. Childe *Jesus, Emanuel God with US.* VI. That God by his Prerogative Power, hath elected the Seed of *Adam* to be saved, and hath pre-ordained the Seed of the Serpent, such as *Penn the Quaker* is, to be damned, without any other Inducement, but his own Prerogative Will and Pleasure. VII. A Reply to the Discourse between *Penn* and me. VIII. What is meant by the Armour of God, the Wilderness, and the wilde Beasts I fought with in the Wilderness. By LODOWICK MUGGLETON.
      4to. London, Printed in the Year, 1673. 19 ½

Reprinted. . . 4to. *No Printer's name, place, or date,* [1753?] 18

----- The same.
>London: *Re-printed by Subscription, in the Year* 1835, *by E. Brown, St. John St., Clerkenwell.* . 4to. 19

----- *Here followeth a Declaration what the whole Armour of God is, and what is meant by the Wilderness; and a description of the Wilde Beasts I fought with after the manner of men in the Wilderness, as I was journeying and travelling towards the heavenly* Canaan, *in those 6 years time, from the year 1662 to the year 1668. Concerning my Travels through the Spiritual Wilderness of Mens hearts in Mortality, towards the spiritual and heavenly Land of* Canaan. *By Lodowick Muggleton.*

4to. *No date.* 2 ¾

> Note -- This Declaration Is the latter part of the "Answer to Penn," and the following is an Extract from a Letter to Thomas Tomkinson, January 19, 1678. concerning Penn's book.

"Now I shall write a few words to satisfy you, that my answer to William Penn's book is got safe out of the press, but with great charge and difficulty; the volume is pretty large, nineteen sheets and an half, and there is variety of matter in it that is new, never written before, very pleasant to read: the books are half a crown a-piece, I will not let one go under to friend nor stranger, therefore if you please to make those friends acquainted with it that will go to the price of it, let them send money, and I will send as many of them as the money doth amount to at half a crown a-piece."—*Spiritual Epistles,* 2nd edition, p. 386.

----- The 𝔄cts of the 𝔚itnesses of the SPIRIT. In Five Parts; By Lodowick Muggleton, One of the Two Witnesses, and True Prophets of the only High, Immortal, Glorious God, *Christ Jesus. Left by him, to be publish'd* after's death.
In the latter days two Bright Stars shall arise, *raising up men being dead in their Sins, which shall resist the Beast, and the Waters of the Dragon; testifying and preaching the Law of the Lamb, and the Destruction of Antichrist, and shall diminish his Waters; but they shall be weakened in the Bread of Affliction, and they shall rise again in stronger force; and after Truth shall be revealed, and the Lamb shall be known: After this shall be but a small Space.*
Fox in his *Book* of *Marters.* [With an "Epistle Dedicatory," by T. T. [Thomas Tomkinson]. (Written 1677) (With a Portrait by Caffeel).

4to. *London : Printed in the Year of our Lord God,* 1699. 23 ½

(Brit. Mus. 699.t.g./1-5)

> Note.—Few copies of this edition have the original title page and *Epistle Dedicatory,* containing ten lines respecting the fate of "Judge Jephreys;" even in perfect copies these lines are usually found crossed out with a pen,

----- The *same,—London: Printed in the year of our Lord God* 1699: *and Re-printed in the Year* 1764,

4to. 23 ½

----- 𝔖acred 𝔑emains: or, a DIVINE APPENDIX; being a COLLECTION of several TREATISES Epistolary and Publick. Originally

Written above Fifty Years since, By the Lord's last Immediate Messenger, JOHN REEVE, and Now, after careful Examination by the most correct Copies communicated for the Consolation and Establishment of the Church of Christ, by their Brethren, whose Faith in these and all other his irremandable Declarations, doth (and by Divine Protection) will remain unshaken to Eternity. [Written 1652-1657.]
> 4to. *Printed by Subscription in the Year* 1706. *The rest are to be sold at Two Shillings per Book, against the Sign of the Pidgeon in Lamb-Alley in Bishopsgate-Street, London.*

(*Brit. Museum*, 699t/2)

> Note.—This book contains nothing by Muggleton, and was probably published by the *Reevites.*

Reprinted, ... 4to. *No date.* 14

Reprinted, entitled,—" Sacred Remains, or, A DIVINE APPENDIX; being a Collection of Five Spiritual Epistles, originally written about the year 1654: also William Sedgwick's Replies to several Queries sent to him, by the Lord's Last immediate Messenger JOHN REEVE, then residing in London. Third Edition.
> *London: Re-printed for Joseph Frost,* 17, *Half Moon Street, Bishopsgate Street; By Andrew T. Roberts,* 2, *Hackney Road, opposite Shoreditch Church.*
> 4to.   1856.   10

Contents of "Sacred Remains," 1st edition.
> Queries sent to Mr. Sedgwick, by the Prophet Reeve, p. 1.
> Mr. Sedgwick's *Replies,* p. 3.
> *The Prophet's Answer to* Mr. Sedgwick's *Replies,* p. 6.
> Of the *One Personal Uncreated Glory,* p. 20.
> *The Prophet's Answer to a Letter sent him by Esquire* Pennington, P. 29.
> An EPISTLE *to the* Earl of Pembrooke, p. 38.
> An EPISTLE to a KINSMAN, p. 47.
> *What was* from *Eternity,* p. 51.
> A General TREATISE of the *Three Records,* or D*ispensations,* p. 62.
> A CLOUD of Unerring Witnesses Plainly Proving there neither is, nor ever was, any other GOD but *Jesus Christ* the LORD, p. 74.

----- An EPISTLE to a QUAKER. (By John Reeve.,
> 8v. *[Printed* in *the Year* 1711 ?]

Reprinted in, "A Stream from the Tree of Life, &c.," p. 49.
> 4to.   1758.

----- An EPISTLE *of the Prophet* REEVE. Written in the year 1656. With, *"An Occasional Discourse from the First and Second Verse of the Second, Chapter of the* Divine Looking-Glass, *concerning the Prophet* Reeve, &c. *By the Prophet* Muggleton, *Septem.* 28. Anno Dom. 1668.

4to. [*Printed* 1719.] 1

<blockquote>Note—The Epistle, as above was reprinted in " Stream from the Tree of Life, &c," 1768. The Occasional Discourse," has been reprinted separately.</blockquote>

----- *An Occasional Discourse from the First and Second Verse of the Second Chapter of the* Divine Looking-Glass, *concerning the Prophet* Reeve, *that* Darkness, Death and Hell, *lay secretly hid in the Spiritual Earth eternally with God. By the Prophet* Muggleton, *Septem.* 28. *Anno Dom.* 1668.

4to. [*London, Printed in the Year,* 1719.]

<blockquote>Note.—Printed at the end of "An Epistle of the Prophet Reeve."</blockquote>

Reprinted, at the end of "A Divine Looking-Glass, the 4th edition."

4to. 1760.

Reprinted, at the end of "A Divine Looking-Glass, the 5th edition.

8vo. 1846.

----- *Lodowick Muggleton's* Letter to *Robert Peirce, concerning the Holy Ghost.* (Written *August 2nd,* 1680.) With, "The Testimony of the Prophet Muggleton concerning the Death of Moses."

4to.   [*Printed in the Year,* 1719?] 1

<blockquote>Note.—The Letter to Robert Peirce, was reprinted in the "Volume of Spiritual Epistles," see page 826, 1st edition, 1755, and p. 484, 2nd edition, 1820, and "The Testimony concerning the Death of Moses," was reprinted In the "Stream from the Tree of Life." 1768.</blockquote>

----- AN ANSWER to ISAAC PENINGTON, *Esq.:* His Book Intituled, *Observations on some Passages of* Lodowick Muggleton's *Interpretation of the* llth *Chapter of the* Revelations. *Also some Passages of that Book of his Intituled,* The Neck of the Quakers Broken. And in his Letter to *Thomas Taylor.* Whereby it might appear what Spirit the *said Lodowick Muggleton* is of, and from what God his Commission is. As by what Authority his Spirit is moved to write against the People called Quakers. Written to inform those that do not know the Antichristian Spirit of False Teachers in these our Days. By *Lodowick Muggleton.* Written in the YEAR, 1669.

London Printed by Subscription in the Year 1719. 4to.   3 ½

The same,—

<blockquote>*London: Printed by Subscription in the year* 1719 *And Re-printed in the year* 1831, *by R. Brown,* 26, *St. John-street, Clerkenwell*</blockquote>

4to.   4 ½

<blockquote>Note.—Muggleton sent this book to the press in the year 1699, but only *one sheet* was set up, the copy and proof being seized out of the Printer's hands, the particulars of which are given as follows, in a Letter to Thomas Tomkinson, dated January 31, 1669.</blockquote>

" This is to certify you that I have sent seven books of the Interpretation of the Witch of Endor. I did intend the Answer to Isaac Pennington should have been printed also; but it did miscarry in the Press.

" I never was so crossed in all the books as I have printed, as in these two; for this of the Witch of Endor hath been for six months in the Printer's hands; but with much difficulty, and trouble, and charge, I have got it safe out of the press: but because this Printer was so base, and kept it so long, I put the other to another Printer, thinking to have it done before this, and so it would; but through the forgetfulness of the Printer, not taking the copy in his pockets as he thought to do, he went out and left the copy and proof of one sheet upon the press with his servants, and the searchers came immediately up stairs and took it, and would have carried it to the Council; but the printer made friends for money, else he would have been utterly undone; for it cost the printer seven pounds, and me five pounds to pacify the matter, and not get it done neither. But I have preserved the copy, most part of it, and hereafter I do think to print it, but not at present, it will be no ways convenient."—*Spiritual Epistles,* 2nd edition, 1820, p. 279.

A COLLECTION OF EPISTLES AND LETTERS, VIZ.

‖ ----- *The Prophet* Reeve's *Epistle to his Friend, discovering the dark Light of the* Quakers; *written in the Year* 1654 *September the 20th.*

----- *An Epistle of* John Reeve *to Mr.* Hill. *(June* 11. 1656.)

----- *Another Epistle of* John Reeve's *to the same Person.*—For his Loving Friend *Christopher Hill, Heel-maker* in *Stone street in Maidstone,* in *Kent. These.—London, June* the last 1656.

----- *Another Epistle of* John Reeve's *to the same Person.*

*----- *A Copy of a Letter wrote by the Prophet* John Reeve *to Mrs.* Alice Webb, *containing her Blessing and the Six Principles, on August* 15. 1666.

*----- *An Epistle of* John Reeve *to a Friend, written in* May 1657.

*----- *Another Epistle of* John Reeve's.

*----- *An Epistle wrote by the Prophet* JOHN REEVE *to* ISAAC PENNINGTON, *Esq; dated 1658, concerning an Answer to a Book of his, with several Mysteries and Divine and Spiritual Revelations declared by the Prophet, concerning God's visible appearing in the Flesh.*

Note—The foregoing Epistles and Letters are printed at the end of the 2nd *edition* of "The Witch of Endor," and these marked (*)are reprinted in "A Stream from the Tree of Life, &e." Those marked (‖) are reprinted is "A Volume of spiritual Epistles, &c.-

----- A DISCOURSE, between *John Reeve* and *Richard Leader,* MERCHANT. *Recited by* Lodowick Muggleton, *One of the Two Last* WITNESSES and PROPHETS *of the Most High* GOD, *the Man* CHRIST JESUS *in Glory.—With,—*"A *Copy of a Letter, by* the PROPHET LODOWICK MUGGLETON, to Mr. *James Whitehead of Brantry (Braintree) in Essex,* Bearing Date, *the 13th* of *June* 1682. "
       4to. *No Printer's name or place,* [about 1724?] 2

Reprinted in, "A Stream from the Tree of Life,"   4to. 1758

Reprinted in the "Two Systems of Astronomy, &c." By Isaac Frost.—p. 75.

[Epistle Showing "The Cause of the Excommunication of William Meadgate, &c. and Letters, viz.---}

----- *The Prophet* Muggleton's *Epistle to the Believers of the* Commission, *touching the Rebellion occasioned by* the Nine Assertions.---1671. *Here followeth the Copy of a Letter to* Walter Bohenan, a Scotchman, *another Rebel in the same Conspiracy with the rest, in Answer to his Rebellious Letter,* —A *Copy of a Letter written by the Prophet* Lodowick *Muggleton, to Colonel* Phaire, *and the rest of the Believers of the Commission of the Spirit, living in the Kingdom of* Ireland, *dated in* London, February *the* 16th, *1680.-- The Prophet* LODOWICK MUGGLETON'S *Blessing to Mrs.* SARAH SHORT, *transcribed from a Copy drawn form Original given to her by him, June the* 2d 1662.
            4to. [*Printed in* 1724?] 2 ¾

Note.--Muggleton's Blessing to *Sarah* Short, is reprinted in the "Volume of Spiritual Epistles, &c." all the others are reprinted in "A Stream from the Tree of Life, &c." 1758. The first paragraph in the first piece is omitted in the reprint.

----- VeræFidei Gloria est Corona Vitæ—A VOLUME of SPIRITUAL EPISTLES: being The *Copies* of several LETTERS Written *by* The two last PROPHETS and MESSENGERS of God, *John Reeve* and *Lodowicke Muggleton;* containing Variety of Spiritual Revelations, and deep Mysteries, manifesting to the Elect Seed the Prerogative Power of a true Prophet; who, by Virtue of their Commissions, did truly give Blessings of Life Everlasting to those that believed their declarations.; and to all despising Reprobates the Curse or Sentence of Eternal Damnation. COLLECTED By the great Pains of *Alexander Delamaine* the Elder, a true Believer of God's last Commission of the Spirit. INTENDED At first only for his own spiritual solace; but finding they encreased to so great a Volume, he leaves it to his posterity, that Ages to come may rejoice in the comfortable View of so blessed and heavenly a treasure. Transcribed from *Alexander*

Delamaine's Original Copy by *Tobiah Terry,* a true Believer of the like precious Faith in the true God the Man *Christ Jesus,* which most holy Faith the reprobate World despises. Written 1653-1691. This printed by Subscription in the Year 1755. The *Sacred Remains,* with the *Soul's Mortality,* and the *Answer to William Penn,* was re-printed by Subscription in the Years 1751, 1752, and 1753, which is an Example for Generations to come.

4to. 1755. 66 ½

----- The same,—Printed *by Subscription, in the Year* 1755: *Reprinted, by Subscription, in the Year* 1820, *by W. Smith, King Street, Long Acre.*

4to. 1820. 77 ½

Note.—This Volume contains, besides other matter :—

"The Prophet Reeve's Epistle,—discovering the dark Light of the Quakers, 1654."

Muggleton's Epistle to Christopher Hill, concerning Laurence Claxton,-1660.

The Quakers religion seemeth to Muggleton to be the purest of all the seven Churches in respect of practice, but the worst of all in matter of true doctrine, see p. 69. 2nd edition.

Elizabeth Hooton, a Woman Devil, see p. 231. Geo. Fox, Geo. Fox, the Younger, Edward Burrough, Francis Howgil, damned Devils, p. 71, 388.

"A Relation of some Passages in a discourse with Geo. Whitehead and Josiah Cole, in the year 1668, also some relation of that cursed Devil, Thomas Loe, Speaker of the Quakers."

A Testimony against John Reeve & Lodowick Muggleton, by the Quakers of *Cork,* signed by Wm. Morris, Wm. Edmondson, Robert Sandham and 23 others with Muggleton's Sentence of damnation upon them, p. 379-401. And the names of many other Friends & things concerning Friends are scattered throughout the vol.

A Letter to Elizabeth Atkinson, Feb. 12. 1671.

Muggleton's Letter to Isabella Malum, Quaker, of Nottingham, 1674. on her return to the Quakers.

Muggleton's Letter to Rice Jones, in Nottingham.

Muggleton's Letter to William King a Quaker, who came from *New-England,* 1672.

Muggleton's Letter to William Penn, 1673.—Muggleton here calls Penn, "that blaspheming, reprobate Devil."

Muggleton's Letter to John Grattan, 1669.—

----- A STREAM from the TREE OF LIFE: or, the THIRD RECORD vindicated being the COPIES of several Letters and Epistles wrote by the Two last Witnesses of *Jesus* Christ. Wherein Truth rides triumphant, and Imagination is confounded. These were not included in the Volume of SPIRITUAL EPISTLES, because of the great Expence. [Written 1654-1682.] (Edited by JOHN PEAT.)

4to. *Printed from the Original Manuscript in the Year of Our Lord* 1758. . . . . .11 ½

Contents.—The Prophet Muggleton's Epistle to the Believers of the Commission, touching the Rebellion occasioned by the Nine Assertions. p. 1.

A Letter written by the Messenger of God, Lodowick Muggleton to Walter Bohenan, of Condemnation for Apostacy, January 23, 1671. p. 9.

A Copy of a Letter written by the Prophet Lodowick Muggleton, to Mr. James Whitehead of Braintree in Essex, bearing Date, June 13, 1682. p. 17.

A Copy of a Letter written by the Prophet Lodowick Muggleton, to Colonel Phaire, and the rest of the Believers of the commission of the Spirit. Dated in London, February, 16, 1680. p. 25.

A Copy of a Letter written by the Prophet Lodowick Muggleton, to Mr. Edward Fewterell of Chesterfield, bearing date from London, March 29, 1660. p. 30.

A Discourse between John Reeve and Richard Leader, Merchant; recited by Lodowick Muggleton one of the two last Witnesses and Prophets of the most high God, the Man Christ Jesus in Glory.p. 88.

A Letter from the Prophet Muggleton, to Thomas Tomkinson.— From the Press-yard, Newgate, April 23, 1677. p. 48.

An Epistle To a Quaker. By John Reeve.—Begins, Dear and Loving Friend." p. 49.

An Epistle written by the Prophet Lodowick Muggleton. p. 55.

An Epistle of John Reeve to his loving Friend Christopher Hill, p.63.

A Copy of a Letter wrote by the Prophet John Reeve to Mrs. Alice Webb, containing her Blessing, and the Six Principles, on August 15, 1656. p. 64.

An Epistle of John Reeve to a Friend, written in May, 1657. p. 66.

Another Epistle of John Reeve's. p. 69.

An Epistle wrote by the Prophet John Reeve to Isaac Pennington, Esq.; dated 1658. Concerning an Answer to a Book of his, with several Mysteries and Divine and Spiritual Revelations declared by the Prophet, concerning God's visible appearing in the Flesh. p, 74.

The Testimony of the Prophet Muggleton, concerning the Death of Moses. p. 80.

An Epistle of the Prophet Reeve Written in the Year, 1656. p. 81.

A Copy of a Letter written by the Prophet Lodowick Muggleton, to Ann Adams of Orwell, in Cambridgeshire, bearing Date from London, March the 27th, 1663. p. 86.

----- SUPPLEMENT to The Book of Letters, written by John Reeve and Lodowicke Muggleton, the Two 𝔍ust 𝔓rophets of the only true 𝔊od, our Lord Jesus Christ.

BELOVED BRETHREN.

With the authority of the Church we have made diligent search through the Manuscript Records of the Church, and have found the following Letters, not in print in the "Book of Letters." The following Letters may be considered the conclusion of all the Writings of the Prophets REEVE and MUGGLETON, both of spiritual matter and temporal advice, as far as the Church is in possession of.
JOSEPH & ISAAC FROST.

London: Printed by R. Brown, 26, St. John Street, Clerkenwell. . . . . .4to. 1831. 7 ½

----- The WORKS of John Reeve and Lodowicke Muggleton, the Two Last Prophets of the *Only true God, our Lord Jesus Christ.* In three volumes. (With a Portrait to each vol.)
London : Printed by Subscription. 4to. 1882.
(Brit. Museum, 1012. b.)

----- GENERAL INDEX to John Reeve & Lodowicke Muggleton's Works. Intended for Three volumes. By Joseph and Isaac Frost.
R. Brown, Printer, 26, St. John Street, Clerkenwell.
4to. 1831. 5

☞ In the Year 1654, an order was made in the Colony of Massachusetts Bay, that every inhabitant who had in their custody any of the books of John Reeve's and Lodowick Muggleton, "who pretend to be the two last witnesses and Prophets of Jesus Christ," which books were said to be full of blasphemies, should bring or send them in to the next Magistrate, within one month on pain of £10 for each book remaining in any person's hands after that time.— *Hutchinson's History of the Colony of Massachusetts Bay.*

ANSWERS TO MUGGLETON AND REEVE, BY FRIENDS.

BURROUGH, Edward, of *Underbarrow, Westmoreland.*
----- and FRANCIS HOWGIL.—Answers to several QUERIES put forth to the despised People, called Quakers, by *Philip Bennet,*— Also, Answers to *several* other subtil Queries put forth by one *John Reeve,* who lives in the City of LONDON, who cals himself, the last *Messenger* and Witnesse unto the true God, but is found a false Witness, and a Lyar, and a Perverter of the right way of God. Answered by *Edward Burrough,* and *Francis Howgil,* who are Witnesses unto the Truth against this subtil serpent-like generation.
London, Printed for Giles Calvert, at the Black-Spread-Eagle, at the West end of Paul's.
4to. 1654. 2

Reprinted in Burrough's Works, p. 29. Folio. 1672.

COALE, Josiah, of *Winterburne, (near Bristol) in Gloucestershire.*
----- A Testimony concerning Lodowick Muggleton.—In J. C.'s Works, p. 343; also in "Piety Promoted."

FARNWORTH, Richard, of *Balby in Yorkshire.*
----- TRUTH ASCENDED, or, *The Annointed and Sealed of God defended:* in an ANSWER written by Richard Farnsworth, as TESTIMONY against a Counterfeit Commission and all Injustice and false Judgement done and pronounced under pretence of the same.
4to. London, Printed in the Year, 1663. 4

Note.—This piece is addressed to Lodowick Muggleton.

FOX, George, Founder of the Society of Friends.
----- Something in ANSWER to *Lodowick Muggleton's* Book, which he calls, *The Quakers Neck-Broken.* Wherein in Judging others he hath Judged himself.
4to. London, Printed in the Year, 1667. 4 ½

FRIENDS OF CORK, viz., WILLIAM MORRIS, WILLIAM EDMUNDSON, ROBERT SANDHAM, and 23 others.-- See Muggleton's Volume of Spiritual Epistles, p. 379, 2nd Edition, where the answer is inserted.

GRATTON, John.--See his Journal, 1st Edition, p. 23 and 73.

HARWOOD, John, answer to Claxton.—See LAWRENCE CLAXTON.

PENINGTON, Isaac, Son of Alderman PENINGTON, of *London.*
----- OBSERVATIONS on some Passages of *Lodowick Muggleton, in his* Interpretation of the 11th Chapter of the *Revelations.* As also on some Passages in that Book of his, stiled, *The Neck of the Quakers Broken,* and in his letter to *Thomas Taylor.* Whereby it may appear what Spirit he is of, and what god his Commission is from, &c,
4to. Printed in the Year, 1668. 3 ½

Reprinted in the *1st edition of his Works, Part 2, Page 36.*

Folio, 1681.

PENN, William, Founder *of Pennsylvania.*
----- The NEW WITNESSES proved Old Hereticks: or Information to the Ignorant; in which the Doctrines of *John Reeve and Lodowick Muggleton,* which they stile, Mysteries never before known, reveal'd, or heard of from the Foundation of the World, are proved to be mostly Ancient Whimsies,

Blasphemies and Heresies, from the Evidence of *Scripture, Reason,* and several *Historians.* Also An Account of some discourse betwixt L. M. and myself, by which his Blasphemous, Ignorant and unsavory spirit is clearly and truly manifested, in love to the immortal souls of those few, who are concern'd in the belief of his Impostures. *By a Living true Witness to that one Eternal Way of God, revealed* in the Light of Righteousness. W. P.

4to. Printed in the Year, 1672. 8

Reprinted in his Works, vol. 2, page 152.

> Note.—This book is written chiefly in reply to "The Divine Looking-Glass," the Transcendent Spiritual Treatise," and the "True Interpretation of all the Chief Texts, and Mysterious Sayings, &c., of the Book of the Revelation of St. John."

WHITEHEAD, George.—See his "Quakers' Plainness detecting Fallacy," &c. 8vo. 1674.

> ☞ It is to be noted that though the Muggletonians have reprinted Muggleton's books against Friends down to the present day, yet Friends have not reprinted the foregoing answers; for instance, Edward Burrough's and Josiah Coale's works, have not been reprinted. R. F.'s works were never collected, and the tract never reprinted. When G. Fox's works were collected the tract against Muggleton was not included; and though Isaac Penington's have been reprinted, the part about Muggleton is omitted; the same with Wm. Penn's.

MUGGLETONIANS. —

Books by Believers in the Doctrines of John Reeve and Lodowick Muggleton, (including some favourable to their principles or friendly towards them by Non-Believers.)

ANONYMOUS.—

----- An Elegy on the Death of Mr. Lodowick Muggleton, Great Teacher and Chief Pillar of a Society of People from him so call'd, who departed this Life on Monday, the 24th of March having passed the 88th year of his Age, and bore the Character of a Mighty Prophet among his own people.

Broadside, 1698.

----- The same.—Printed at the request of some of their followers, 1698.

Reprinted, 1754.	Broadside.
Reprinted.	Broadside, 1831.

> Note. This "Elegy" written by a Non-Believer, was printed at the request of Muggleton's Followers.

B. (T. H.)

----- An ODE. (on his belief in MUGGLETON)

4to. *(No Printer's name, place, or date.)* ¼

BROWN, John, of

----- THE SAINT'S TRIUMPH AND THE DEVIL'S DOWN-FALL. Being a Short and True DEMONSTRATION OF ELECTION, REPROBATION, AND FREE-WILL. By JOHN BROWN, a Brother to the *Saints,* and a Friend to the *Elect.* By way of QUESTION AND ANSWER.
  Norwich: Printed by S{tephen} White, Magdalen-street.
              4to. [1771.]   7 ½

CLAXTON, Lawrence, of *Cambridgeshire.*

FROST, Joseph, and ⎫ of St. John's Square, Clerkenwell, London,
FROST, Isaac,   ⎭   Brass Founders.

----- DIVINE SONGS of the 𝔐uggletonians, in grateful Praise to the only true God, the Lord. Jesus Christ.—Printed by Subscription. (Portrait.)
  London: Printed by B. Brown, 26, St. John Street, Clerkenwell.
              16mo. 1829. 20 ¼
  Note. The 197th Song in this Collection is by Elizabeth Henn.

----- A LIST OF THE BOOKS, with part of their title pages and the price of each book, of the THIRD AND LAST TESTAMENT of the only God, our Lord Jesus Christ. Written by JOHN REEVE AND LODOWICK MUGGLETON, the Two Witnesses prophecied of in the Eleventh chapter of the Revelations of Saint John the Divine.
  London: Printed by R. Feeny, 26, St. John Street, Clerkenwell.
                  16mo. 1848.

----- 𝔄 𝔏ist of 𝔅ooks and GENERAL Index to John Reeve & Lodowick Muggleton's WORKS: being the Third and last Testament of the only God our Lord Jesus Christ.
  London : Printed by Feeny and Co., 26, St. John Street, Clerkenwell.
              8vo. 1846.   1 ½

FROST, Isaac.

 ----- Two Systems of ASTRONOMY: 𝔉irst, THE NEWTONIAN SYSTEM, showing the Rise and Progress thereof, by a short Historical Account: the General Theory, with a variety of Remarks thereon. 𝔖econd, The System in accordance with THE HOLY SCRIPTURES, showing the Rise and Progress from Enoch, the Seventh from Adam: The Prophets, Moses and others, in the First Testament: Our Lord Jesus Christ, and his Apostles, in the New or Second Testament Reeve and Muggleton, in the Third and Last Testament; with a variety of remarks thereon. By ISAAC FROST. (With 11 plates.)

"Nevertheless we, according to His Promise, Look for New Heavens and a New Earth, wherein dwelleth Righteousness." —2 *Peter* iii. 13.

𝕰ntered at 𝖘tationers' 𝕳all.
London: Printed by Catchpool & Trent, 5, St. John's Square; Published by Simpkin, Marshall, & Co., Stationer's-Hall-Court.

Large 4to. 1846. 4 ¼

FROST, Joseph.
----- A Printed Letter, dated, January, 1858,—respecting there being no "List of the Subscribers, to the *4th edition,* of "The Divine Looking-Glass; &c." 1760.

4to. ½

PEAT, J., and others.
----- SONGS 𝔒f 𝔊rateful 𝔓rais𝔢 to t𝔥e Ever-Blessed, Glorious King of Saints And Merciful Immortal God, *Our* LORD JESUS CHRIST. (First Edition of the Song Book.) 16mo. [1790?] 57 pages?

   First SONG, by J. PEAT.
   Second SONG, by *James Miller.*
   Third SONG by *James Miller.*
 • Fourth SONG, Made on WILLIAM RINGER, ROBERT INGRAM and EDMUND TOULMAN receiving the Truth, by *Robert Ingram.*
 • Fifth SONG, by ROBERT INGRAM.
   Sixth SONG, by WILLIAM WOOD, *Joiner.*
   Seventh SONG, by *Boyer Glover.*
   Eighth SONG, by *George Hermitage.*
   Ninth SONG, by *Rebecca Batt.*
   Tenth SONG, by *J. Miller.*
   Eleventh SONG, by *B. Glover.*
   Twelfth SONG, *Made by John Gates, once Clerk of Eggam in Berkshire.*
   Thirteenth SONG, by *Boyer Glover.*
   Fourteenth SONG, by *Boyer Glover.*
   Fifteenth SONG, by *William Wood, Painter.*
   Sixteenth SONG, by *Robert Pickard.*
   Seventeenth SONG, by *James Miller.*
   Eighteenth SONG, by *Boyer Glover.*
   Nineteenth SONG, by *John Williams.*
   Twentieth SONG, by *William Wood, Painter.*
   Twenty-first (miscalled Twenty-fifth) SONG, by *Boyer Glover.*
       Note.—The 4th and 5th Songs, by Robert Ingram, who became a *Birchite*, are omitted in the Song Book of 1829.

POWELL Nathaniel.
----- A true Account of the Trial and Sufferings of LODOWICK MUGGLETON, *One of the two last Prophets and Witnesses of the Spirit,* left by our Friend Powell, who witnessed the Trial and all his Sufferings, therefore He gives a more full and particular Account of the Whole Proceedings than the

Prophet has left on Record, which is the Cause of my Printing it, *That Believers may see how patiently our Prophet bore those sufferings* on *Truths Account.* Knowing when time is ended, he should meet his God, his King and Redeemer, with all those that truly believe Jesus Christ, that was Crucified, was the only and alone eternal God, one Glorious distinct Person in the form of a Man, who now reigns in the highest Heavens, where we shall behold his glorious Face, to live with him, and praise his Holy Name for ever!

     4to. *Printed for T. Fever, (a Birchite.) 1808.* 3 ¼

----- An Answer to James Hurst, *alias* Patteson, (an apostate), in M.S.

SADDINGTON, John, born at *Arnesby* in *Leicestershire,* about 1634, died in *London,* September, 1679.

----- A Prospective Glass for SAINTS and SINNERS: whereby may appear and be seen, 1. The Author's Life expressed in the first Epistle. 2. That there is no true peace of mind in those that account themselves Believers, so long as they lead a corrupt life. 3. What great Enemies the Riches of this World, and Poverty are to Truth. 4. What that truth and true knowledge is, which giveth satisfaction to the mind of Man in this life. And several other things necessary to salvation. By *John Saddington,* A true Believer of the Witnesses of the Spirit, sent forth by the immediate voice of God Almighty, in the year 1651.

     4to. *Printed in the Year* 1678. 12 ½

----- The same.
 Printed in the Year 1673, *and reprinted for J. May, by T. B. Underdown, Deal.*

     8vo. 1823. 7 ¾

 Note.—This book is not specially written against Friends, but the Author charges them with being of an anti-christian spirit "in denying the Resurrection of the Body of Christ".

----- The ARTICLES of TRUE FAITH, depending upon the COMMISSION OF THE SPIRIT. Drawn up into Forty-Eight Heads, by JOHN SADDINGTON, An Ancient Believer; for the Benefit of other Believers, *That now are, or hereafter shall come to believe;* and to confound and disprove all despisers, that say, "We know not what we believe." Anno M.DC.LXXV.

 London: Printed by R. Brown, 26, St. John Street, Clerkenwell.

     8vo. 1830. 1

 Note.--On a separate paper (one leaf), pasted on the cover of the above pamphlet, "I do believe that there is a God full of all Spiritual Glory above or beyond the Stars."

----- THE WORMES CONQUEST, (M.S) . . . . . . 1677.

 Note.--This is an allegory in poetry, referring to the trial of Muggleton, who is the "Worme."

TENNANT, James.

----- 𝔗𝔥𝔢 𝔄𝔯𝔢𝔢𝔡. Signed J.T. . . . . . . 4to. No date. ¼

    Reprinted, with the Author's name.
                        4to. *(No Printer's name, place* or *date.)* ¼

TOMKINSON, Thomas, of *Sladehouse, Staffordshire,* born 1631, died about 1710.

----- The HARMONY of the THREE COMMISSIONS; or, *None but* CHRIST: Wherein is infallibly declared that all *Prophets* in the Time of the *Law,* or under the *first Commission,* and all *Apostles* and *Ministers* in the Time of the *Gospel, do* each of them unanimously agree in their Doctrine concerning GOD. And that according to the Doctrine of the *third Commission,* which Doctrine was in the two first *Commissions,* and is more fuller in this, being the *Commissions* of *the Spirit;* namely, that there is *None but* CHRIST, *None but* CHRIST; no other GOD but our *Lord Jesus Christ,* now in Heaven glorified. The first RECORD evidenced. *Unto us a* child *is born: unto us a* Son *is given: He shall be called the* mighty God *and the* everlasting Father.—Isa. ix. 6. The second RECORD evidenced. Great is the mystery *of* Godliness; God *manifested in Flesh. There are* three *that bear Record in* Heaven, &c.--1 *John.* v. 7. The third RECORD evidenced. *In the Days of the Voice of the* seventh Angel, *when he shall begin to sound, the* Mystery *of* GOD *shall be finished. By* THOMAS TOMKINSON. First written in the Year of our *Lord God* 1692; Revised and abridged by the *Author,* and printed in the Year M.DCC.LVII.
                                              8vo. 1757.

----- The Muggletonians Principles PREVAILING: Being An Answer in full to a Scandalous and Malitious Pamphlet, Intituled A 𝔗𝔯𝔲𝔢 𝔎𝔢𝔭𝔯𝔢𝔰𝔢𝔫𝔱𝔞𝔱𝔦𝔬𝔫 of the Absurd and Mischievious Principles of the Sect called MUGGLETONIANS; Wherein the aforesaid Principles are vindicated, and proved to be infallibly True. And The Author of that Libel, his Scandalous Title and Subject proved as False to Truth, as Light is to Darkness: And that he knows no more what the true God is, nor what the right Devil is; nor any true Principle or Foundation of Faith, for *all* his great Learning he so much bosts of, then those *Jews* that put the Lord of Life to Death: For learned and taught Reason is but natural, and so falls short of the Glory of God; as will appear in the following Discourse. By T. T.
                4to. *Printed in the Year of our Lord God,* 1695. 10

----- The same,—*Reprinted by T. Hayward, Beach Street, Deal.*
                                              4to. 1822. 10

----- *Truth's Triumph:* OR A WITNESS To the Two WITNESSES, Together with an EXPLANATION or the Torments of HELL.

Written by *Thomas Tomkinson,* Deceas'd. And now published by *T. B.* PART VII.
      4to. *Printed in the Year MDCCXXIY.* 26 pp.

----- (The Running Title:)—Truth's *Triumph: Or, the Devils* TORMENT. (John Middleton, his book, 1769.)

----- *Truth's Triumph:* OR A WITNESS TO THE TWO WITNESSES; Written by *Thomas Tomkinson,* Deceas'd. And now Published By Some FRIENDS. PART VIII.
      Printed in the Year MDCCXXI.
(John Middleton, his book, 1769.)

----- (The Running Title:)—*Truth's Triumph: Or, the Saints* JOY.
      4to. 24 pp.
  Note.—This appears to be the whole of Truth's Triumph as printed previous to 1828.

----- TRUTH'S TRIUMPH; or, A Witness to the Two Witnesses; from that unfolded Parable of Our Lord and Saviour, Jesus Christ, the High and Mighty god, Matthew, chap. 13, verse 30 to 42 wherein the Fundamentals of Faith are clearly discussed, Opened and Examined; Being drawn up into these Eight heads following: That is to say,

First.........*Of the True God.*	Fifthly......*Of the Laws nature.*
Secondly...*Of the Two Seeds.*	Sixthly.....*Of the Soul's Mortality.*
Thirdly......*Of the Right Devil*	Seventhly.*Of the Devil's Torments.*
Fourthly....*Of Predestination.*	Eighthly...*Of the Saint's Joys.*

By THOMAS TOMKINSON, A Believer and true Lover of the Commission of the Spirit, being written for the benefit of himself and others, who are of the Seed of the Son of Man, the Lord Jesus Christ, the High and Mighty God, being both Father, Son, and Spirit, in one single Person, blessed for ever. Amen.
 Be not forgetful to entertain strangers, for by that means some have received Angels unawares, and have not known it.—Heb. 18. 2.
Written in the Year of our Lord God, 1676; Transcribed by the Author, with some Alterations, 1690, and Printed by Subscription, 1823.
 London: *Printed by W. Smith, King Street, Long Acre.*
      4to. 1823. 61 ¾

----- A Practical DISCOURSE upon The Epistle, by Jude. Originally Written by THOMAS TOMKINSON, Gent. Being a copy of a Manuscript left with Thomas Tomkinson Jun. his Grandson.
 Deal: Printed for James May, & Joseph Gandar, by J.B. Underdown.
      8vo. 1828. 14
  Note.---There are two distinct editions of this work in the Author's Autograph, the first being dated 1704.

----- The MYSTERY of FAITH, by Thomas Tomkinson, 𝕮𝖔𝖕𝖎𝖊𝖉 𝖇𝖞 SAMUEL MORRIS BAILY, May, 1823.

----- A SYSTEM of RELIGION, Singular and Surprising: Treating of the following Heads. I. Of the Nature of GOD, and that Jesus Christ is the Only One and True GOD. II. Of the TRINITY, in a Manner wholly differing from either the *Athanasians* or *Arians,* nearer to the plain literal Text of the Scripture, and less liable to philosophical objections. III. Of the Devil; that he is no where to be found, but incarnate in Man. IV. Of the SOUL'S dying with the Body till the Resurrection, shewing that the Notion of an immaterial Soul distinct from the Body, is an inconceivable philosophical Absurdity, and against the whole Tenor of the Scripture. V. Of PREDESTINATION. VI. That there are in Man two *Principles* natural to his Constitution, a good and a bad, which *Necessarily* determine his Actions, and are at Enmity with each other; and how to know which is predominant. VII. A Philosophical Manner of accounting for the RESURRECTION. *Faithfully Collected from a curious Manuscript, found among the Papers of* THO. TOMKINSON, Gent.

        8vo. *London : Printed in the Year,* 1729. 9 ½
        Price Sticht 2s. Bound 2s. 6d.

----- Reprinted *by T. Goode, 80 Aylesbury Street, Clerkenwell.*

              4to.   1857.   16 ½

----- Zion's Sonnes, 1679. M.S. Autograph. 4to. 115 leaves and appendix of 16 leaves.

----- The Soul's Struggle, 1681. MIS.
      Note.—Transcribed by Arden Bonell.

----- The Christian Convarte, or Christianytie Reviewed,1692.M.8.
    Note.—An autobiographical work. Transcribed by Arden Bonell.

----- The White Divell Uncased, 1704, in M.S.
     Note.—There are two editions of this is the same year is the author's autograph.

----- Joyful News from Heaven, *for the Jews are called,* N.D. in M.S.
     Note.—A Poem in 20 stanzas, transcribed by Arden Bonell.

----- A Brief Concordance of all the Chief Heads of all the writings of John Reeve and some of the writings of Lodowick Muggleton, in M.S.

                12mo. N.D. 70 pp.

    Note.—Transcribed by William Chair. Probably composed between 1664 and 1665.

TURNER, Robert.

----- An INDEX To the Three Witnesses on EARTH, to the One Personal God CHRIST JESUS. *Moses* and the *Prophets* to the Work of Creation, CHRIST and the *Apostles* to the Work of Redemption, *Reeve* and *Muggleton* to the Work of Resurrection. By ROBERT TURNER.
London, Printed for the Author. [Price Ninepence.]
4to. 1739.   4 ¾

BOOKS REGARDED AS AUTHENTIC BY THE *MUGGLETONIANS.*

The TESTAMENT of the Twelve PATRIARCHS, The Sons of JACOB. Translated out of Greek into Latin, by ROBERT GROSTHEAD, sometime Bishop of Lincoln: And out of his Copy, into French and Dutch by others; and now Englished. *To the Credit whereof, an Ancient Greek Copy, written in Parchment is kept in the University Library of Cambridge.*
London: Printed by Benja. Harris for the Company of Stationers.
12mo.   6

Note.--This book was first printed in 1577.

The BOOK of ENOCH the Prophet: an Apocryphal production, supposed for ages to have been lost; but discovered at the close of the last century in Abyssinia; now first translated from an Ethiopic MS. in the Bodleian Library. By RICHARD LAURENCE, LL.D., Archbishop of Cashel, late Professor of Hebrew in the University of Oxford. Third Edition, revised and enlarged.
Oxford, Printed by S. Collingwood, Printer to the University, for John Henry Parker. Sold also by J. G. and F. Rivington, London.
8vo.   1838.   19 3/8

Note.—The date of the 1st edition is 1821, and the 2nd edition, 1828.

LIBRI ENOCH Prophetæ versio Æthiopica, quæ seculi sub fine Novissimi ex Abyssinia Britanniam Advecta vix Tandem Litterato orbi innotuit; Edita A Ricardo Laurence, LL.D. Archiepiscopo Cassiliensi.
(Ethiopic.)
Oxoniæ, Typis Academicis, impensis Editoris. Prostat venalis apud J. H. Parker, Oxoniæ et J. G. et F. Rivington, Londini.
8vo.   1838.   10 ½

BOOKS RELATING TO THE MUGGLETONIANS,
PRO AND *CON.*

ADAMS, Hannah.

----- A VIEW OF RELIGIONS, in Three Parts. A New Edition, By Andrew Fuller.
  London: Printed for T. Williams el Co., &c.
  8vo. 1805. 32

AIKIN, M., LL.D.

----- Memoirs of Religious Impostors from the Seventh to the Nineteenth Century.
  London: Printed for Jones & Co., Warwick Square, and sold by all Booksellers.
  12mo. 1823.
  Note.—Containing, "Memoirs of Lodowick Muggleton."

ANONYMOUS.

----- A true NARRATIVE of the Proceedings at the Sessions-house in the OLD-BAYLY, At a Sessions held there on *Wednesday,* the 17th of *January,* 1676/7. Giving a full Account of the true Tryal and Sentence of LODOWICK MUGGLETON For Blasphemous Words and Books. As also the Tryals and Condemnation of a Woman for killing her Bastard Child; and of a man for personating another person in giving Bayl before a Judge. With an Account how many are Condemned, Burn'd in the Hand, to be Whipt, and Transported. With Allowance, *Roger L'Estrange.*
  London : Printed for D. M.
  1676/7. 1
  (*Brit. Museum,* P.P. 1349. a.)

----- A Modest Account of the wicked Life of that grand Impostor Lodowick Muggleton: wherein are related all the remarkable Actions he did, and all the strange Accidents that have befallen him, ever since his first coming to London, to this Twenty fifth of January, 1676. Also a Particular of those Reasons, which first drew him to these damnable Principles: with several pleasant Stories concerning him, proving his Commission to be but Counterfeit, and himself a Cheat; from divers Expressions which have fallen from his own Mouth. Licensed according to order.
  Printed at London for B. H. in 4to. 1676. 6 pages
  Reprinted in *The Harleian* Miscellany, Vol. 1. p. 610.
  4to. 1808.
  Note.—Quakers are mentioned and also misrepresented in this pamphlet.

----- A True REPRESENTATION of the Absurd and Mischievous PRINCIPLES of the SECT, Commonly known by the Name of MUGGLETONIANS. (By JOHN WILLIAMS, afterwards *Bishop* of *Chichester.*)
  London, Printed for *Ric. Chiswell, at the Rose and Crown*

  in St. Paul's Church Yard.

4to. 1694.   4 ¼

 (Brit. Museum, 696.J.15/4).

   Note. --Answered by THOMAS TOMKINSON.

----- *Dictionarium Sacrum sen Religiosum.* A. DICTIONARY of all RELIGIONS,—whether *Jewish, Pagan, Christian,* or *Mahometan.* More Particularly comprehending 1. The Lives and Doctrines of the Authors and Propagators, &c. [By DANIEL DEFOE?]

 The 2nd edition, *with very large* Additions.   8vo. *London,* 1723.

  Note.—Contains, an account of Lodowick Muggleton, and his Tenets. (adverse to him)

------ OBSERVATIONS on some ARTICLES of the *Muggletonians* CREED: viz. I. That *Matter* existed without Beginning. II. That a *Good,* and also an *Evil Principle* did eternally exist; and that the Devil had a carnal knowledge of *Eve.* III. That God existeth in the form of an *old Man* about Six Feet high. IV. That God became an Infant. V. That whilst *Jesus Christ* was upon Earth, there was no God in *Heaven.* VI. That when Jesus Christ died, God died; and there was then no God either in *Heaven* or on *Earth.* VII. That MUGGLETON and REEVES (Two Sectaries, who liv'd in the time of OLIVER CROMWELL'S Protectorship,) were *two* Divinely inspired Prophets from whose Direction we can only understand the true Sense of Scripture. Proposed more immediately To the Considertion of the PRINCIPAL of the Modern MUGGLETONIANS.

 London : Printed for the Authors, And sold by R. Hat, at the Bible and Crown in the Poultry, [Price Six-pence.]

8vo. 1735.

 (Brit. Museum, 105. b. 88.)

----- The PRINCIPLES of the MUGGLETONIANS asserted, under the following Heads. I. On the Eternity of Matter. II. On the Existence of Two Eternal Beings, On the Angels Fall and the Fall of Man. III. On Gods eternal existence in the form of Man. IV. That God became a man, and manifested himself in the Flesh: and the Scripture doctrine of the Trinity considered. V. That Jesus Christ was God the Creator of the World. VI. When Christ dyed God dyed: Enoch, Moses and Elias were taken up into Heaven and left with deputed power there, while God was performing the work of redemption here on Earth. VII. Concerning John Reeve's and Lodowick Muggleton's Commission, with some observations thereon.

Price One Shilling. 8vo. *London,* 1735. 50 pages

  Note.--This is s reply to the foregoing. The "Advertisement" is signed A. B. (i.e. Arden Bonell.] April 1735.

----- *A* CONFERENCE betwixt a MUGGLETONIAN and a BAPTIST, On these Propositions: 1. There was no God in Heaven

when Christ Jesus was on this earth. II. God became as a Creature, Sin excepted. III. God dyed.
  London: Printed for T. Cooper, at the Globe in Paternoster-Row.
            8vo. 1789. 1

  Note.---This pamphlet is "a Defence of certain Propositions, contain'd in the Writings of JOHN REEVE, which were taken out by a Baptist, and asserted to be false, and contrary to the Scriptures." -- Introduction.

----- The Amorous HUMOURS and Audacious Adventures of one WH ††††††††D. By a MUGGLETONIAN.
  London: Printed for the Author, and sold by M. Watson next the King's Arms Tavern, Chancery-Lane; at the corner of Cock Court, facing the Old Bailey, Ludgate-Hill, and at the Pamphlet shops of London and Westminster. (Price 6d.)
         8vo. No date. 1 3/8

(*Brit. Museum,* 1077. K. 84.)
  Note.--(A Satire in verse upon George Whitefield.)

BAILEY, Nathan, an English Grammarian and Lexicographer, who kept a School at Stepney, where he died in 1742.

----- An Universal Etymological English Dictionary. 2nd edition.
         8vo. *London,* 1724.
  Article" Muggletonians"

BARLOW, Thomas, Bishop of Lincoln.
----- The Genuine Remains, p. 318. . . . . . . 1698.

*BUGG, Francis, (An Apostate from the Quakers.)
----- The 𝔓ilgrim'𝔰 𝔓rogre𝔰𝔰 from Quakerism to *Christianity,* &c.
        4to. *London,* 1698. 23

Reprinted.---The 2nd edition. 8vo. 1700. 26
 • See my Catalogue of Friends' Books, vol.1, p. 388.

----- *A Catalogue of Books wrote by* Fran. Bugg. . . 8vo. [1700.] ¼

  Note.—In this Catalogue is an "Advertisement," and F. B. *says* therein, "That in the Library of *Christ* Church Colledge in *Oxford,* there is by a Worthy Gentleman, a Divine of the Church of England, bought of me, and given by him for the Service of the Church, of Quakers' Books, wrote by the most approved Authors of that Sect, which I think are thus Chained up (from doing any more hurt). First, *G. Fox's Journal,* next to it *Muggleton's Journal* or Works, (containing more than 1,000 pages,4to.); and I think the best Quaker of the two; next to that *G. Fox's Great Mystery,* &c.. *Fol.,* with near 20 more of his Books, &c., &c.

CARLILE, Richard, of *London*.
----- The Lion. 4 vols.
𝔏𝔬𝔫𝔡𝔬𝔫: *Printed and Published by Richard Carlile, 62, Fleet Street.*
8vo. 1828-1829.
Note.--See concerning Muggleton in Vol II., No. 13. p. 886, and in Vol 3.

BROWN, Tom.
----- Works,--The Widow's Wedding, 9th Edition, 1760. Vol.4, p. 142-6.

CHAMBERLAYNE'S, Edward.
----- Angliæ Notitia, 17th Edition. . . . . 1691.
----- " " 18th Edition. . . . . 1694.
. Muggletonians, p 378.

CHAMBERS, E., F.R.S.
----- Cyclopædia: or, An Universal Dictionary of Arts and Sciences, 5th Edition, 2 vols.
London, Printed for D. Midwinter, (and others).
Large folio. 1741-1743.
Article, "Muggletonians."

CHAMBERS, Robert,
----- The BOOK of DAYS a Miscellany of Popular Antiquities in connection with the Calendar including Anecdote, Biography, & History, Curiosities of Literature and Oddities of Human Life and Character. Edited by R. Chambers. In 2 vols.
W. & R. Chambers, London and Edinburgh. Large 8vo. 1864.
See—History of Lodowick Muggleton, vol 1. p. 362.

DUNTON, John, Printer, of *London*.
----- Post Boy robb'd of his Mail, (pp. 422-482) 2nd editn.   1706.

DYCHE, Thomas, Schoolmaster at *Stratford-le-bow, Middlesex*.
----- A New General English Dictionary, the 11th Edition.
London: 8vo. 1760.
Article, "Muggletonians."

EVANS, John, Master of a Seminary, *Islington*.
----- A Sketch of the Denominations of the Christian World, &c. The 13th Edition. . . . . . . 12mo. *London,* 1814.
. Muggletonians, p. 295, 6.

FRISWELL, James Hain.

----- VARIA: Readings from Rare books. By J. Hain Friswell. Author of "The Gentle Life," etc.
  London: Sampson Low, Son, and Marston, Milton House, Ludgate Hill. 8vo. 1966. 22
   _{*} Muggletonians, p. 237-250.

GORDON, Alexander, of *Norwich*, late of *Liverpool.*

----- The Origin of the Muggletonians: a Paper read before the Liverpool Literary and Philosophical Society. April 5th, 1869. By Alexander Gordon, MA.
  D. Marples, Printer, Lord Street, Liverpool. . 8vo. [1869.] 21

----- Ancient and Modern Muggletonians: a Paper read before the Liverpool Literary and Philosophical Society, April 4th, 1870, by Alexander Gordon, M.A.
  Liverpool: Printed by D. Marples, Lord Street. 8vo. [1870.] 4

GRANGER, J., Vicar of *Shiplake in Oxfordshire.*
----- Biographical History of England. Vol. 4, p. 200. 4th Edition.
                 8vo. 1804
  _{*} Containing, an Account of Lodowick Muggleton (and his Portrait).

HENDERSON, William, Brother of PATRICK HENDERSON, of *Dublin.*

----- Truth and Reason defended against *Error* and *Burning Envy,* in a PUBLICK DISPUTE, held at the *Magpie* in the *Borough, Southwark,* on the 16th and 18th days of Dec., 1728, between John Rawlinson, *a Muggletonian,* and William Henderson, *a Quaker,* in the presence of some Hundreds of *People, &c.*—*Published by* WILLIAM HENDERSON
            8vo. *London,* [1728.] 5 ½
  See my Catalogue of Friends' Books, vol.1, p. 933.

HUTCHINSON, Thomas.
----- The History of the Province of Massachusetts Bay [1628 to 1760]. 2 vols.
           Boston. 8vo. 1764-67.
----- Inquirer (The). . . . . 1868.

LESLIE, Charles, of *London,* born in *Ireland.*
----- The Snake in the Grass, or Satan transformed into an Angel of Light.
           8vo. *London.* 1696. 89
  Reprinted.---See CHARLES LESLIE, p. 267 of this Catalogue.

MACAULAY, Thomas B., of *London.*

\----- History of England, vol. 1. p.164. . . . . . 8vo. 1848.
    Reprinted.--See THO. B. MACAULAY, p. 278 of this Catalogue.

REES, Abraham, D.D.F.R.S. of *London. Son of Lewis Rees,* a dissenting Minister in *Montgomeryshire.*

\----- The New Cyclopædia; or, Universal Dictionary of 𝔄rts, 𝔖cience, 𝔏iterature: formed upon a more enlarged Plan of arrangement than the Dictionary of Mr. Chambers. Large 4to. *London.*

SCOTT, Sir Walter, Son of WALTER SCOTT *of Edinburgh.*

\----- Woodstock (a Novel) vol. 3. (p. 205.) . . . . . .1826.

SEWEL, William, of *Amsterdam.*

\----- The History of the Rise, Increase, and Progress of the Christian People called Quakers, &c.
                                                 Folio. *London,* 1722. 188

    Repd. —See my Catalogue of Friends' Books, vol. 2. p. 561.

SHARPE. I., A.M., of *Stepney, London.*

\----- A New-Years-Gift to the Ratcliff Convert, (against the Muggletonians).
                                                                                 8vo. 1717.

\----- *The Spirit of Two Pretenders,* John Reeve *and* Lodiwick Muggleton: Or, some SHORT REMARKS Upon this Year's Edition of The *Divine Looking-glass:* or, *Third and Last Testament of our Lord and Saviour Jesus Christ.* In a Letter to a Friend. Part II. By I. SHARPE of *Stepney.*

> *And they had a king over them, which is the Angel of the Bottomless Pit, whose Name in the Hebrew Tongue is* Abaddon; *but in the Greek Tongue hath his Name* Apollyon.
> *Come out of her, my People, that ye be not Partakers of her Sins, and that ye receive not of her Plagues; for her Sins have reached unto Heaven, and God hath remembred her Iniquities.*
>   Rev. 9, 11. 18, 4. 5.

> *London, Printed for R. Wilkin at the King's Head in St. Paul's Church-Yard, and G. Strahan at the Golden Ball in Cornhil; and sold by J. Morphew near Stationers-Hall, Edward Baldwin and Paul Sorrel, Stationers in Ratcliff.* Price Six Pence.
>   8vo. 1720 3 1/8

>> Note.—A copy of the above bitter pamphlet is in the Library of Alexander Gardyne, Richmond Road, Dalston, London. The anonymous one on page 328, "A Conference betwixt a MUGGLETONIAN and a BAPTIST," is also in the same

gentleman's library. Both these pamphlets are scarce, and the latter only came to my knowledge whilst passing this Catalogue through the press.

THOMPSON, Thomas.

----- The QUAKERS QUIBBLES, in Three Parts. First set forth in an EXPOSTULATORY EPISTLE to WILLIAM PENN —Also the Pretended Prophet, LOD. MUGGLETON, and the Quakers compared.

8vo. *London,* 1675. 16 ½

VAUGHAN, Robert Alfred, B.A.

----- HOURS WITH THE MYSTICS. A Contribution to the History of Religious Opinion. By Robert Alfred Vaughan, In 2 Volumes.
London: John W. Parker and Son, West Strand. 8vo. 1856.

Note.—In vol. 2. p. "The Muggletonians, Fifth Monarchy men, and Ranters of those days were the exceptional mire and dirt cast up by the vexed times, but assuredly not the Representatives of English Mysticism.

Reprinted.—The Second Edition Revised and Augmented by the Author. 2 vols.

8vo. 1860.

WHITEHEAD, George, of *Orton, Westmoreland,* last of *London.*

----- The Quaker's Plainness Detecting FALLACY, In Two Short Treatises, I. The *First* in Answer to an abusive Epistle, styl'd *The Quakers' Quibbles;* and the comparison therein between the *Muggletonians* and *Quakers,* proved *Absurd* and *Unjust,* &c.

8vo. *Printed in the Year,* 1674. 5 ½

WILLIAMS, John, Bishop of Chichester.

See under Muggletonians. Anon., p. 327.

WYETH, *Joseph,* of *London.*

----- Anguis Flagellatus: or, a Switch for the Snake. Being an ANSWER to the Third and Last Edition of the SNAKE IN THE GRASS, &c.

8vo. *London,* 1699. 35 ½

PORTRAITS OF MUGGLETON.

1. An Oval painting of the Head and Bust, in the Bird Gallery at the British Museum.

2. Painting full length by Muggleton's Friend, William Wood, of Braintree.—In the possession of the Muggletonian Body.

3. Caste of the Prophet's features taken after death.—From this cast a 4to. Copper plate engraved was executed by G. V. Caffeel. It bears the following inscription: "Lodowick Muggleton. Dyed the 14th of March, 1697/8, then aged 88 years 7 months and 14 days. An original impression of this, 4to., Mezzotint, was priced by a London Printseller a few years ago as Extra Rare £1. 11. 6. Later impressions were published by Caulfield and Herbert, 4to. 1794.

4. A Small Oil Painting from the same, by Richard Pickersgill in 1813.

5. A half length engraving was executed by J. Kennerley, from the full length Portrait, in 1829. Prefixed to the "Song Book," at the expense of Joseph and Isaac Frost.—This engraving *has* been Photographed Carte-de-Visite size.

> Note.—There are Collections of Muggleton's works, and also of his followers, in the Library of the British Museum; in the Bodleian Library, at Oxford; in Sion College, London Wall; in Dr. Williams's Library, Queen Square, Bloomsbury; in the Friends' Library, Devonshire House, Bishopsgate Street, Without; in the *Friends' Library of Biblical Literature*, 5, *Bishopsgate Street*, without, and in the Library of St. Paul's Cathedral is a Volume of Pamphlets in which is written,
>
> "30th August 1676.
> Seized at Lodowick Muggleton's house by
> Samll. Mearne
> &
> Richard Clark } Wardens."
>
> Another Volume is in the Library of Lambeth Palace, also seized by the Wardens of the Stationers' Company, in which is endorsed on the back of the title page of the first tract,
> "Aug. 30th, 1676.
> Seaz'd att Muggleton's house, in the Posterne, by
> Samuell Marne
> Richard Clarke } Wardens"

REEVE, John, was born in *Wiltshire,* his Father, Walter Reeve, was Clerk to a *Deputy* of *Ireland,* his Cousin L. Muggleton says "A Gentleman, But fell to decay, so he put John Reeve Apprentice to a Tailor in *London.* He was of an Honest, Just nature, and Harmless, but a Man of no great wit or Wisdom, no Subtilty, nor no great store of Religion. He died about the latter end of *July,* in the year 1658, in the 49th year of his age, and was buried in Bethlam Churchyard."

----- An Epistle from the Mighty JEHOVAH, or Jesus the only LORD, and God of the Elect Israelites, from one, whose name *is* John Reeve, Pilgrim, &c.

1654 ?

----- *An* Epistle *of the Prophet* Reeve. Written in the Year, 1656. With, "An Oceasional Discourse, &c., by the Prophet Muggleton.
        4to. *No Printer's name or place,* [1719.] 1
      See LODOWICK MUGGLETON.

----- *The Prophet* Reeve's *Epistle to his Friend, discovering the dark Light of the* Quakers; *written in the year* 1654, September *the* 20th, after some other Epistles, is the following, at the end, viz.

----- *An Epistle wrote by* the *Prophet* JOHN REEVE *to* ISAAC PENNINGTON, *Esq.; dated* 1658, *concerning an Answer to a Book of his, with several Mysteries and Divine and Spiritual Revelations declared by the Prophet, concerning God's visible appearing in the Flesh.*
        4to. No *Printer's name or place,* [1658 ?] 2 ½

----- Sacred Remains, &c.
        4to. *Printed by Subscription in the Year 1706.*
Reprinted. . . . . .4to. No date. 14

 Reprinted again. See LODOWICK MUGGLETON.

----- An Epistle to a Quaker. By John Reeve.
        8vo. *No Printer's name, place or Date. [1711?]* ¾

   See also LODOWICK MUGGLETON.

THE PROPHET OF WALNUT-TREE YARD.

By
Rev. Augustus Jessopp, DD.

"Did you ever hear tell of Lodowick Muggleton?"
"Not I."
"That is strange. Know then that he was the founder of our poor society, and after him we are frequently, though opprobriously, termed Muggletonians, for we are Christians. Here is his book; I will sell it cheap."— LAVENGRO.

SCRUPULOUS veracity was hardly a characteristic of the late George Borrow. A man of great memory, he was also a man of fertile imagination, and where the two are found in excess, side by side in the same intellect, they are apt to twine round one another, so to speak, and the product is something which the matter-of-fact man abhors. I do not doubt that Borrow did meet a Muggletonian at Bristol—I think it was there—some sixty years ago; but I am pretty sure that he knew very little indeed about the Muggletonians, and that he could have hardly opened the book which he implies that he purchased, and which I am almost certain he never read. I have a strong suspicion that he very much antedated the incident which he narrates, for I myself knew an old secondhand bookseller in a back street at Bristol, who was a Muggletonian, with whom I made acquaintance when a lad. He was a slow-speaking, wary, suspicious, and dirty old man, and as I had not sufficient funds to be a good customer, I daresay he did not think it worth his while to be communicative, but he told me one day that he had been one of the original subscribers to the Spiritual Epistles which were reprinted in quarto years before I was born; though, as he confessed, his name does not appear on the list of names printed at the end of the preface, which list, he assured me, was very incomplete, as he from his own knowledge could certify. This old man would have been very old indeed if he had been old when Borrow was a youth; and yet, as I say, I suspect he was the very man of whom mention is made in the extract I have given above. He was the only Muggletonian I ever knew, but he certainly was not the last of his sect, and I should not be at all surprised to hear that it is a flourishing sect still, and that it still has its assemblies, its votaries, its literature, and its propaganda. It is true that the name Muggletonians does not appear in that astonishing list of religious denominations which the Registrar-General was enabled to compile for the year 1883; but that proves little, inasmuch as the closer a religious corporation is, the more exclusive, the less does it care to register the name of the building in which it may choose to assemble for worship; and I observe that the Southcotians are no longer to be found upon that list, though I happen to know that they are not extinct yet, nor has their faith in their prophetess and her mission quite died out from the face of the earth.

This is certain, that as late as 1820 an edition of the Spiritual Epistles, which must have cost at that time two or three hundred pounds to print, was subscribed for, and that nine years afterwards appeared Divine Songs of the Muggletonians—they were not ashamed of the name—printed also by subscription, filling 621 pages, and showing pretty clearly that there had of late been a strange revival of the sect: an outburst of new fervour having somehow been awakened, and an irrepressible passion for writing "Songs" having displayed itself, which had not been without its effect in resuscitating dormant enthusiasm. The vagaries of the human mind in what, for want of any better designation, we call "religious belief" have always had for me a peculiar fascination, as they have for others. Epiphanius, whose name is and used to be a terror to her Royal Highness in days gone by, when I insisted upon reading to her about the peculiar people who made it a matter of faith to eat bread and cheese at the Eucharist—Epiphanius is to me positively entertaining, and Pagitt's Heresiography is none the less instructive because it is a vulgar catchpenny little book, made up, like Peter Pindar's razors, to sell. To me it seems that to dismiss even the wildest and foolishest opinion which makes way, as if it were a mere absurdity that does not deserve notice, is to show a certain flippancy and shallowness. Do not all thoughtful men pass through certain stages of intellectual growth, and are not the convictions of our youth held very differently from those which we find ourselves swayed by in our later years? The beliefs which the multitude take up with are such as the untrained and the half-trained are always captivated by, whether individually or in the mass. There are limits to our powers of assimilation according as our development has been arrested or is still going on, and he who hopes to understand the course of human affairs or to make any intelligent forecast of what is coming can never afford to neglect the study of morbid appetites or morbid anatomy in the domain of mind.

There is a strong family likeness among all fanatics; and this is characteristic of them all, that they are profusely communicative and absolutely honest. Prophets have no secrets, no reserve, no doubts, they are always true men. John Reeve and Lodowick Muggleton are no exception to the general rule. We can follow their movements pretty closely for some years. The book of The Acts of the Witnesses of the Spirit furnishes us with quite as much as we want to know about the sayings and doings of the grotesque pair and their early extravagances; and Muggleton's letters cover a period of forty years, during all which time he was going in and out among the artisans and small traders of the city, obstinately asserting himself in season and out of season, and leaving behind him in his eccentric chronicle such a minute and faithful picture of London life among the middle—the lower middle—class during the last half of the seventeenth century as is to be found nowhere else. The reader must be prepared for the most startling freaks of language, for very vulgar profanity, the more amazing because so manifestly unintended. When people break away from all the traditions of the past and surrender themselves to absolute anarchy in morals and religion the old terminology ceases to be employed in the old way, ceases indeed to have any meaning. The prophet or the philosopher who sets himself to invent a new theory of the universe or a new creed for his followers to embrace, can hardly avoid shocking and horrifying those who are content to use words as their forefathers did and attach to these words the same sort of sacredness that the Hebrews did to the Divine name. There is no need to do more than allude to this side of the Muggletonian writing. What we are concerned with is the story of the prophet's life, which has been told with the utmost frankness and simplicity; a more unvarnished tale it would be difficult to find, or one which bears more the stamp of truth upon its every line.

The *Acts of the Witnesses of the Spirit* is a posthumous work written by Muggleton when he was very old, and left behind him in manuscript with directions that it should be published after his death. It is a quarto volume of 180 pages and is a book of some rarity. It was published in 1699, with an epistle dedicatory to all true Christian people, apparently written by Thomas Tomkinson, one of the chosen seed. After preparing us for what is coming by dwelling upon the wonderful stories in the Old Testament and the New, Muggleton plunges into his subject by giving us a brief account of his own and his brother prophet's parentage and early biography. Let the reader understand that here beginneth the third chapter of *The Acts of the Witnesses* at the third verse:—

"3. As for John Reeve, he was born in Wiltshire; his father was clerk to a deputy of Ireland, a gentleman as we call them by his place, but fell to decay.

"4. So he put John Reeve apprentice here at London to a tailor by trade. He was out of his apprenticeship before I came acquainted with him; he was of an honest, just nature, and harmless.

"5. But a man of no great natural wit or wisdom; no subtlety or policy was in him, nor no great store of religion; he had lost what was traditional; only of an innocent life.

"7. And I, Lodowick Muggleton, was born in Bishop-gate Street, near the Earl of Devonshire's house, at the corner house called Walnut-tree Yard.

"8. My father's name was John Muggleton; he was a smith by trade—that is, a farrier or horse doctor; he was in great respect with the postmaster in King James's time; he had three children by my mother, two sons and one daughter, I was the youngest and my mother loved me."

His mother died, his father married again, whereupon the boy was sent into the country—boarded out as we say—and kept there till his sixteenth year, when he was brought back to London and apprenticed to a tailor—one John Quick—"a quiet, peaceable man, not cruel to servants, which liked me very well." Muggleton took to his trade and pleased his master. The journeymen were a loose lot, "bad husbands and given to drunkenness, but my nature was inclined to be sober." Hitherto the young man had received no religious training; when he had served his time, however, "hearing in those days great talk among the vulgar people and especially amongst youth, boys, and young maids, of a people called Puritans ...... I liked their discourse upon the Scriptures and pleaded for a holy keeping of the Sabbath day, which my master did not do, nor I his servant."

This must have been about the year 1630—for Muggleton was born in June 1610—when the Sabbatarian controversy was at its height, and the feeling of the country was approaching fever heat, and when Charles the First had resolved to try and govern without a Parliament, and when Archbishop Abbot was in disgrace, and Laud had begun to exercise his predominant influence. Muggleton was but little impressed by "the people called Puritans," and he went on his old way. When he had nearly served his time, he began to look about him. The tailor's trade did not seem likely to lead to much, unless it were combined with something else, and a brilliant opening offered itself, as he was at work for a pawnbroker in Hounsditch. "The broker's wife had one daughter alive. The mother, being well persuaded of my good natural temper, and of my good husbandry, and that I had no poor kindred come after me to be any charge or burthen to her daughter ..... proposed to me that she would give me a hundred pounds with her to set up .... So the maid and I were made sure by promise, and I was resolved to have the maid to wife, and to keep a broker's shop, and lend money on pawns, and grow rich as others did." Muggleton had not yet been admitted to the freedom of the city, and the marriage was arranged to take place after he should have done so. In the meantime he found himself working side by side with William Reeve, Prophet John Reeve's brother, at this time a "very zealous Puritan," with whom he talked of his prospects. "I loved the maid, and desired to be rich," he tells us; but these Puritan people were horrified at his deliberately intending to live the life of a usurer, and they "threatened great judgments, and danger of damnation hereafter."

It is clear that the frightful eschatology of the time was exercising a far greater power upon the imagination of the masses than anything else. People were dwelling upon all that was terrible and gloomy in the picture of a future life; the one thought with the visionaries was this— Save yourselves from the wrath to come. "I was extremely fearful of eternal damnation," says Muggleton, "thinking my soul might go into hell fire without a body, as all people did at that time."

There was evidently a struggle between conviction and inclination, and it ended as we should have expected—the marriage was broken off. Then followed some years of vehement religious conflict; "Neither did I hear any preach in these days but the Puritan ministers, whose hair was cut short. For if a man with long hair had gone into the pulpit to preach, I would have gone out of the Church again, though he might preach better than the other." All through this time visions of hell and torment, and devils and damnation troubled him; now and then there were "elevations in my mind, but these were few and far between; a while after all was lost again." He soon consoled himself for his matrimonial disappointment; he married and had three daughters, then his first wife died. He throve in his calling, "only the spirit of fear of hell was still upon me, but not so extreme as it was before." He took a second wife, and the civil war began.

"And generally the Puritans were all for the Parliament, and most of my society and acquaintance did fall away and declined in love one towards another. Some of them turned to Presbytery, and some turned Independents; others fell to be Ranters, and some fell to be mere Atheists. So that our Puritan people were so divided and scattered in our religion, that I was altogether at a loss; for all the zeal we formerly had was quite worn out. For I had seen the utmost perfection and satisfaction that could be found in that way, except I would do it for loaves, but loaves was never my aim."

The civil war ran its course, but Muggleton cared nothing for the general course of events. What were kings and bishops and Lords and Commons to him? he was living in quite another world. As for Laud and Strafford, and Pym and Hampden, he does not even once name them. He makes not the slightest allusion to the death of Charles the First, though he was living within half a mile of Whitehall when the king's head fell on the block. Prophets of the Muggleton type are so busied about their own souls and their own spiritual condition, that the battles, murders, and sudden deaths of other men, great or small, give them no concern whatever.

A couple of years or so after the execution of the king, "it came to pass I heard of several prophets and prophetesses that were about the streets .... Also I heard of two other men that were counted greater than prophets—to wit, John Tannye and John Robins. John Tannye, he declared himself to be the Lord's High Priest, therefore he circumcised himself according to the law. Also he declared that he was to gather the Jews out of all nations, ... with many other strange and wonderful things. And as for John Robins, he declared himself to be God Almighty. Also he said that he had raised from the dead several of the prophets, as Jeremiah and others. Also I saw several others of the prophets that was said to be raised by him, *for I have had nine or ten of them at my house at a time, of those that were said to be raised from the dead."*

Is madness contagious? Or is it that, while the sane can exercise but a very limited power over the insane, there is no limit to the influence which the insane can gain over one another? Living in a world of their own, where delusions pass for palpable facts, where the logical faculty accepts the wildest visions as of equal significance with actual realities, these dreamers have a calculus of their own which includes the symbols in use among the sane, but comprehends besides a notation which these latter attach no meaning to, reject, and deride.

"Would you be so kind as tell me, sir, what's a ohm?" said the worthy Mr. Stiggins to me the other day. "It's a modern term used in electricity, which I am too ignorant to explain to you." He looked full at me for more than five seconds without a word, then he said, "I'm thinking that this man was a fool to talk about ohms when not even you knew what a ohm means. And he came from Cambridge College too, and he's got a vote! I reckon when a man can't talk the same as other folks he'd ought to be shut up." Indignant Stiggins! But are we not all intolerant?

John Robins had acquired an almost unlimited ascendency over his crazy prophets, and speedily acquired the like ascendency over Muggleton. What specially fascinated him was that all John Robins's prophets "had power from him to damn any that did oppose or speak evil of him. So his prophets gave sentence of damnation upon many, to my knowledge, for speaking evil of him, they not knowing him whether he was true or false." Muggleton was profoundly impressed, but according to his own account he was a silent observer, and waited. One of the prophets often came to his house and was welcome; he "spake as an angel of God, and I never let him go without eating and drinking," for Muggleton was a man of large appetite and demanded large supplies of food, nor did he stint himself of meat and drink or withhold creature comforts from those he loved.

Just at this time Muggleton "fell into a melancholy." He had arrived at the prophetic age; he had completed his fortieth year. "Then did two motives arise in me and speak in me as two lively voices, as if two spirits had been speaking in me, one answering the other as if they were not my own spirit." So that our noble laureate was anticipated by two centuries, unless indeed the "two lively voices" make themselves heard at times to most men who have cars to hear them. Muggleton's voices were not very high-toned voices; they were voices that spake of heaven and hell, nothing more. Love and duty never seem to have formed the subject of his meditations. "For I did not so much mind to be saved, as I did to escape being damn'd. For I thought, if I could but lie still in the earth for ever, it would be as well with me as it would be if I were in eternal happiness ..... for I did not care whether I was happy so I might not be miserable. I cared not for heaven so I might not go to hell. These things pressed hard upon my soul, even to the wounding of it."

The battle within him went on fiercely for some time, and it ended as we should have expected. "I was so well satisfied in my mind as to my eternal happiness, that I was resolved now to be quiet and to get as good a living as I could in this world and live as comfortably as I could here, thinking that this revelation should have been beneficial to nobody but myself." The "motional voices," and visions, and questionings, continued from April 1651 to January 1652; and it was during this time that the intimacy between Muggleton and Reeve became more closely cemented, for "John Reeve was so taken with my language that his desires were extreme earnest that he might have the same revelation as I had. His desires were so great that he was troublesome unto me, for if I went into one room, into another, he would follow me to talk to me." His persistence was rewarded, and just when Muggleton's visions ceased "in the month of January 1652, about the middle of the month, John Reeve came to me very joyful and said, Cousin Lodowick, now said he, I know what revelation of Scripture is as well as thee." Reeve's revelations increased, and never ceased for two weeks. "First visions, then by voice of words to the hearing of the ear three mornings together the third, fourth, and fifth days of February, 1652, and the year of John Reeve's life forty-two, and the year of my life forty-one."

Two men in this curious ecstatic condition obviously could not stop at this point. It was a critical moment—would they enter into rivalry or spiritual partnership? If the latter, then who was to be the leader, who would make the first move? It was soon settled.

"The first evening God spare to John Reeve he came to my house and said, Cousin Lodowick, God hath given thee unto me for ever, and the tears ran down both sides his cheeks amain. So I asked him what was the matter, for he looked like one that had been risen out of the grave, he being a fresh-coloured man the day before, but the tears ran down his cheeks apace." John Reeve was not yet prepared to deliver his commission with authority; it was coming, but not yet. Meanwhile he turned to Muggleton's children and pronounced them blessed, "but especially thy daughter Sarah, she shall be the teacher of all the women in London." Sarah was hiding on the stairs and was not a little afraid; she was a girl of fourteen, but she accepted her mission there and then.

She proved to be a valuable helper, "and several persons came afterwards to my house more to discourse with her than us, and they marvelled that one so young should have such knowledge and wisdom." Next day John Reeve came again, and Muggleton was pronounced to be the mouth of the new revelation, "as Aaron was given to be Moses' mouth."

The first thing to be done was to depose the other two prophets, Robins and Tannye, and to hoist them on their own petard. It had to be seen who could damn hardest. For one moment even Muggleton's stout heart failed, he would take another with him to be present at the great trial of strength. He called upon a certain Thomas Turner to accompany him, "else you must be cursed to all eternity. But his wife was exceeding wroth and fearful, and she said, if John Reeve came again to her husband that she would run a spit in his guts, so John Reeve cursed her to eternity." Whereupon Turner, appalled by the sentence, complied with the order and went. The three presented themselves before the other madman, and John Reeve uttered his testimony, denouncing him as a false prophet and gave him a month to repent of his misdeeds. When the month had elapsed Reeve wrote the sentence of eternal damnation upon him "and left it at his lodging, and after a while he and his great matters perished in the sea. For he made a little boat to carry him to Jerusalem, and going to Holland to call the Jews there, he and one Captain James was cast away and drowned, so all his powers came to nothing."

The day after the interview with Tannye, the prophets proceeded to deal with John Robins. He had been thrown into Bridewell by Cromwell, and there he lay, his worshippers still resorting to him, for any one with money could visit a prisoner in gaol as often as he pleased. When the prophets appeared at the gate empty handed, the keeper as a matter of course refused them admittance. Then said John Reeve to the keeper, "Thou shall never be at peace." By and by they were shown where Robins's cell was; they summoned him to the window, and a strange interview took place, which is minutely described. It ended by Reeve delivering his charge and pronouncing his sentence. Many had been the crimes of John Robins. He had ruined and deceived men in a multitude of ways; among others "thou givest them leave to abstain by degrees from all kinds of food, thou didst feed them with windy things, as apples and other fruit that was windy, and they drank nothing but water; therefore look what measure thou hast measured to others we will measure again to thee."

John Robins was utterly mastered; "he pulled his hands off the grates and laid them together and said, It is finished; the Lord's will be done." In two months he had written a letter of recantation, was released from durance, and is heard of no more.

"Thus the reader may see that these two powers were brought down in these two days' messages from the Lord."

The world was all before them now. It remained that the new prophets should have some distinctive dogma, and that the printing press should be called in as an accessory to spread their fame. Again John Reeve took the lead, and in 1652 he wrote an account of his divine commission and published his first work, A Transcendant Spiritual Treatise, which told of his last revelation of the message to Tannye and Robins.

While the book was passing through the press the prophets lived by their trade, and made no attempt to preach before any assembly.

They talked incessantly, and they cursed liberally. At last the children in the streets began to follow Reeve and pelt him, crying after him, "There goes the prophet that damns people!" Muggleton, meanwhile, was always ready to meet an inquirer, and to eat and drink with him. "On one occasion an old acquaintance would needs have me drink with him, that he might have some talk with me, and there followed a neighbour of his, a gentleman, as we call them; his name was Penson, and he sat down in our company." Soon Penson began to deride and abuse the prophet; whereupon Muggleton calmly "did pronounce this Penson cursed to eternity." Penson did not like being damned under the circumstances. "'Then he rose up, and with both his fists smote upon my head ...... But it came to pass that this Penson was sick immediately after, and in a week or ten days after he died, much troubled in his mind, and tormented insomuch that his friends and relations sought to apprehend me for a witch, he being a rich man, but they couldn't tell how to state the matter, so they let it fall."

It is pretty clear that John Reeve was from the first disposed to go beyond his brother prophet; and shortly after the incident of Penson's death Reeve made a grand coup, which produced a profound impression. Muggleton had damned a gentleman. Reeve tried his power upon the same class, and succeeded in actually converting two of them, who were influential men among the Ranters. The Ranters were startled and puzzled. "And it came to pass that one of these Ranters kept a victualling house and sold drink in the Minories, and they would spend their money there. So John Reeve and myself came there, and many of them despised our declaration. So John Reeve gave sentence of eternal damnation upon many of them, and one of them, being more offended than all the rest, was moved with such wrath and fury that five or six men could hardly keep him off, his fury was so hot. Then John Reeve said unto the people standing by, 'Friends,' said he, 'I pray you stand still on both sides of the room, and let there be a space in the middle, and I will lay down my head upon the ground and let this furious man tread upon my head and do what he will unto me. .....' So John Reeve pulled off his hat and laid his face fiat to the ground, and the people stood still. So the man came running with great fury, and when he came near. him, lifting up his foot to tread on his neck, the man started back again and said, 'No, I scorn to tread upon a man that lieth down to me.' And the people all marvelled at this thing."

Though Muggleton does not make much of this incident, it appears to have been a very important one in the early history of the sect, for from this moment the numbers of Muggletonians began to increase, and they began to absorb a small army of wandering monomaniacs who were roaming about London and talking about religion, and visions, and revelations, and attaching themselves first to one body and then to another, according as they could get admission to the meeting-houses and be allowed to preach and harangue. Astrologers too, came and conferred with the prophets, and drunken scoffers laid bets that they would get the prophet's blessing; and on one occasion a company of "Atheistical Ranters" made a plot to turn the tables upon Muggleton, and damn him and Reeve. Three of "the most desperatest" agreed to do it. "So the time appointed came, and there was prepared a good dinner of pork, and the three came ready prepared to curse us." Part of the agreement was that the dinner should follow upon the cursing. But whether it was that the rogues could do nothing until they were fortified with drink, or that a sudden spasm of conscientiousness came upon them, or that they were like superstitious people who with blanched lips loudly protest that they do not believe in ghosts, but decline on principle to walk through a churchyard after dark, these three fellows all ran away from their engagements at the eleventh hour. "So they departed without their dinner of pork."

The prophets were becoming notorious. The Ranters and John Robins had been vanquished; their first book was published and was selling; they were advertising themselves widely, and being advertised by friends and foes; but as yet they had not been persecuted, and as yet they had not put very prominently forward any distinctive or special theology. They claimed to be prophets, but their mission, What was it? What were they charged to proclaim?

It was just about this time that the works of Jacob Boehm had begun to exercise a very great influence upon the visionaries in England. The *Mercurius Teutonicus* was first published in an English translation in 1649, and the *Signatura Rerum* had appeared in 1651. Muggleton had certainly read these books, and as certainly turned them to account. The jargon of the German mystic was exactly what he wanted in his present state of mind, and there was that in the new philosophy which commended itself vastly to him. Not that he, as an inspired prophet, could for one moment admit that he had received any light from man or was under any obligation to anything but the divine illumination enlightening him directly and immediately; but the obligation was there all the same, and to Jacob Boehm's influence we must attribute the evolution of the distinctive doctrine of the Muggletonians, which just about this time comes into obtrusive prominence.

It was at the beginning of the year 1653 that the prophets made their first important convert. Up to this time they had been heard of only in the back streets of London. But now a New England merchant named Leader, who had made a fortune in America, and had come back in disgust at the intolerance and persecution that prevailed among the colonists, made advances to Muggleton. Leader was in a despondent state of mind, and on the lookout for a religion with some novelty in it. He too had, it seems, been a student of Jacob Boehm, and the *Signatura Rerum* had opened out a new line of speculation to him. "His first question was concerning God—whether God, that created all things, could admit of being any form of Himself?"

Prophets are never at a nonplus, and never surprised by a question; the more transcendental the problem, the more need for the prophetic gift to solve it. In fact, the prophet comes in to help when all human cunning is at fault.

Accordingly Mr. Leader's question led to a discussion which is all set down at full for those who choose to read it, and as the result of that discussion comes out into clearness the astounding declaration which henceforth appears as the main article of the Muggletonian theology.

"God hath a body of His own, as man hath a body of his own; only God's body is spiritual and heavenly, clear as *christial*, brighter than the sun, swifter than thought, yet a body."

Hitherto the prophets had been groping after a formula which might be their strength, but they had not been able to put it into shape. Jacob Boehm's mysticism, passing through the alembic of such a mind as Leader's, and subjected to that occult atmosphere which Muggleton lived in, came forth in the shape of a new theology, transcendental, unintelligible, but therefore celestial and sublime. The prophets from this moment made a new departure.

Meanwhile, the unhesitating and authoritative damning of opponents exercised a strange fascination over the multitude. Reeve and Muggleton lived among the blackguards at their first start, and they damned the blackguards pretty freely. In numberless instances the blackguards were to all intents and purposes damned before Muggleton's sentence was pronounced. They were fellows given over to drink and debauchery, sots who had not much life in them, scoundrels who were in hiding, skulking in the vilest holes of the city, whom the plague or famine would be likely to rid the world of any day. They died frequently enough after the sentence was pronounced, and it is quite conceivable that the sentence may have hastened the end of many a poor wretch who had nothing to live for. Nay, in more cases than one a timid man, when the sentence was passed, was so terrified that he took to his bed there and then, and never rose from it, or became insane, neglected his business, and so was ruined; and as the number of the damned was always increasing, the chances of strange accidents and misfortunes would go on increasing also. People heard of these, and of these only.

What the prophets themselves did, it was only natural that their followers would try to do also; indeed, it is wonderful that the damning prerogative was not invaded much oftener than it was. It was very rarely intruded upon, however. Once, indeed, a misguided and too venturous believer named Cooper took upon him to usurp authority, and pronounced the sentence of damnation upon a small batch of fifteen scoffers who had jeered at him and the prophet's mission. The precedent was a dangerous one, there was no telling what it would lead to if such random and promiscuous damning was to go on. Next day Cooper fell grievously sick, and conscience smote him; he could not be at peace till he had confessed his fault and been forgiven. He was forgiven accordingly, but he was admonished to lay to heart the warning, and to presume no more. "Not but that I do believe," says Muggleton, "they will all be damned," all the whole fifteen!

The movement was becoming a nuisance by this time, and Reeve got a hint, and no obscure one, that a warrant would be issued against him, "either from General Cromwell, or the Council of State, or from the Parliament." So far from being deterred by the prospect—was there ever a prophet who was frightened into silence?—he declared that if Cromwell or the Parliament should despise him and his mission, "I would pronounce them damned as I do you!" Though no warrant came from the Council or Cromwell—a matter much to be regretted—yet a warrant was taken out by five of the opponents, and the prophets were brought before the Lord Mayor. As usual, a detailed account is given of the proceedings, which are valuable as illustrating the method pursued in those days in the examination of an accused person, and the procedure of the court—so very different from our modern practice. The prophets were committed for trial; they refused to give bail, and were thrown into Newgate. It was the 15th of September, 1653, one of the great festivals among the believers. The hideous picture of prison life in Newgate deserves to be read even by those who have some acquaintance with the horrors of our prisons at this time. The prophets were well supplied with money, and so were spared some of the worst sufferings of the place; but it was bad enough, in all conscience, and one night the two narrowly escaped being hanged in their own room, and were only saved by five condemned men, who came to the rescue. Muggleton says the highwaymen and the boys were most set against him; one of the highwaymen, whenever he saw him in the Hall, "would come and deride at me, and say, 'You rogue, you damn'd folks.' And so it was with the boys that were prisoners; they would snatch off my hat, and pawn it for half-a-dozen of drink. So the boys did, and I gave them sixpence every time they did it, to please them." Highly gratifying to the boys!

While the two were in Newgate John Reeve wrote a letter to the Lord Mayor and another to the Recorder, mildly damning them both. If we are to believe Muggleton, the Recorder was somewhat disturbed and alarmed by the sentence. When the day of trial came, Reeve bade the Lord Mayor hold his peace and be silent, as became a damned man in the presence of the prophets, and we are told the Mayor obeyed and said nothing more. The two were condemned, nevertheless, and thrown into Bridewell for seven months. Under the horrors of that dreadful imprisonment Reeve's constitution broke down. He was never the same man again. He languished on, indeed, for four years more, but he was a dying man, and he spent his time in writing books, his followers kindly ministering to him in his broken health and feebleness. The end came to him while visiting some convents at Maidstone—good women, of course. "The one was Mrs. Frances, the eldest; the second, Mrs. Roberts; the third, Mrs. Boner. This Mrs. Frances closed up his eyes, for he said unto her, Frances, close up mine eyes, lest my enemies say I died a staring prophet.'"

While Reeve and Muggleton were lying in Newgate, another mystic—are we to call him a prophet too?—was lying in Carlisle gaol. George Fox, the Quaker, had fallen into the hands of Wilfrid Lawson, then High Sheriff for the county, who had not spared him. Just about the time that the London prophets were discharged, Fox arrived in London under the custody of Captain Drury, and had that memorable interview with Cromwell which readers of Fox's Journal are not likely to forget, though Carlyle has gone far to spoil the story by slurring it over.

It was a great event to the Quakers to have their leader in London. He had only once before been in the Metropolis—that was nine years ago—and then he had been "fearful," had done nothing, was tongue-tied, and had 'gladly escaped to itinerate among the steeple houses in the north. This time he had gained acceptance with the Protector. No man would meddle with him from henceforth or let them look to it! The Quakers were, of course, elated; they were going to carry all before them; they met to organize a grand campaign for proselytizing all England. The two commissionated prophets were by no means dismayed, by no means inclined to be outdone by the Quakers; they invited them to a disputation—a trial of the spirits, in fact. It came off, accordingly, in Eastcheap, and George Fox was there, and with him two or three of his "ministers whom the Lord raised up." It is not a little significant that Fox makes no mention of this meeting in his Journal—significant because he never omits to speak of his successes, and never tells us anything of his failures. Nay, he studiously omits all mention of Muggleton's name throughout the Journal, and in his books against him indulges in really violent language. Muggleton, on the other hand, speaks of this discussion at Eastcheap as if it had been a serious check to the Quakers, and from this time to his death he never ceased to assail them with a resolute aggressiveness which indicates no sort of misgiving in his power to deal with his antagonists. The discussion, however, ended in Fox and his supporters—five in all—receiving the sentence of damnation from the two prophets, and from this moment there was internecine war between the Quakers and the Muggletonians; each denouncing the other fiercely, and issuing books against the other by the score—works which have happily been long ago forgotten, to the great advantage of mankind. If, however, any one, curious in such lore, is desirous of finding out what cursing and swearing, regarded as one of the Fine Arts, may achieve when skilfully managed by adepts, let him by all means turn to the pamphlets of Pennington, Richard Farnsworth, and others of the Quaker body, while delivering their souls against Muggleton, and the counterblasts of Muggleton, Claxton, and their friends in reply. One of the choicest diatribes of these *esprits forts*, as we may well call them, was hurled at the prophet by William Penn.

Muggleton had some very zealous converts at Cork—for there were believers everywhere by this time—and as they were people of substance and much in favour, they were making some way. Of course they came into collision with the Quakers, and not without success. Penn had early fallen under the influence of Richard Farnsworth, whom Muggleton had damned in 1654, and Penn's father had sent him over to manage his Irish estates, in the hope of getting the new notions out of the young man's head. The experiment failed, and young Penn, now only twenty-four years old, had returned to England in 1668 as staunch a Quaker as ever. There was a leading man among the Quakers, Josiah Cole by name, whom Muggleton had solemnly damned; he was in failing health, and he died a few days after the sentence was pronounced. The Muggletonians were jubilant, and some of the Quakers were disturbed and alarmed. Penn's heart was moved within him, and with all the fervid indignation of youth he stepped forward to draw the sword of the Lord. He printed a letter to Muggleton which should reassure the waverers. It thundered out defiance. "Boast not," he says, "thou enemy of God, thou son of perdition and confederate with the unclean croaking spirits reserved under chains to eternal darkness. ..... I boldly challenge thee with thy six-foot God and all the host of Luciferian spirits, with all your commissions, curses, and sentences, to touch and hurt me. And this know, O Muggleton: on you I trample, and to the bottomless pit are you sentenced, from whence you came, and where the endless worm shall gnaw and torture your imaginary soul."

Muggleton replied with his usual coolness, and pronounced his sentence upon the young enthusiast. Neither was a man easily to be put down; but whereas the prophet's followers were wholly unmoved by all the attacks upon them, the Quakers found the Muggletonians extremely troublesome, and it is impossible to resist the conviction that large numbers of the Quakers were won over to join the opposite camp. Nay, it looks as if Muggleton had really some strange power over the weaker vessels among the Quakers, and had actually frightened some of them. Writing in 1670, he says: "You are not like the people you were sixteen years ago; there were few Quakers then, but they had witchcraft fits, but now of late I do not hear of any Quaker that hath any fits, no, not so much as to buz and hum before the fit comes. But if you, Fox, Both know of any of you Quakers that have any of those witchcraft fits as formerly, bring them to me, and I shall cast out that devil which causeth those fits." The Quakers could hardly have been as angry as they were, nor their books have been so many and their writers so voluble during twenty years and longer, if Muggleton had not been a disputant to be dreaded, and a prophet with the faculty of drawing others after him.

In the whole course of his career, which extended over nearly half a century, Muggleton never found any difficulty in maintaining his authority over his followers. There were indeed two attempts at mutiny, but they were promptly suppressed, and they collapsed before they had made any head. The first was in 1660, shortly after the death of John Reeve. Lawrence Claxton, a "great writer" among the Muggletonians, had during Reeve's long illness come very much to the fore as an opponent of the Quakers, and his success had a little turned his head. In one passage of his writings he had taken rank as Reeve's equal and representative, and had put himself on a level with "the Commissionated." It was an awful act of impiety. "For," says Muggleton, "as John Reeve was like unto Elijah, so am I as Elisha, and his place was but as Gehazi, and could stand no longer than my will and pleasure was." Claxton had been formally blessed, therefore he could never be damned, but excommunicated he could be and was. He at once dropt out and we hear of him no more.

The second revolt was much more serious. "There were four conspirators in the rebellion ..... for which I damned two of them, and the other two I did excommunicate." This time the fomenter of discord was a busy Scotchman. Muggleton calls him Walter Bohenan, which appears to be only a phonetic representation of Walter Buchanan. That so sagacious a seer as Muggleton should have been betrayed into associating himself intimately with a canny Scot is truly wonderful, and illustrates the eternal verity that "we are all of us weak at times," even the prophets. Bohenan's self-assertion led him on to dizzy heights of towering presumption, until at last "he acted the highest act of rebellion that ever was acted." It was all in vain; he was cut off for ever—perished from the congregation; utterly damned, and thereupon disappears, swallowed up of darkness and silence.

Muggleton lived twenty-six years after this last revolt, exercising unquestioned authority; an autocratic prophet to whom something like worship was offered even to the last. He was far advanced in his eighty-ninth year when he died. He was far on towards seventy when he was brought before Jeffreys, then Common Serjeant, and other justices, on a charge of blasphemy. Jeffreys was as yet a novice in those arts of which he became the acknowledged master a few years after, but already he quite equalled his future self in his savage brutality to the poor monomaniac. "He was a man," says Muggleton, "whose voice was very loud; but he is one of the worst devils in nature." The jury hesitated to bring in their verdict, knowing well enough what would follow, but Jeffrey's look and manner cowed them. The prophet was condemned to pay a fine of £500, to stand in the pillory three times for two hours without the usual protection to his head, which those condemned to such a barbarous punishment were allowed. He was to have his books burned by the common hangman, and to remain in Newgate till his fine was paid. Only a man of an iron constitution could have come out of the ordeal with his life. Muggleton bore it all; remained in Newgate for a year, compounded for his fine in the sum of £100, which his friends advanced, and was a free man on the 19th of July, 1677, a day which the Muggletonians observed as the prophet's Hegira.

As early as 1666 he had many followers on the Continent, and in that year the Transcendant Spiritual Treatise was translated into German by a convert who came over to London to confer with the sage. Except on very rare occasions he never left London, nor indeed the parish in which he was born. He pursued the trade of a tailor till late in life, but his books had sold largely, and he managed to get together a competence, and was at one time worried by his neighbours and fined for refusing to serve in some parish offices. There was a fund of sagacity about the man which appears frequently in his later letters, but an utter absence of all sentiment and all sympathy. He had no nerves—staid, stern, and curiously insensible to physical pain. He was absolutely fearless, with a constitution that could defy any hardships and bear any strain upon it.

When we come to the teaching of Muggleton, we find ourselves in a tangled maze of nonsense far too inconsequential to allow of any intelligible account being given of it. Jacob Boehm's mistiest dreams are clearness itself compared with the English prophet's utterances. Others might talk of the divine cause or the divine power or the divine person, "fumbling exceedingly" and falling back in an intellectual swoon upon the stony bosom of the Unknowable. Muggleton grimly told you that there was a personal Trinity in the universe—God, man, and devil—and each had his body. If you pressed him for further particulars he poured forth words that might mean anything, a metallic jargon which you were ordered to receive and ponder. Such as it was, however, you had to accept or reject it at your peril. Why should an inspired prophet argue?

Something must be set down to the circumstances in which he found himself, and to the dreadfully chaotic condition which the moral sentiments and religious beliefs of the multitude had been reduced to during the wild anarchy of the seventeenth century. There were two men in England who were quite certain—George Fox was one, Muggleton was the other. Everybody else was doubting, hesitating, groping for the light, moaning at the darkness. These two men knew, other people were seeking to know. George Fox went forth to win the world over from darkness to light. Muggleton stayed at home, he was the light. They that wanted it must come to him to find it. All through England there was clamour and hubbub of many voices, men going to and fro, always on the move, trying experiments of all kinds. Here was one man, "a still strong man in a blatant land," who was calm, steadfast, unmovable, and always at home. He did not want you, whoever you were; he was perfectly indifferent to you and your concerns. Preach? No! he never preached, he never cared to speak till he was spoken to. If you went to him as an oracle, then he spake as a god.

Moreover, when the Restoration came and the high pressure that had been kept up in some states of society was suddenly taken off, there was a frantic rage for pleasure, which included the wildest debauchery and the most idiotic attempts at amusement. Then, too, the haste to be rich agitated the minds of all classes; Westward ho! was the cry not only of Pilgrim Fathers but of reckless adventurers of all kinds. From across the sea came the ships of Tarshish bringing gold, and silver, and ivory, and apes, and peacocks, and a thousand tales of El Dorado. Muggleton the prophet, with that light brown hair of his and the dreamy hazel eye and the resolute lips, waited unmoved. Pleasure? If he wondered at anything it was to know what meaning there could be in the word. Riches? What purpose could they serve? To him it seemed that the Decalogue contained one wholly superfluous enactment; why should men covet? There would have been some reason in limiting the number of the commandments to nine; nine is the product of three times three. Think of that! This man in that wicked age must have appeared to many a standing miracle, if only for this reason, that he was the one man in London who was content, passing his days in a stubborn rapture, as little inclined for play or laughter as the sphinx in the desert, which the sand storms can beat against but never stir.

So far from Muggleton's influence and authority growing less as he grew older, it went on steadily increasing; there was a mystery and an awe that gathered round him, and latterly he was regarded rather as an inspired oracle than as a seer. The voice of prophecy ceased; he had left his words on record for all future ages, but from day to day his advice was asked, and people soon found it was worth listening to. In the latter years of his life his letters dealt with the ordinary affairs of men. People wrote to inquire about their matrimonial affairs, their quarrels, their business difficulties, whether they must conform to this or that enactment of the State, how they might outwit the persecutors and skulk behind the law. Muggleton replies with surprising shrewdness and good sense, and now and then exhibits a familiarity with the quips and quirks of the law that he can only have acquired by the necessity which suffering had laid upon him. His language is always rugged, for he had received little or no education; he is very unsafe in his grammar, but he has a plain, homely vocabulary, forcible and copious, which, like most mystics, he was compelled to enrich on occasion, and which he does not scruple to enrich in his own way. His style certainly improves as he gets older, and in these letters one meets now and then with passages that are almost melodious, the sentences following one another in a kind of plaintive rhythm, and sounding as you read them aloud, like a Gregorian chant. He died of natural decay, the machine worn out. His last words were, "Now hath God sent death unto me." They laid him on his bed, and he slept and woke not. Nearly 250 of the faithful followed him to his grave. It is clear that the sect had not lost ground as time moved on.

Not the least feature in this curious chapter of religious history is that the Muggletonians should have survived as a sect to our own days. As late as 1846 an elaborate index to the Muggletonian writings was issued, and the Divine Songs of the Muggletonians, written exclusively by believers, show that there has been a strange continuity of composition among them,. and that, too, such composition as ordinary mortals have never known the like of. Yet Muggleton never broke forth into verse. Joanna Southcott could not keep down her impulse to pour forth her soul in metre; Muggleton is never excited, the emotional had no charm for him. So, too, he never cared for music, he makes no allusion to it. Nay, he speaks slightingly of worship, of prayer and praise, especially of congregational worship. It was allowable to the little men, a concession to the weak which the strong in the faith might be expected to dispense with sooner or later. For himself, isolated and self-contained, he could do without the aids to faith which the multitude ask for and find support in. He held himself aloof; he had no sympathy to offer, he asked for none; nay, he did not even need his followers, he could do without them. The question for them was, Could they do without him? For more than two centuries they have kept on vehemently answering No!

Of late years a class of specialists has risen up among us who have treated us to quite a new philosophy—to wit, the philosophy of religion. To these thinkers I leave the construction of theories on Muggleton's place in the history of religion or philosophy; to them, too, I leave the question of what was the secret of his success and power. Much more interesting to me is the problem how the sect has gone on retaining its vitality. Perhaps the great secret of that permanence has been that Muggleton did not give his followers too much to believe or too much to do. He disdained details, he was never precise and meddlesome. If the Muggletonians wished to pray, let them; to sing, there was no objection; to meet together in their conventicles, it was a harmless diversion. But they must manage these things themselves, and provide for difficulties as they arose. It was no part of the prophet's office to make bye-laws which might require to be altered any day. Thus it came about that the sect was left at Muggleton's death absolutely unfettered by any petty restraints upon its freedom of development. The believers must manage their own affairs. There is one God and Muggleton is His prophet—that was really the sum and substance of their creed. That followed on a small scale which is observable on a large scale among the Moslems, the prophet's followers found themselves more and more thrown back upon their prophet till he became almost an object of adoration. The creed of

Islam without Mahomet would be to millions almost inconceivable; the Muggletonian God without Muggleton would not be known

Says her Royal Highness, looking over my shoulder, "You have written quite enough about those crazy, vulgar people. It's all old world talk. There are no prophets now; there never will be any more."

No more prophets! The prophetical succession never stops; never will stop. When Muggleton died Emanuel Swedenborg was a boy of ten; twenty years afterwards the new prophet was walking about London just as the old one had done, living the same lonely life, conversing with the angels and writing of heaven and hell and conjugal love, and—well, a great deal else besides; and, odd coincidence, it was in that same Eastcheap where Muggleton had damned the Quakers in 1653 that the Swedenborgians held their first assembly in 1788, just about the same time that Joanna Southcott came to London, and before Joseph Smith and Brigham Young were born or thought of. No, no. The prophets are not improved off the face of the earth. They never will be. They will turn up again and again. You can no more hope to exterminate them by culture than you can hope to produce them by machinery. *Propheta nascitur non fit.* For once her Royal Highness was wrong.

Privately Printed Opuscula issued to Members

of ye Sette of Odd Volumes

No. LXXI

LODOWICK MUGGLETON

A PAPER READ BEFORE YE SETTE OF

ODD VOLUMES, AT YE 337TH

MEETING, JANUARY 27, 1915

BY

BRO. GEORGE CHARLES WILLIAMSON

Horologer to ye Sette

1919

PRIVATELY PRINTED OPUSCULA

ISSUED TO MEMBERS

OF YE

SETTE OF ODD VOLUMES

No. LXXI

LODOWICK MUGGLETON

MINIATURE PORTRAIT OF LODOWICK MUGGLETON
BY SAMUEL COOPER
Now in the Pierpont Morgan Collection
See pages 243 and 262
Photograph by Hallett Hyatt

Lodowick Muggleton

A PAPER READ BEFORE YE SETTE OF

ODD VOLUMES, AT YE 337TH

MEETING, JANUARY 27, 1915

BY

BRO. GEORGE CHARLES WILLIAMSON

HOROLOGER TO YE SETTE

LONDON: IMPRYNTED FOR YE AUTHOR AT
YE CHISWICK PRESS
AND TO BE HAD OF NO BOKESELLERS
1919

Academic Literary and Scientific Interest

OPUSCULUM LXXI

1919

This Edition is limited to 199 copies, and is imprynted for private circulation only.

Copy No. ....

PRESENTED UNTO

....

BY

....

𝔍𝔪𝔭𝔯𝔦𝔪𝔞𝔱𝔲𝔯

Let this be imprynted.

E. SULLIVAN (*Bookbinder*).
Chairman of ye Publication Committee

WITH GRATEFUL THANKS TO ALL WHO
HELPED IN ITS COMPILATION, ESPECIALLY
TO ALL KIND FRIENDS AT 7, NEW STREET,
BISHOPSGATE, LONDON
NOTABLY TO
MR. RICHARD W. HUNTLEY
AND
MR. JOHN H. CATER

TABLE OF CONTENTS

	Page
CERTIFICATE	233
IMPRIMATUR	237
DEDICATION	239
YE BOKE	242
APPENDIX	268

ILLUSTRATIONS

TO FACE PAGE

MINIATURE PORTRAIT OF MUGGLETON, by Samuel Cooper, now in the Pierpont Morgan collection .... Frontispiece

HALF-LENGTH PORTRAIT, in oil, representing Muggleton, in the possession of his followers at New Street, Bishopsgate, London 244

ENGRAVING OF MUGGLETON, by G. V. Casseel. Frontispiece to "Interpretation of the Revelation of St. John " 248

FULL-LENGTH PORTRAIT, in oil, done from life, by his friend William Wood of Braintree. In the Reading Room at NewStreet, Bishopsgate 257

ENGRAVING OF MUGGLETON, by J. Kennerley, after the portrait by William Wood, used as a frontispiece to three of Muggleton's Works 261

DEATH MASK OF MUGGLETON, preserved by his followers at New Street, Bishopsgate 263

THE MUGGLETONIAN READING ROOM AT NEW STREET, BISHOPSGATE 265

LODOWICK MUGGLETON

THE middle of the seventeenth century was in England a time of great revival of religious thought, and it was responsible for the creation of numerous strange and mysterious sects, the leaders of which entertained very strong and definite opinions respecting one another, and did not fail to express those opinions, both by word of mouth, and in their writings, in the forcible manner, mingled with much personal abuse, which appears so strange to us at the present day. Of the various bodies which arose in this time of tempestuous movement, many have disappeared, and of the Commonwealth sects, practically only two now survive, the highly respected Society of Friends, and the exceedingly small and obscure body known as Muggletonians. There may perhaps be a few persons remaining who hold to the strange ideals of the Seventh Day Baptists, but practically all those persons who believed in what was known as the Millenium doctrine, the doctrine of the Fifth Monarchy, and other people who were called Behmenists, Bidellians, Coppinists, Salmonists, Dippers, Traskites, Tryonists, Philadelphians, Christadelphians, Shakers, and Ranters, have disappeared, and to all intents and purposes, the only body which is well known to students of religious history in Commonwealth times, and which flourishes at the present day, is the great Society of Friends.

The Muggletonians have been forgotten by very many persons who are students of religion. They exclude from their church meetings the usual exercises of public worship, and therefore do not appear in the lists of the Registrar-General.[1] They have no preachers, consequently

---

[1] There is no allusion to them in the London Post Office Directory, nor are they mentioned in the Religious Census of London undertaken

there are no persons regarded as their leaders whose names would be printed in any list of eminent religious persons at the head of a definite organization, but there is still a small body of people who hold to the opinions laid down by Lodowick Muggleton in the middle of the seventeenth century, and who meet together in one place in London, in a building which occupies part of the site of the birthplace of their leader, and who read his works and hold his name in great repute, and it is concerning these people that I propose to set down certain statements of fact.

It may be, perhaps, a matter of wonder why I, a Catholic, should have been induced to look into the history of Lodowick Muggleton, and to make any inquiry respecting his followers, but the whole subject arose from the purchase by Mr. Pierpont Morgan of a miniature representing Lodowick Muggleton, which had remained in the possession of his descendants and followers until the time it came into Mr. Morgan's possession, and had been practically unknown to the various persons who were familiar with the features of Muggleton, and who knew about his portraits. This portrait was handed over to me that I might study it.

Its purchaser knew nothing of who Muggleton was, except that he was a seventeenth century religious leader, and from his appearance was supposed to be of Puritan ideas. The only point of information available concerning him at the moment—was one which is wholly inaccurate and very unfair, the remarks made by Macaulay about Muggleton in his "History of England" (1848). This quotation Mr. Morgan had heard of, and his secretary turned it up, handing a copy of the extract over to me, as the sole information that was known respecting the man, and I was thereupon asked to find out whether this statement was a correct one, and if not, to investigate Muggleton's history, in order that, in the catalogue I was then preparing, I might give such details concerning him and his followers, if any existed, as I thought fit.

Macaulay speaks of Muggleton in the following words. He says: "A mad tailor named Lodowick Muggleton wandered from pothouse to pothouse, tippling ale, and denouncing eternal torments against all those who refused to believe, on his testimony, that the Supreme Being was only six feet high, and that the sun was just four miles from the earth." (Hist, 1848, i, 764.)

Almost every piece of information in this statement is entirely inaccurate. The only thing that has anything of the real truth about it is the fact that Muggleton was inclined to denounce eternal torments against those who refused to believe, not the ridiculous statements that Macaulay makes, but in Muggleton's own authority as a

---

by the Daily News in 1904, nor in the similar volume by Mr. Charles Booth issued in 1902.

preacher. It was not easy to find out where the Muggletonians carried on their religious meetings, but eventually I was able to locate the building in the East End of London, near to Bishopsgate, and after some little time, I made the acquaintance of various members of this strange and obscure sect, had many conversations with them, visited the room in which they held their meetings, examined the portraits which they possessed representing their founder, and had them photographed for the first time. I also introduced to their notice this particular portrait of Muggleton, which was new to them, although it had belonged for over two hundred years to persons who had accepted him as a true prophet. As soon as I began to learn something of the doctrines held by the Muggletonians, it impressed me as a very curious fact in the history of this remarkable sect, that the only two sects which have survived from the stormy times of the Commonwealth should be those which held doctrines absolutely

PORTRAIT OF MUGGLETON AT NEW STREET, BISHOPSGATE
Inscribed "Lodowick Muggleton Dyed 14 of March 1698 then aged 88"
Photographed by Hallett Hyatt

antithetical to one another, the two bodies which were in their day the bitterest in opposition to one another, because certainly no one opposed Fox and Penn so strongly in their own time as did Lodowick Muggleton, and no one, was more strenuous in his opposition to the entire theory of religion held by those two great leaders than was this same Muggleton.

The very forcible opinion which Muggleton held respecting the Quakers, who were his great opponents, especially in the position he adopted with regard to prayer, is set out upon the titles of the various books which he wrote against the Society of Friends. The principal work is entitled "The Neck of the Quakers Broken, or cut in sunder by the two-edged Sword of the Spirit, which is put into my mouth."

Another work on the same lines is entitled "A Looking-glass for George Fox the Quaker and other Quakers, wherein they may see themselves to be right Devils, and wherein is set forth the ignorance and blindness of the Quaker doctrine of Christ within them, and that they cannot nor doth not understand the meaning of the Scripture, neither have the gift of the true interpretation of the Scripture, as will appear in the pages following." This book was written in reply to one which was issued by George Fox, and which he called "Something in Answer to the Muggleton book which he calls 'The Quaker's Neck Broken.'" A little later on, Penn issued a book against Muggleton called "The New Witnesses proved Old Heretics," and then Muggleton replied by a book which he called "The Answer to William Penn, Quaker, wherein he is proved to be an ignorant spatter-brained Quaker, who knows no more what the true God is, nor His secret decrees, than one of his coach-horses does, nor so much, for the ox knoweth his owner, and the ass his master's crib, but Penn doth not know his Maker, as is manifest by the Scripture, which may inform the reader, if he mind the interpretation of the Scripture in the discourse following." In this latter book Muggleton attacked Penn in language that even at that time was accounted rather startling and virulent, because Penn would not accept the materialistic teaching which Muggleton at that particular period of his life was announcing. The Friends, however, despite these attacks, multiplied and grew, but the Muggletonians never became more than an exceedingly small sect.

Lodowick Muggleton was born in Walnut-Tree Yard, now called New Street, in Bishopsgate Without, and the present meeting of the Muggletonians is in a small modern built private residence, which occupies, as I have stated, as near as possible the site of his birthplace. He first saw the light in July 1609, and was baptized in the Church of England faith in that same month, at St. Botolph's Church, which was close at hand. He was of a Northamptonshire family, and the name still survives in the little village of Wilbarston, from whence the Muggletons originally came. His father was a farrier. His mother died in 1612, when the boy was only three years old, and then his father sent him away into the country, it is not known exactly where, and he was brought up, he says, by strangers. It would appear that the father was rather more than an ordinary smith or farrier, and carried on the business also of a veterinary surgeon, and was a man of some considerable repute. The family was a good one, it had been in the same place for three centuries, at least, and Lodowick himself speaks of his forefathers as "plain men yet downright honest, men of no great repute in the world, nor of base report as ever I could hear." He also speaks in terms of great endearment of his mother, although he, as the youngest, and only three years old when she died, could not have remembered very much about her. His father appears to have married again almost immediately, and hence it was that, on his mother's death, Lodowick was sent away to a distance from all his relations, to live with other people, and appears to have seen very little of his father, or of his father's second wife, between the death of his mother, and his return to London when he was fifteen or sixteen years old. When he came back to London he was apprenticed to John Quick, a tailor in Walnut-tree Yard, who must have lived close to where the Muggletons were residing, probably within a door or two, because Walnut-tree Yard was at that time a very small entry. Quick was a tailor who did a good business in livery gowns, and appears to have been in some ways an interesting person. Lodowick speaks of him as quiet and peaceable, and "able to teach his apprentices the trade well," and he also says that he himself learnt his trade quickly, and pleased his master more than did any other of the apprentices. He began very early in life to interest himself in religious movements; he heard about the Puritans, and some of them came to talk with his master, pleading that the Sabbath day should be kept holy, and trying to persuade John Quick not to open his shop on that day, as he had been in the habit of doing. They did not, however, have very much success with the tailor, nor at that time with his apprentices, and when the term of apprenticeship ran out, Muggleton, who had a great desire to get on in the world, and who said that he thought the trade of a tailor would not gain much riches, changed his occupation and went to work in a shop in Houndsditch, with a man whose name was Richardson, who "made clothes to sell," and who also carried on the business of a pawnbroker. Muggleton there fell in love with the daughter of his employer, and as he pleased Mrs. Richardson by his managing power, and by the skill with which he looked after the business, she agreed to the match, her husband being a distracted, hare-brained sort of man, not of very much importance in the household. She promised to give her daughter a hundred pounds, with which Muggleton was proposing to start in business as a pawnbroker and clothier, but suddenly an entire change of opinion took place in his ideas. He went as journeyman in 1631 to his cousin, John Reeve, the tailor, who lived in a street in the City known as St. Thomas Apostle. Reeve, who was a very zealous Puritan, took

Muggleton to task upon the question of the lawfulness of lending money upon pawn, and pleaded that it was usury and extortion, and forbidden to religious people. He pressed home the argument with such great force that he brought Muggleton round to his opinion, with the result that he made up his mind that if he lent money upon usury and extortion, his future life would be in danger, and he thereupon became a zealous Puritan, and an ardent student of Holy Scripture. So he continued until his own more extraordinary opinions remodelled the conditions of his religious life. The change, however, involved the loss of the girl to whom he was engaged, because Mrs. Richardson refused to let him have the money unless he started as a pawnbroker, and he had to forsake the Richardsons, and says later on, in his own journal, with a certain bitterness of feeling that the girl was still living, and then was worth £700 a year, as she and her mother had developed the old business to such an extent that it had become one of considerable importance.

However, Muggleton did get married, and more than once during this part of his career, each time, he says, to a girl of about nineteen. His first wife, Sarah, he married in or about 1635, and she died three or four years afterwards. We know nothing of her, except that she was the mother of two children who survived him. His second wife, Mary, he married in 1642 and she died in 1648. He speaks of her as "a comely woman to see to, yet of a melancholy, dropsical nature and humour," given to much melancholy and discontent of mind, especially "if things did not go well in this world." She left behind her one only surviving child, a boy, who was very scrofulous, and who died in 1653. As to his disease, Muggleton wrote, " I was glad, (though I used means to help him, but all in vain,) knowing that all the children I had by her did partake of her melancholy and dropsical nature."

We thus come to the period of about 1650, which was so full of strange religious movements, and Muggleton seems to have been attracted by the declamations of two men who were styled Ranters, John Robins and Thomas Tany, and also to have read some of the publications of an even better known person, Jacob Behmen, a shoemaker of Gorlitz, who believed that he had visions and revelations concerning religion, and stated that he was in a position to declare the true faith. Behmen influenced George Fox very largely, and many of Fox's spiritual ideas were derived from the writings of that man. Robins and Tany were of quite a different sort. They were wild and outrageous fanatics with strangely disordered imaginations, full of all sorts of extraordinary ideas, but they both of them affected Reeve and Muggleton, and eventually, in 1652, Reeve announced that he had received personal communications by "voice of words from Jesus Christ, who was the only God," appointing him to be the messenger of a new dispensation, and Muggleton to be his preacher or mouth. The

ENGRAVING BY G. V. CASSEEL.
Frontispiece to "Interpretation of the Revelation of St. John"

two men came forward as prophets, identifying themselves with the two witnesses who are spoken of in the Revelations, xi, 3, said that they were empowered to declare a new system of faith, and had authority to pronounce on the eternal fate of individuals. They called themselves the Witnesses of the Spirit, and gathered about them considerable crowds of people. Many of their strange ideas they put into print, the first book that was issued being the work of John Reeve, and entitled "A Transcendant Spiritual Treatise." Reeve appears to have been a person of some moment, a man of personal holiness and a quiet, courteous, kindly-natured fellow, but he was ever in poor health, and he only lived for six years after this announcement in 1652. He, however, seems to have started the movement, and to have first laid down the absolute cardinal principles of Muggletonianism, leaving it to Muggleton to define and declare their definite details. Reeve and Muggleton entirely rejected any doctrine of the Trinity, considering that that there was but one God, and He a glorified body of flesh like unto a man in compass and substance and that the references to the Mediator and to the Holy Ghost were simply various methods of alluding to the same Deity. They did not believe in a personal Devil; they said that the Devil and Human Reason were synonymous expressions, but practically the Devil was Human Reason itself. They believed in the sleep of the soul, and in its physical resurrection with the body; a doctrine at one time accepted by Unitarians and in 1562 by the original articles of the Church of England. They taught that there was an actual heaven, a place beyond the stars, but that there was no actual hell at present, although there would be one later on, after the last judgement, and it would be situate on the earth. They furthermore laid down the statement that the angels were the only beings of pure reason, and then they started all sorts of strange ideas in opposition to the science of astronomy, trying to point out that Holy Scripture contradicted the theory of astronomy, that the sun travelled round the earth, that heaven was only a very short distance off, just above the stars, and various other curious ideas, which were more opposed to science than to revealed religion.[1] The strangest position, however, which they took up, was

---

[1] The Six Principles of the Muggletonian faith may thus be summarized:
1. There is no God but the glorified Man Christ Jesus.
2. There is no Devil but the unclean Reason of men.
3. Heaven is an infinite abode of light above and beyond the Stars.
4. The place of Hell will be this Earth when sun, moon, and stars are extinguished.
5. Angels are the only beings of Pure Reason.
6. The Soul dies with the Body and will be raised with it.

their opposition to prayer, and here it was that the great divergence between them and the Quakers was first marked. The Muggletonians said that prayer was a mark of weakness, a remnant of the corrupt nature, and that as God lives in regal state,[1] and does not interfere with things below, outward worship of any kind was a folly and a mistake, and all ideas connected with prayer or with preaching were heresy. The Quakers, of course, whom the Muggletonians in their forcible manner termed "spawn of Hell," took up an entirely opposite opinion as to prayer and worship. The Muggletonians attached no importance whatever to forms or ceremonies, to ordinances or consecrations, and in that respect they coincided with the teaching of the Quakers. They considered that salvation was the effect of a spiritual principle, which was quickened by God, and which had nothing whatever to do with outward professions or creeds, and further, in common with the Quakers, they objected to bear arms, and to take an oath; but their most strenuous opposition was reserved for the accepted type of religious worship, and for the doctrine of prayer.

Muggleton and Reeve were very speedily charged with blasphemy, were brought up before the Lord Mayor, detained in Newgate for a month, and then kept in the Old Bridewell for six months. They were liberated in April 1654, and immediately proceeded to carry out their religious work in very strong and enthusiastic fashion; but the death of Reeve in July 1658 left Muggleton practically in charge of the movement, and he began to sum up the principles of his special doctrine, and to put them into more definite and concrete form.

His supremacy as a religious teacher was very quickly questioned by a man named Laurence Claxton, who was a beneficed clergyman and a friend of Reeve's, and who after Reeve's death aspired to be the leader of the movement, but Muggleton was by far the stronger man, and eventually Claxton became his follower. There were several other

---

[1] "God, the Muggletonians maintain," says Dr. Gordon, "exercises no immediate oversight on affairs. He has made the world a going machine, he has supplied every human being with a working conscience, etc." "Whoever doth not act well, by that law written in his heart, and doth not stand in awe of that, and fear to offend that law of conscience as if God himself did stand by, all his well doing is but eye service." "God has, no doubt, on rare occasions intervened to makerevelations of truth; these have been completed; he will take no further notice of the world until the Judgement Day."

"The system of belief," Dr. Gordon adds, "is [in its entirety] a singular union of opinions which seem diametrically opposed. It is rationalistic on one side, credulous on another. In some respects one of the most purely spiritual, in others it is one of the most rigidly dogmatic of systems."

efforts made to prevent Muggleton from being regarded as the leader of this special religious movement, but he overcame all those who opposed him. His vehemence was extraordinary, and he spoke with such plainness of speech about those who differed from him, that he crushed their opposition, and brought them into line with himself. Immediately after Reeve's death, he commenced his strenuous attack upon the Quakers, for whom he entertained a great contempt. Their spiritual ideas did not appeal to him, because he regarded God as a Person, having all the attributes of human nature, although transfigured, and not in any sense as a spirit. Muggleton came into contact with the law very frequently. He was arrested at Chesterfield in 1663 on the instance of John Coope the Vicar, and although this Vicar pronounced him to be "the soberest, wisest, man of a fanatic that ever he had talked with," yet he was obliged to take action against him for what he regarded as blasphemy, and Muggleton was committed to Derby gaol, and was there imprisoned for nine days.

Muggleton never had any patience with people who opposed him. He pronounced against them what he called the curse of God, calling down a sentence of eternal damnation upon every person who refused to accept his religious opinions.

When he was at Derby, he had an interesting interview with Gervase Bennet, a magistrate, whose sarcasm had given rise to the fixing of the name of Quakers upon the persons who up to that time had been called the Society of Friends of Truth, or by others, the followers of George Fox. Muggleton discussed many points of theology with Bennet. Bennet was unwise enough to allow an audience, which included the other magistrates, the Sheriff's men, and the jailer, to be present at the interview. Muggleton was far better acquainted with Holy Scripture than was Bennet, and was able with great shrewdness to make use in the controversy of various passages from the Bible which he had at his fingers' ends. The result was that Bennet was nonplussed in his arguments, and had met with his match. On the whole, it was a fairly good-humoured controversy, but Bennet himself was rather indignant at the way in which those who were listening to the arguments expressed their great satisfaction when the magistrate was defeated by Muggleton in the controversy, and who rejoiced at seeing him vanquished in argument. The only point that the two men held in common was that "the soul of man was mortal and doth die," but in every other respect they bitterly opposed one another.

Soon after he returned from Derby, Muggleton married for the third time. His wife was one Mary Martin, the daughter of John Martin, a tanner, of East Mailing in Kent. He had then been a widower for sixteen years, and was fifty-three years old. His wife was twenty-five. The marriage seems have been a very happy one, and she survived him for twenty years. She brought him a little property, and devoted herself to his interests to the day of his death, and often, says Dr.

Gordon, "by her quickness of wit, stood between him and danger, and tended his latter years with the most patient care."

In 1670, his books were seized in London, were pronounced to be blasphemous, and were destroyed,[1] and Muggleton had to hide for a long time. In 1675, he had to take action in a court of law against a certain Sir John James in respect to some house property, formerly belonging to a friend of his, one Mrs. Brunt, the widow of John Brunt, for whom he was executor, and who, with her husband, had been one of his most faithful followers. In connection with proving the will, he was obliged to appear in what was then called the Spiritual Court, and as soon as it was known who he was, he was again arrested on the charge of blasphemy. He was tried at the Old Bailey in 1677, before Sir Richard Rainsford, Chief Justice of the King's Bench, but it was not easy to prove the crime for which he had been apprehended, because he had printed nothing since 1673, and that brought him within the Act of Indemnity of 1674. However, a copy was found of his principal book, called "The Neck of the Quakers Broken" with the imprint "Amsterdam 1663," and it was proved that this was a false impression as the book was really printed in London and not in Holland. It was then argued that the book was antedated, to put it under the protection of the Act and had really been printed in 1676. This was not true, and the whole trial in many respects was unfair. The prosecution were, however, determined to bring in a verdict of "Guilty," and they succeeded in doing so, and Muggleton was fined for what was called "a malicious, scandalous, blasphemous, seditious and heretical book, unlawfully, wickedly, maliciously, scandalously, blasphemously, seditiously, schismatically and heretically printed, sold, uttered, and published." He was fined £500, a fine that was quite impossible for him to pay, and he was thereupon sent to prison. There he remained for six months, and was then released after paying £100, and finding two sureties for his behaviour during his life. Meantime, before being sent to prison, he had to stand upon the pillory in three places in the city, the Exchange, Temple Bar and Smithfield, on three several days, and while there, his books were burned with fire before his face. This pillory punishment was a cause of great suffering to him and he was much knocked about while within the pillory, dirt, mud, and rotten eggs being thrown at him. He was released from gaol on July 19th, 1677, and the memory of that day is still kept sacred by his followers although, since the alteration of the calendar, the date has been regarded as the 30th of July, and the two festivals which the Muggletonians keep, are the 30th of July, "a day of joy to his people," and the 14th, 15th and 16th of February, the latter dates being to commemorate the day upon which Reeve announced that he had

---

[1] At Lambeth Library and in St. Paul's Library are two of the actual books that were seized, having inscriptions in them to that effect.

received the commission from God, and was one of the two true Prophets of Witness.

There is in the British Museum a very rare tract concerning Muggleton, a quarto of six pages, which was printed in London in 1676, for an anonymous author, who styles himself B. H.

I am indebted to Sir Ernest Clarke for a reference to this extraordinary document, which was evidently prepared by someone who was in bitter opposition to Muggleton. It is full of hard statements respecting him, and contains a great deal of information which later investigation has proved to be wholly inaccurate. The writer calls it "A Modest Account of the wicked life of that Grand Impostor." It speaks of his principles as damnable, and says that his commission was but counterfeit and himself a cheat, and it professes to prove all these statements from Muggleton's own words, but, as a matter of fact, it does not quote a single word of Muggleton's from beginning to end. It is merely a vulgar attack upon Muggleton, calling him a poor, silly, despicable creature in one place, in another an infamous blasphemer, further on, a flatterer of Oliver Cromwell, and at the end, a man who poisoned the minds of people with a hodgepodge of rotten tenets, who was worthily rewarded with dirt and rotten eggs. Everything that Muggleton preached was regarded by this writer as an imposture, and as a piece of impertinence, and the vindictive character of the pamphlet is shown by the fact that Muggleton is declared as "humouring his sensualities with any sort of recreation," and as encouraging licentiousness and the use of wine and strong drink, whereas these were the actual vices which Muggleton preached against in the most forcible manner. The tract has some considerable interest, as showing the strong feeling that there was against Muggleton in his own time, and as an example of the way in which his enemies stooped to any kind of statement in order to injure him.

By this time Muggleton was sixty-eight years old and we do not hear very much of his vehemence afterwards. The degradation of his cruel punishment had eaten into his soul. He was not willing again to expose himself to the jeers and violence of the mob, but he devoted the remaining twenty years of his life to his followers and to his own family, to the preparation of his autobiography, and to a very extensive correspondence with his friends.

His letters are of considerable interest. They are full of clever expressions and wise utterances. They possess also a considerable amount of humour, and show every sign of having been written by a man who was decidedly conscientious, firm in his belief, and from his point of view religious in every action of his life. Throughout his career Muggleton was a bitter opponent of all forms of vice and uncleanness. He spoke strenuously against drunkenness and gambling, and would have nothing to do with any games of chance or cards in any form. Contrary to the then universal superstition he also refused to believe in witchcraft.[1] He had a strange antipathy to Scottish people, and to Scotland as a whole, having once had a Scottish friend, Buchanan, who proved to be a traitor and thereafter he would have little or nothing to do with anyone who came from that country. He strongly opposed, however, what is now termed passive resistance, and insisted upon his followers obeying the law and paying taxes, even though they might consider the law an unjust one, and were all the time working for its repeal. He had a great belief in the inspiration of his own writings, and that belief is accepted by his followers in the present day, who regard his chief book, the "Third Testimony," as quite equal in inspiration and in importance, to the Testaments, Old and New, and who read it with as much care and discretion as they do the accepted Bible.[2]

However much we may differ from the opinions which Muggleton taught and preached, and however we may regard them as distinctly heretical, it is difficult not to admire many of the personal characteristics of the man himself. He rejected early in life the opportunity of a prosperous marriage, entirely on a point of conscience. Later on, he lost a considerable amount of business because he could not follow his Puritan friends and relations in their ideas. He claimed that he never lived by his preaching, that he always supported himself by hard work as a tailor throughout the whole of his career, and when he gave up business, he affirmed "I owe the world nothing, I never wronged any in the world to the value of sixpence in my life to my knowledge." He took considerable pride in his own calling, and in one of his spiritual epistles he refers to the fact that the prophets of old were herdsmen, and that the Apostles were fishermen, and he argued that it was not altogether a strange thing that God should choose two tailors to be his two last prophets and witnesses of the Spirit, and that their witness ought not to be scorned because of the business with which they were concerned.

There is another very attractive side to the character of this interesting man. He was a staunch Englishman. He declared himself as "a free-born Englishman, a freeman of London by birth, and was never out of England in all my life." On many occasions he was particularly stalwart in his nationalism, and in his desire to exalt England and Englishmen by every constitutional method. He was also

---

[1] See his clever treatise on the "Witch of Endor" in which he traces the popular belief to disordered imagination.

[2] It must not be supposed that it is any part of the religious system to hold that only Muggletonians will be saved. The Founders held no such opinion. Reeve believed that while all children would be saved most men and women would be lost, but Muggleton says that, counting children, probably half the world's population could be saved.

a great believer in the freedom of the Press, and in the freedom on the part of a man to select his profession in life, but at the same time he was a strong opponent of war, regarding the profession of a soldier as an unlawful one. He went even further than that, because three other professions he regarded as unlawful. He objected to all clergy, of whatever type. He refused to believe in the necessity for physicians, claiming that God had given in Nature sufficient remedies to preserve Nature, and he opposed all lawyers, saying that they "keep the keys of the knowledge of the law, and will neither enter into truth and honesty themselves, nor will suffer others to enter in that would." He declared that almost all persons in the world had been deceived by either a lawyer, a physician, or a priest. His language was often exceedingly coarse and vehement, especially when he was opposing the Quakers, and he seasoned his writings with many expressions that can only be termed virulent abuse, but it was very much the manner of the day, the things that people opposed were reprobated at that time in words that were unsavoury and objectionable. He was responsible for a great deal of literature, and many of his books are still to be obtained by those who follow him, and who have carefully kept them in type for their own use and reference. Several of these volumes I purchased as curiosities and have them in my possession.

Muggleton was eighty-nine years old when he died, at his house in the Postern close to his birthplace on March 14, 1698, after only a fortnight's illness.[1] At the time of his death there existed a large number of his followers, and his body lay in state at Loriner's Hall for one day and was visited by those persons who had accepted his teaching. It was then buried on March 17 at Bethlehem New Churchyard in Liverpool Street close beside the body of his cousin John Reeve, but the tomb could not now be identified, as part of the churchyard is covered by the street, and part by the railway station. His funeral was attended by a group of 248 friends and followers.

By his first wife Muggleton had three children: Sarah, who was the first person to believe in her father's mission, and is proclaimed as the first Muggletonian, Elizabeth who married a Mr. Whitfield, and a third child who died young, the other two daughters surviving him. As already mentioned, by his second wife, only one son survived, the others having died in infancy. By his third wife, he does not appear to have had any issue.

---

[1] A very rare and scurrilous pamphlet on Muggleton was published in 1676-7. Printed for D. M. 8 pp. It is entitled "Muggleton's Last Will and Testament setting forth His Legacies to his followers and Gifts bequeathed to the World together With his particular bounty to Oliver's Porter and his gratitude to the Hangman whom he makes sole Executor." I have a copy of it in my possession.

The room in which the Muggletonians now meet bears on its wall a large tablet with the following inscription:

THIS TABLET
WAS ERECTED ON THE 16TH DAY OF MAY
1869,
To commemorate the opening of the
NEW READING ROOM,
Nº. 7, New Street, Bishopsgate. But more especially to denote the place as formerly called
WALNUT TREE YARD,
WHERE THE LORD'S LAST WITNESS WAS BORN.
ALSO,
To record the names of a few of our Christian Brethren who as believers in
THE THIRD COMMISSION,
declared by
JOHN REEVE, & LODOWICK MUGGLETON,
have greatly aided the Church, & partly endowed the present building.

and on this tablet are the names of the various benefactors of the sect and of the Trustees. Near by hangs the full-length painting of Muggleton, which is placed in a bad light, and has also suffered greatly by reason of the decay of the varnish. I had considerable difficulty in obtaining a photograph of it, and had to give it a very long exposure, with the result, however, that I was able to show in my photograph what cannot be seen in the painting, by reason of the decay of the varnish; the various details of the figure, and the whole appearance of the face. The Muggletonians themselves were astonished at the way in which the original painting was revealed by this photograph, and were very pleased to have had it done: They also possess an interesting death-mask of Muggleton, a cast taken after death, and that I had photographed as well as various portraits[1] of the author, which appeared as frontispieces to his writings.

The room in which the members meet is not known as a church or a chapel or a preaching-place, but is merely called a reading-room,

---

[1] There is also an important portrait of him in the National Portrait Gallery.

FULL-LENGTH PORTRAIT IN OIL BY WILLIAM WOOD
OF BRAINTREE
See pages 256 and 266
Specially photographed by Hallet Hyatt for this book

and the Muggletonian services consist in the members reading aloud the writings of their founders from beginning to end, and in singing certain spiritual songs, also composed by the two persons who were responsible for the foundation of the sect, the volume being called "Christian Hymns and Spiritual Songs, for those who follow the Third Commission." From the very beginning, the Muggletonians proclaimed the most absolute toleration of free will and the fullest liberty of opinion; while in some of their writings there are passages which may be fittingly called noble and dignified with respect to free speech, liberty of conscience, and liberty of opinion in religion. With all this liberty there was a strong flavour of English common sense about their teaching. It was sober and solid, and it protested in many places against luxury or extravagance, even in conversation, and against the extravagance of language into which the Quakers were at times led. It is a dogmatic faith, very matter-of-fact, and opposed in religious matters to what is often called superstition, and yet it has to do with matters which are entirely spiritual, and its followers believe very thoroughly in the spiritual teaching of Scripture in contradistinction to the inspired letter. On the other hand, as has been pointed out, the Muggletonians accept the most extraordinary ideas concerning science. They disbelieve in all the rules of modern day astronomy, and decline to accept either the ordinary laws of gravity, or the ordinary rules of mathematics, while some of them profess to accept quite definitely the doctrine of the resurrection of animals. There does not appear to have been at any time, except immediately after the prophet's death, a very large number of followers who accepted his teaching, and at the present day, those who call themselves believers in the Third Commission of the Spirit are quite few in number and are persons belonging to a very small group of families who have handed down this particular faith from generation to generation.[1]

To the student of religions it is distinctly interesting to find still surviving a body of men who accept this very sturdy person Muggleton as their teacher, and who read with the utmost diligence the writings which he prepared in the seventeenth century and which they still regard as holy. As to the Bible they do not receive the Apocrypha as an inspired work and have never done so, and they also exclude from the canon of Holy Scripture the writings of Solomon—Ecclesiastes, the Book of Proverbs and the Canticles—believing indeed that Solomon was a very wise man, but not accepting him in any sense as a prophet, nor even regarding him as a holy person. They also venerate a strange apocryphal work which is said to date from the second

---

[1] Dr. Gordon says: "They are, I believe, about as numerous now as ever they were." The Society is now 263 years old.

century and is certainly older than Origen's time, called the "Testament of the Twelve Patriarchs," a book introduced into England by Grosseteste, Bishop of Lincoln, 1240, first printed in 1577, a very popular religious manual of the sixteenth and seventeenth centuries. Furthermore, they receive the Book of Enoch as an inspired volume, and they read it as part of Scripture, in this way copying the early Christian Fathers who also accepted it; and then, side by side with it, and with Holy Scripture, they read the writings of Reeve and Muggleton, which they regard as the Third Testament. Their only collection of hymns is the volume already mentioned, the Divine Songs or Song Book, and that is their sole devotional manual, for while they do not accept nor believe in prayer, yet they do sing songs of gratitude and thanksgiving, although they expressly state that it is not done by way of worship.

They retain in their possession a considerable quantity of MSS. which have belonged to their founders, the originals of some of the treatises, a large collection of letters, and quantities of bills and account books, from 1760, specially relating to the sale of their printed books, and the expenses of their social meetings. Their original minute-books in Muggleton's thick, tremulous, and laboured handwriting are also in their possession. The officials of the headquarters in London furthermore possess a small amount of property, which is intended for the relief of the suffering, and which is exceedingly carefully managed and distributed amongst the deserving poor of their own body. Their meetings are not necessarily either monthly or weekly, but are arranged according to the convenience of the persons who can be accommodated. As a rule the Muggletonians meet every month, and they have two great yearly gatherings, on the dates that have already been mentioned. On these occasions they have tea, and later on, supper together. The room in which they meet would hold perhaps fifty to seventy people, and in the same building there are cloak-rooms and dressing-rooms, and apartments for the man and his wife who look after the house. At their two great festivals they drink toasts to absent friends and to the household of faith, and these are taken in port wine negus, which is made according to an old and well-established receipt, is handed round in some very interesting wine-glasses, and ladled by means of a beautiful antique silver ladle which belonged to a former believer.

One of the reasons why the Muggletonians were so bitterly opposed in early days was their habit of passing—in their phrase—sentence of damnation upon their fellow-creatures who did not accept their teaching. This was regarded by the early Muggletonians as a duty, as a mark of faith, and as a means of strengthening faith. It was the ultimate weapon to which they resorted, and it was held quite strenuously, for they believed that it was the right thing to make use of this weapon, and the sentence could either be pronounced by word of mouth, or by letter. The use, however, of this habit of passing sentence upon their fellow-creatures has for many years been dropped, and is now practically obsolete. It did exist, however, down to the middle of the last century, and was exercised especially against Swedenborgians, whose doctrines and tenets the Muggletonians bitterly opposed.

To one author, who has devoted himself with much care to studying the history of the Muggletonians, and to his writings, the Rev. Alexander Gordon, of Belfast, I owe a great deal of the information which I have obtained concerning these people. He is not only the author of the article on Muggleton in the "Dictionary of National Biography" (vol. xxxiv[1], p. 264) and of other articles relating to persons who founded similar sects, or who were associated more or less with Muggleton; but he prepared in 1868 and in 1870 two important papers on Muggleton which were read before the Literary and Philosophical Society in Liverpool, and which are now somewhat difficult to obtain.[2] He is one of the few persons who have been associated with the Muggletonians in their present work, and appears to have understood them very thoroughly.

In one or two respects, however, I have been able to go beyond Dr. Gordon. He states in his articles that he was never able to procure a copy of the song-book, but he only saw the copies that were in use at the meetings that he attended. Apparently the Muggletonians were not anxious to let him have a copy of this very strange religious manual, but I am glad to say that I have been able to obtain a copy of it, and have it in my own library. It is a scarce book, and exceedingly difficult to procure, while I should think it is absolutely unrivalled in the very extraordinary nature of its rhymes, more especially perhaps the hymn (148) which is sung on 19 July, and which appears to have as little real poetry in it as any hymn could very well possess.

Another pamphlet which Dr. Gordon was unable to obtain is entitled "The Articles of True Faith." It contains what is practically the creed of the Society, forty-eight articles of what they term the True Faith. This also, although a very small pamphlet, is of the greatest rarity, and it was only by the kindness of a Muggletonian lady that I was able to obtain a copy of it.

The anti-Quaker books are also very rare, as they were seized and destroyed, and one of the very scarcest of the Muggletonian pamphlets is the account of the trial and sufferings of Muggleton himself, which was issued in 1808, privately printed for the Muggletonians, with the understanding that it should never pass out of their hands. It is a pathetic document, and also almost impossible to procure, except by

---

[1] The article in respect of Lodowick Muggleton in the D.N.B can in fact be found at p. 264 of vol. XXXIX

[2] April 5, 1869, "The Origin of the Muggletonians"; April 4, 1870, "Ancient and Modern Muggletonians."

ENGRAVING BY J. KENNERLEY AFTER THE PORTRAIT
BY WILLIAM WOOD

Frontispiece to three books " Divine Songs," "Divine Looking Glass,"
and "Transcendent Spiritual Treatise"

the assistance of the Muggletonians themselves. I am glad to own a copy of it also.

Finally, I was presented with a little pamphlet, which is scrupulously kept to the Muggletonians, and issued for their own use only, containing a list of the Muggletonian books which are used and read by them, together with the prices at which those that are still in print can be obtained, but they can be so obtained only by Muggletonians, and it was as a special favour, in consideration of the assistance I had given them with regard to their portraiture, that they permitted me to purchase some of the books which were still in use, and are comparatively modern, from their headquarters at the prices at which they are sold to Muggletonians only.

Another clergyman who had written about the Muggletonians was the late Rev. Augustus Jessop, who in 1884 wrote an article for the "Nineteenth Century " on the person whom he terms "The Prophet of Walnut-tree Yard." Beyond these articles there is little information in print regarding this small sect, and the Muggletonians themselves, very naturally, are not anxious to talk, to the man in the street, respecting their belief, for fear that the result should be either unpleasant comment or ridicule. Although I was by no means in sympathy with their peculiar opinions, they received me with extreme kindliness and charity, and I was able to gather up from the lips of the leaders of the body a certain amount of information to supplement that which Dr. Gordon had issued. I believe that, with the exception of the Rev. Alexander Gordon, who visited them in 1868, I am almost the only person who has ever been admitted into the confidence of the members of this strange, mysterious, and somewhat pathetic sect, but I was able to place them under an obligation with regard to the portraiture of their founder, which they very generously recognized to the best of their ability. They were particularly interested in seeing the portrait of Muggleton, and in comparing it with the mask, the engravings, and the oil painting which had always been in their possession, and as I was able, by the kindness of Mr. Morgan, to supply them with a copy of this portrait of their great leader, they were not slow to express their gratitude for this gift.

Comparison of the newly discovered miniature with the old portrait enabled one to see that the attribution was correct, and to understand that Muggleton was a tall man with an aquiline nose, high cheekbones, long and very straight hair, hazel eyes, and a stern, yet suave, expression. It was curious that the miniature portrait had not been known to those who had accepted Muggleton's teaching in London, but had remained hidden away in one of the very few families in Derby where Muggleton had been received as a prophet, and it was not until the death of one member of this family that the miniature, fully authenticated by contemporary documents, came into the market, and was secured by the great collector whom I have already mentioned. It was undoubtedly a contemporary portrait and most certainly the work of Samuel Cooper, the formost painter of miniatures in England.

THE DEATH MASK OF LODOWICK MUGGLETON
Preserved at New Street. Bishopsgate
Photographed by Hallett Hyatt

As regards the persons who are members of this strange sect I cannot do better than quote the words of the Rev. Alexander Gordon:

"It is not very difficult," he says, "to estimate the extent to which the Muggletonian doctrines have met with success. Their influence has been confined almost entirely to the small body which professes them; for their writings have seldom been published in the ordinary way; they have never invited converts, and have found no opportunity, and looked for none, of bringing their opinions before the notice of the world. Neither Reeve nor Muggleton were preachers; they disseminated their views in conversation and by letter; and this has ever been the habit of the body. Persons of influential position have rarely been attracted to their community, but the personal character of its members has always stood high; few in numbers, they are and have been an industrious, and, in the main, a well-to-do and thriving set of people." (ii. 45.)

It may finally be of some interest to reproduce Dr. Gordon's account (taken from the "Christian Life" for 28 February 1914) of the last visit he paid to the Muggletonians in New Street, upon which occasion he had the unique privilege of attending their annual festival. "It was," Dr. Gordon writes, "in 1860 that he first came across a Muggletonian in the flesh, in the person of the late William Ridsdale, of Mansfield, a very courteous old gentleman, who in March, 1863, wrote to the 'Inquirer' correcting some remarks by W. H. [Dixon] in the previous January. Not, however, till he picked up on a Liverpool bookstall, in 1865, one of Muggleton's printed works, did he become at all interested in these people Through Mr. Ridsdale he became introduced to the then leaders of the body in London; in the first instance to Joseph Gandar (who died in 1868) and John Dymock Aspland (nearly related to John Dymock, the Latin lexicographer). It so happened that till May, 1869, 'the Believers in the Third Commission' had no meeting-place of their own. Place of worship, of course, they never had. They met at private houses or at friendly inns, where their book-closet was stored. On February 14th, 1870, they met to celebrate their Great Holiday for the first time on their own leasehold premises in what was once Walnut Tree Yard, where Lodowick Muggleton was born in 1609."

"This Great Holiday commemorates their foundation date, the delivery of the word of the Lord Jesus' to John Reeve, on 3rd, 4th, and 5th February, 1651-2 (Old Style), i.e., 14th, 15th, and 16th February, 1652 (New Style). From that date the Great Holiday has been continuously kept; and in 1870, for the first time in the history of the body a stranger (in the person of the present writer) was permitted to attend the festival on the three evenings of its celebration. It began on a Monday, and during the week which then followed the present writer was engaged in examining and arranging the curious store of manuscripts in the possession of this singular survival from the numerous sects of the Commonwealth period. He has never been present at the Little Holiday, on July 30th, commemorating Muggleton's release from prison on July 19th, 1677 (Old Style). Once only, in the interval between 1870 and the present year, had he revisited the Muggletonian premises, and on no festive occasion. This year, however, he felt moved to make another visit. His old friends, he knew, were all gone, and he wondered what successors they had, for these believers do not proselytize, nor do they attempt to bias their children in favour of their tenets.

"The first move was a preliminary visit to 'Walnut Tree Yard.' The caretaker at the meeting-place proved to be the grand-daughter of the guardian of the place on former visits. This worthy man, Robinson by name, a friendly and kindly old soul, had the repute of being a very firm believer. One remarkable proof of this was found in the fact of his having passed damnatory sentence on a certain Swedenborgian lecturer. Muggleton had laid down the principle: 'If a man give sentence, and afterwards doubts, that sentence returns on a man's own head, and the party so sentenced is freed from the power of his curse.' Robinson was untroubled by doubts. His grand-daughter explained that there was now no admission to view the premises without a pass; a rather surprising innovation, accounted for subsequently by some annoyances received from the ill-behaving. A short conversation in the doorway gave the information required for the next move. Accordingly, on the Friday evening, the present writer took steps to make the acquaintance of a recognized leader of the little community. The visitor's name, not entirely forgotten, secured for him

THE MUGGLETONIAN READING ROOM IN NEW STREET,
BISHOPSGATE, LONDON
Showing the full-length portrait by Wood and the notice-board
See page 256
Photograph by Hallett Hyatt

a hearty welcome, and an invitatation to 'a cup of tea' at the opening of the Great Holiday next day, i.e., last Saturday week, known in the ordinary calendar as Valentine's Day.

"The invitation was duly honoured. As for the meeting-room, upstairs, it looked to the eyes of seventy-two exactly as it had done to those of twenty-seven. The full-length portrait of Lodowick Muggleton, painted by his friend William Wood, dominated the apartment from its situation beside the fireplace. Confronting it on the opposite wall was the oil painting, enlarged from the figure on the well-known gem, which exhibits in profile the supposed likeness of our Lord, as his visage is portrayed in the Lentulus letter. A few names had been added on the tablet which record the benefactors, otherwise all was as before. The same cannot be said of the company present. From about two score they had dwindled to about a score. Some thirty years back there was an accession to the London fellowship, but the present numerical decline was freely admitted. Yet the number of those who meet together has never been an indication of the total tale of believers. It may be mentioned as a curious circumstance that in 1869 an inquiry in the Library of St. Paul's Cathedral for one of Muggleton's books (seized on his arrest in 1676, and there preserved) was immediately responded to by the lay official then in charge, who went at once to the right shelf for the book, and with little or no hesitation accounted for his knowledge of its whereabouts by saying he had learned the truth from it. In like manner conversions have from time to time been made, often in entire ignorance of the existence of any persons entertaining the same belief. The present London contingent appears to know little of the historic fortunes of the body. The one serious inroad on the Muggletonian forces occurred in 1772 by the defection of the Birchites. A reference to an acquaintance of years back as having been 'the last of the Birchites' was met by the inquiry, 'And who were the Birchites?' These minor heresies are soon forgotten. Dr. Martineau in 1859 referred to Charles Wellbeloved as having been known of old as a votary of Cappism. Even then the question arose: 'What was Cappism?' Few to-day could tell.

"After the enjoyment of an ample and pleasant social meal, enlivened by much friendly converse, the Believers in the Commission of the Spirit' were left to sing the Commission Song ('Arise, my soul, arise!') and complete the customary programme of their Great Holiday—with a promise to rejoin them on their next 'reading day.'"

I may add finally that I have adopted the spelling of Muggleton's Christian name without a final e because it is so spelled in his various works and is still so spelled by his followers. In the entry of his baptism at St. Botolphs Church, it appears with an e, thus:

"Lodowicke the sonne of Johne Muggleton bapt ye 30 of Julye," and he himself frequently signed his letters Lodowicke. There are instances, however, of the adoption in his signature of the word Lodowick without the final e.

The Muggletonians appear to have always used the form Lodowick.

APPENDIX

A LIST OF REEVE AND MUGGLETON'S WRITINGS

A TRANSCENDANT SPIRITUAL TREATISE upon several Heavenly Doctrines from the Holy Spirit of the Man Jesus, the only true God, sent unto all his Elect. 1652. Later editions have an engraved portrait.

A GENERAL EPISTLE FROM THE HOLY SPIRIT unto all Prophets, Ministers, or Speakers in the World. 1653.

A REMONSTRANCE FROM THE ETERNAL GOD; declaring several Spiritual Transactions unto the Parliament and Commonwealth of England; unto his Excellency, the Lord General Cromwell; the Council of State; the Council of War; and to all that love the Second Appearing of the Lord Jesus, the only God, and Everlasting Father blessed for ever. 1653.

A DIVINE LOOKING GLASS; or the Third and Last Testament of our Lord Jesus Christ, whose personal residence is seated on his throne of eternal glory in another world. Being the Commission of the Spirit, agreeing with, and explaining the former Commissions of the Law and the Gospel, differing only in point of worship. Set forth for the trial of all sorts of supposed spiritual lights in the world, until the ever-living true Jesus, the only high and mighty God, personally appears in the air, with his saints and angels. 1656.

AN OCCASIONAL DISCOURSE CONCERNING THE PROPHET REEVE, Sept. 28, 1668; usually bound at the end of "The Looking Glass."

JOYFUL NEWS FROM HEAVEN; or the last intelligence from our Glorified Jesus above the stars; wherein is infallibly recorded how that the Soul dieth in the Body, and lieth in the grave until the day God will raise it from death, with a true description of the Kingdom of Heaven and of Hell. 1658.

A TRUE INTERPRETATION OF THE ELEVENTH CHAPTER OF THE REVELATIONS OF ST. JOHN, and other Texts in that book, as also many other places of Scripture; whereby is unfolded, and plainly declared, the whole council of God concerning Himself, the Devil, and all Mankind, from the foundation of the World to all eternity, never before revealed by any of the sons of men, until now. 1662.

A TRUE INTERPRETATION OF ALL THE CHIEF TEXTS, and Mysterious Sayings and Visions opened of the whole Book of the Revelations of St.

John; whereby is unfolded and plainly declared those wonderful deep Mysteries and Visions interpreted, concerning the true God, the Alpha and Omega, with a variety of other Heavenly Secrets, which have never been opened nor revealed to any man since the creation of the World to this day, until now. With engraved Portrait. 1665.

A TRUE INTERPRETATION OF THE WITCH OF ENDOR, spoken of in the First Book of Samuel, 28th chapter, beginning at the 11th verse, showing—
1st. How she, and all other Witches, do beget or produce that familiar spirit they deal with, and what a familiar spirit is, and how those voices are procured, and shapes appear unto them, whereby the ignorant and unbelieving people are deceived by them.
2nd. It is clearly made appear in this Treatise, that no spirit can be raised without its body, neither can any spirit assume any body after death, for if the spirit doth walk, the body doth walk also.
3rd. An Interpretation of all those Scriptures that doth seem as if spirits might go out of men s bodies when they die, and subsist in some place or other without bodies.
4th and lastly. Several other things needful for the mind of man to know, which whoever doth understand, it will be great satisfaction. 1669.

THE NECK OF THE QUAKERS BROKEN, or cut in sunder by the two-edged sword of the Spirit:
1st. In a Letter to Edward Bourne, a Quaker.
2nd. In answer to a Letter to Samuel Hooton and W. S.
3rd. In a Letter to Richard Farnsworth, Quaker.
4th. In an answer to a printed Pamphlet of the said Richard Farnsworth, entitled, "Truth Ascended; or, the Anointed and Sealed of the Lord Defended." 1663.

A LETTER SENT TO THOMAS TAYLOR, QUAKER; being an Answer to some things of concernment for the reader to know: the particular heads are seven.
1st. That Christ could not make all things of nothing.
2nd. That earth and waters were eternal, and out of that matter God created all living creatures.
3rd. That there was a place of residence for God to be in, when he created this world.
4th. How all Children are saved, though the seed of the serpent, if they die in their childhood.
5th. Of the difference of the fruit of the womb, and the fruit of the flesh; and how they are two several trees, and two several fruits.
6th. How the seed of faith, the elect seed, did all fall in Adam, and therefore made alive in Christ; and how the reprobate seed did not fall in Adam, so not made alive in Christ; and what it is that purifies the Quakers' hearts.

7th. How Adam and Eve were not capable of any kind of death before their fall; and how their fall did procure but a temporal death to all the seed of Adam: but the fall of the serpent did procure an eternal death to all his seed who live to man and woman's estate, and more especially to those that doth deny the person and body of Christ to be now living in Heaven above the stars, without a man, as all the speakers of the Quakers do. 1664.

A LOOKING-GLASS FOR GEORGE FOX, QUAKER; in answer to George Fox, his Book, called, "Something in Answer to Lodowick Muggleton's Book, which he calls 'The Neck of the Quakers Broken;'" wherein is set forth the ignorance and blindness of the Quakers' doctrine of Christ within them, &c. Contents in 36 heads. 1667.

THE ANSWER TO WILLIAM PENN, QUAKER, his Book, entitled, "The New Witnesses proved Old Hereticks;" wherein he is proved to be an ignorant spatter-brained Quaker, who knows no more what the true God is, nor his secret decrees, than one of his coach-horses doth, nor so much ; "For the Ox knoweth his owner, and the Ass his master's crib," but Penn doth not know his Maker, as is manifest by the Scriptures, which may inform the reader, if he mind the Interpretation of Scripture in the Discourse following:

1st. That God was in the form, image, and likeness of man's bodily shape, as well as his soul from eternity.
2nd. That the substance of earth and water was an eternal, dark, senseless chaos, and that earth and water were eternal in the original.
3rd. That the soul of man is generated and begot by man and woman with the body, and are inseparable.
4th. That the soul and body of man are both mortal, and doth die and go to dust until the resurrection.
5th. That to fulfil the prophecy of Esaias, God descended from Heaven into the Virgin's womb, and transmuted his spiritual body into a pure natural body, and became a man child, even the Child Jesus, Emanuel, God with us.
6th. That God by his prerogative power, hath elected the seed of Adam to be saved, and preordained the seed of the serpent, such as Penn the Quaker is, to be damned, without any other inducement but his own prerogative will and pleasure.
7th. A reply to the discourse between Penn and inc.
8th. What is meant by the Armour of God, the wilderness, and the wild beasts I fought with in the wilderness. 1673.

AN ANSWER TO ISAAC PENNINGTON, ESQ. his Book, entitled "Observations on some passages of Lodowick Muggleton's Interpretation of the 11th chapter of the Revelations"; also some passages of that Book of his, entitled, "The Neck of the Quakers Broken;" and in his Letter to Thomas Taylor.—Whereby it might appear what spirit the said Lodowick Muggleton is of, and from what

God his commission is; as by what authority his spirit is moved to write against the people called Quakers. This Answer was Written to inform those that do not know the anti-christian spirit of false teachers, in these our days. By Lodowick Muggleton. 1719 (written 1669).

A STREAM FROM THE TREE OF LIFE; or the Third Record vindicated; being the Copies of several Letters and Epistles wrote by the two last Witnesses of Jesus Christ; wherein truth rides triumphant, and imagination is confounded.

A Copy of a letter to W. Medgate, proving that God takes no immediate notice, except in particular cases.

A Letter to Walter Bohenan on the same subject.

To James Whitehead, answering six queries.

To Colonel Phair, concerning eating the flesh of devils; as also explaining the mustard grain, Luke xiii. 19.

To Edward Fewteril concerning witchcraft.

A discourse between John Reeve and Richard Leader, wherein philosophy is confounded.

To Tomkinson, relating, in part, the Prophets sufferings for declaring truth.

An Epistle to a Quaker, shewing the blindness of those people.

An Epistle of the Prophet Muggleton's, proving his power to give sentences; also explaining how the devil entered the herd of swine.

To Christopher Hill, containing his own Thomas Martin, William Young, and Elizabeth Wyles's blessings.

To Alice Webb, containing the six principles, and her blessing.

To a friend concerning true and false preachers. An epistle concerning spirits.

To Isaac Pennington, Esq., concerning God's visibly appearing in flesh.

The Death of Moses unfolded.

An epistle, proving that Christ had inherent power to die and live again, without assistance from any in heaven or on earth.

To Ann Adams shewing the peace of a pure life. 1663.

SACRED REMAINS; or a Divine Appendix, being a collection of several treatises, epistolary and public, written by the Lord's last immediate Messenger, John Reeve, and after careful examination by the most correct copies, communicated for the consolation and establishment of the Church of Christ by their Brethren, whose faith in these, and all other his irremandable declarations doth (and by divine protection wilt) remain unshaken to eternity.

Questions sent to Mr. Sedgwick, by the Prophet John Reeve.

Mr. Sedgwick's Replies.

The Prophet's Answer to Mr. Sedgwick.

Of the one Personal uncreated Glory.

The Prophet John Reeve's Answer to a letter sent him by Esquire Pennington.
John Reeve's Epistle sent to the Earl of Pembroke.
John Reeve's Epistle to his Kinsman.
An Epistle on what was from Eternity, concerning the only true God; of his glorious throne; and the pure creation, from that which is false.
A General treatise of the three Records or Dispensations.
A cloud of unerring witnesses plainly proving there neither is nor ever was any other God but Christ Jesus the Lord.
Scriptures proving that Christ Jesus is the only God.

A BOOK OF LETTERS, or Spiritual Epistles; being copies of 168 Letters, written by the last Prophets and Messengers of God, John Reeve and Lodowick Muggleton; containing variety of spiritual Revelations, and deep Mysteries, manifesting to the elect seed the prerogative power of true Prophets; who by virtue of their commission, did truly give the blessing of life everlasting to those that believed their declarations; and to all despising Reprobates the curse or sentence of eternal damnation. Collected by the great pains of Alexander Dalamaine, a true believer of God's last commission of the Spirit; intended at first only for his own spiritual solace, but finding they increased to so great a volume, he leaves it to posterity that ages to come may rejoice in the comfortable view of so blessed and heavenly a treasure. 1755 (written 1653-1691).

SUPPLEMENT TO THE BOOK OF LETTERS; being the copies of twenty-three Letters written by John Reeve and Lodowick Muggleton, on various subjects. 1831 (written 1656-1688).

THE ACTS OF THE WITNESSES OF THE SPIRIT, in five parts, by Lodowick Muggleton, one of the two Witnesses and true Prophets of the only high immortal glorious God Christ Jesus; left by him to be published after his death; that after ages may see some of the acts of the two Witnesses of the Spirit, as well as their writings, and their doctrine now in this last age. As they have read of some of the wonderful acts of Moses and the Prophets, and the Acts of the Apostles, so there will be some remarkable acts of the Witnesses of the Spirit left upon record, of their Births, Parentage, Revelations, Disputes, Troubles, Trials by Jury, Imprisonment and Punishment they underwent for declaring the Lord Jesus Christ to be the only God, which declaration of theirs accords with that Prophecy of Isaiah, chap. ix, verse 6th:

> "For unto us a Child is born; unto us a Son is given; and the government shall be upon his shoulders; and his name shall be called Wonderful, Counsellor, the mighty God, the everlasting Father, the Prince of Peace."

1699 (written 1677).

A GENERAL INDEX TO JOHN REEVE AND LODOWICK MUGGLETON'S WORKS, wherein is inserted the contents and subjects of their Works. DIVINE SONGS OF THE MUGGLETONIANS IN GRATEFUL PRAISE TO THE ONLY TRUE GOD THE LORD JESUS CHRIST. 1829. With engraved portrait.

Books Written by the Believers of John Reeve and Lodowick Muggleton's Commission

A TRUE ACCOUNT OF THE TRIAL AND SUFFERINGS OF LODOWICK MUGGLETON. By Nathaniel Powell. 1808 (written 1677).

TRUTH'S TRIUMPH; or, a Witness to the Two Witnesses. By T. Tompkinson.

NONE BUT CHRIST. By T. Tompkinson.

A DISCOURSE UPON THE EPISTLE BY JUDE; together with the MYSTERY OF FAITH. By T. Tompkinson.

A SYSTEM OF RELIGION. By T. Tompkinson.

MUGGLETONIANS' PRINCIPLES PREVAILING. By T. Tompkinson.

PERSPECTIVE GLASS FOR SAINTS AND SINNERS. By J. Saddington.

THE ARTICLES OF TRUE FAITH DEPENDING UPON THE COMMISSION OF THE SPIRIT, by John Saddington. 1830.

Beloved Brethren,

The afore mentioned Books may be considered the whole of the Writings of the Lord's last Prophets, John Reeve and Lodowick Muggleton, as far as the Church is in possession of

We have given the contents of each Book, in a General Index, to make reference more easy to those that would willingly be instructed in the knowledge of the true God and their own eternal salvation.

JOSEPH & ISAAC FROST.

CHISWICK PRESS: PRINTED BY CHARLES WHITTINGHAM AND CO.
TOOKS COURT, CHANCERY LANE, LONDON.

English Sects: An Historical Handbook

By
Arthur Reynolds

MUGGLETONIANS

OF the many sects which sprang into existence during the Commonwealth—Traskites, Shakers, Ranters, Dippers, Behmenists, and the like—probably three only survive, the Seventh Day Baptists, the Society of Friends (the Quakers), and the Muggletonians. Of these three, one only, the Quakers, is of any account; the other two are obscure and numerically negligible.

The Muggletonians derive their name from Lodowick Muggleton, who was born in Walnut-Tree Yard, Bishopsgate Without, in 1609, and was baptized in the Parish Church of St. Botolph. Macaulay (*History of England*) describes him thus:—

"A mad tailor named Lodowick Muggleton wandered from pothouse to pothouse, tippling ale, and denouncing eternal torments against all those who refused to believe, on his testimony, that the Supreme Being was only six feet high, and that the sun was just four miles from the earth."

Muggleton was certainly a tailor, but by no means a mad one, for, apart from his strange heresies, he was particularly sane. So far from being a tippler, he taught the virtue of sobriety. He indulged in imprecations, it is true, on those who rejected his teaching, which, however, was not so monstrously absurd as Macaulay represented it to be, though he ridiculed the conclusions of astronomers, and clung to the belief that the sun revolves round the earth.

When he was about forty years of age he came under the influence of two Ranters, John Robins and Thomas Tany, his cousin, John Reeve, also a tailor, being likewise affected. In 1652 Reeve gave out that he was appointed, "by voice of words from Jesus Christ, Who was the only God," to bring in a new dispensation, with Muggleton for his spokesman. They represented, he affirmed, the two witnesses of the Apocalypse, and a statement of the new doctrines was drawn up by Reeve in *A Transcendant Treatise*. In this it is declared that the deity consists only in a "glorified body of flesh like unto a man in compass and substance"; that the devil is human reason; that astronomy is all wrong, and that heaven is quite near, just above the stars. God, the Muggletonians were taught to believe, having started the world, left it to men to operate, and exercises no immediate control over human affairs, though on a few occasions He has intervened with revelations, the last of which was the Third Commission, declared by John Reeve and Lodowick Muggleton. This revelation, or testament, is regarded by their disciples as inspired equally with the Sacred Scriptures.

The sect has no ministry and no worship. It meets irregularly in the Reading Room of a house built on the site of Muggleton's birthplace, and listens to selections from the Bible, the Book of Enoch, the writings of Reeve and Muggleton, and, strange to say, another old apocryphal treatise, "The Testament of the Twelve Patriarchs." The nearest approach it makes to worship is the singing of its own "Divine Songs," but it is distinctly understood that they express nothing more than thanksgiving. Two festivals are observed, "The Great Holiday," which commemorates on February 16th the founding of the sect, and the "Little Holiday," on July 30th, the day on which Muggleton was released from prison. The Muggletonians make no proselytes. They are a close and exclusive body consisting of a few families. The score or so of members are persons of good character, industrious, and well-to-do.

www.ingramcontent.com/pod-product-compliance
Lightning Source LLC
Chambersburg PA
CBHW061437300426
44114CB00014B/1716